Higher Education and Lifelong Learners

Responding to the emerging needs of lifelong learners arguably represents one of the most fundamental challenges facing higher education systems of the countries of the developed world. At the start of the new century the concept of *lifelong learning* may indeed be counted as one of the key organising concepts underlying public policy in many countries. The interpretation of the concept, however, remains highly contested.

This timely book throws new light on the dramatic changes taking place in higher education through an exploration of the participation of 'non-traditional' students in ten countries. Amongst others, the following areas are explored:

- the complex reality behind the statistics on participation in higher education in five European countries (Austria, Germany, Ireland, Sweden, the United Kingdom) North America, Japan, Australia and New Zealand
- contrasting perceptions of lifelong learning
- changing patterns of participation by adults in higher education
- national and institutional policies and innovations to accommodate non-traditional students and new forms of study
- conclusions for policy, practice and research.

Higher Education and Lifelong Learners will be of interest to academics, researchers and students involved with higher education, lifelong learning, comparative education as well as policy makers, educational managers and administrators. The contributions reveal a remarkable transformation in the student body and in the way learners pursue their studies, highlighting the international impact of increasing marketisation and differentiation on the nature of the higher education accessible to potential lifelong learners.

Hans G. Schuetze joined the University of British Columbia in 1991 as Professor of Higher Education and Research Associate at the Centre for Policy Studies in Higher Education and Training. His research interests and publications are in the fields of post-secondary education and training, comparative and international education. **Maria Slowey** is Professor and Director of Adult and Continuing Education at the University of Glasgow where she is also Vice Dean (Research) in the Faculty of Education. She is involved in research and policy analysis on post-compulsory education, in particular adult participation in education and training. Both authors have worked extensively with intergovernmental bodies, including the OECD, EU, and the Council of Europe.

Higher Education and Lifelong Learners

International perspectives on change

Edited by Hans G. Schuetze
and Maria Slowey

London and New York

First published 2000
by RoutledgeFalmer
11 New Fetter Lane, London EC4P 4EE

Simultaneously published in the USA and Canada
by RoutledgeFalmer
29 West Street, New York, NY 10001

RoutledgeFalmer is an imprint of the Taylor & Francis Group

© 2000 Selection and editorial material Hans G. Schuetze and Maria Slowey;
individual chapters, their contributors

Typeset in Garamond by
Curran Publishing Services Ltd, Norwich
Printed and bound in Great Britain by
St Edmundsbury Press, Bury St Edmunds, Suffolk

British Library Cataloguing in Publication Data
A catalogue record for this book is available from the British Library

Library of Congress Cataloging in Publication Data
Schuetze, Hans G., 1939– Slowey, Maria, 1952–
Higher education and lifelong learners: international perspectives on
change / Hans G. Schuetze and Maria Slowey.
p. cm.
Includes bibliographical references (p.) and index.
1. Continuing education–Cross-cultural studies. 2. Nontraditional college
students–Cross-cultural studies. I. Schuetze, Hans G. and Slowey, Maria
II. Title.
LC5215 .S62 2000
374–dc21   00–046889

ISBN 0–415–24793–4 (hbk)
ISBN 0–415–24794–2 (pbk)

Contents

Figures

Figures

Tables

Contributors

Seth Agbo is Assistant Professor and coordinator of the teacher education programme at the Pacific University in Forest Grove, Oregon, USA.

Karin Agélii is Researcher at the Department of Education, University of Stockholm, Stockholm, Sweden.

David Beckett is Lecturer at the Department of Education, Policy Management, University of Melbourne, Australia.

John Benseman is Lecturer at the School of Education, University of Auckland, New Zealand.

Roger Boshier is Professor at the Department for Educational Studies, University of British Columbia, Canada.

Agnieszka Bron is Professor at the Department of Education, University of Stockholm, Stockholm, Sweden.

Tom Collins is Director at the Centre for Adult and Community Education, St Patrick's College, Maynooth, Ireland.

Tomokazu Fujitsuka is Associate Professor at the Department of Economics, Miyazaki Sangyo-Keiei University, Japan.

Yuki Honda-Okitsu is Researcher at the Japanese Institute of Labour (JIL), Tokyo, Japan.

Richard James is lecturer in the Centre for the Study of Higher Education, University of Melbourne, Australia.

Hans Pechar is Director of the Higher Education Research Programme at the Institute for Interdisciplinary Research, Vienna, Austria.

Hans G. Schuetze is Professor of Higher Education and Research Associate at the Centre for Policy Studies in Higher Education at University of British Columbia, Canada.

Maria Slowey is Professor of Adult and Continuing Education, Vice-Dean Research of the Faculty of Education, University of Glasgow, Scotland.

Andrä Wolter is Professor of Education at the Technical University of Dresden, Germany.

Angela Wroblewski is Researcher at the Centre for the Studies of Higher Education, Vienna, Austria.

Shinichi Yamamoto is Professor of Higher Education and Director of the Research Centre for University Studies, University of Tsukuba, Japan.

Part I

Introduction

Comparative perspectives

1 Traditions and new directions in higher education

A comparative perspective on non-traditional students and lifelong learners

Hans G. Schuetze and Maria Slowey

Adult learners and non-traditional students: background to a comparative study

Higher education in the developed countries underwent significant change, if not transformation, in the last decade of the twentieth century. A massive increase in student enrolment was accompanied by increasing differentiation of higher education systems including, in some countries, the rise of private higher education- trends which appear likely to shape developments for the foreseeable future. The new demand is largely based on two elements. First, structural changes in economic and social systems which are increasingly grounded in scientific and technological knowledge, and are widely perceived as requiring a better qualified workforce. Second, there is a growing acceptance of the principle that education, especially higher education, should no longer be confined to the young but needs to be spread out over the lifetime of individuals. The demand is further fuelled by a continuing focus on issues of access and equity both from a policy perspective and as a response to pressure from social movements.

In the 1990s, student numbers increased by 40 percent on average across developed countries (OECD 1999). For example, in Sweden and New Zealand, enrolment grew by 41 percent, in Ireland by 51 percent, and in the UK by a dramatic 81 percent. Other countries where enrolment had been strong already in the 1970s and 1980s, such as the US and Canada, grew less, proportionally. The growth has been largely driven by youth participation (participation rates of the eighteen to twenty-four population has increased by 70 percent), although demand came also from adults of all ages (the rate of young adults, aged twenty-five to twenty-nine years, increased by almost 50 percent.). For example, Ireland is a case where most first time entrants are young, whereas in Canada, New Zealand and the UK significant numbers of both young and older students enter, a pattern that the OECD analysts (1999 p. 72) call the 'basis of a lifelong learning model'.

In connection with this recent wave of expansion, this volume is concerned with two main themes which dominate the academic, policy and popular debates on higher education at the start of the new millennium. The first of these relates to the thesis that higher education which once served a small segment of the population, the 'elite', has been transformed to a 'mass' or even 'universal' system of higher education (Trow 1973). As a result, the problem of 'access for all' to higher education – for long the unfulfilled promise of an egalitarian society – seems finally to be resolved, and the distinction between 'traditional' and 'non-traditional' student no longer meaningful. The second theme concerns the concept of *lifelong learning* which dominates national and international educational policy discussions. The thesis here is that the perceived universality of access means that the role of higher education in achieving the objectives commonly associated with the concept of lifelong learning is well developed, particularly as higher education comes to be defined more broadly within the context of a 'post compulsory', 'post secondary' or 'tertiary' education system (OECD 1998).

The reality, of course, is not so straightforward, and, as we will show, there are good grounds for challenging both of these contentions.

We set the scene for this volume by outlining the methodology and basis on which the ten country case studies were prepared. As change in higher education cannot be seen in isolation, but is part of a wider transformation associated with debates about the movement from 'industrialised' to 'post-industrialised' societies, we preface our discussion of the key concepts of *lifelong learning* and *non-traditional students* by reference to this broader context. In the light of these discussions, we summarise the main findings from the country reports and make tentative moves towards outlining a framework of how the changes in higher education towards a system of lifelong learning might be conceptualised.

Objectives, methodology and scope

This volume builds on an earlier study undertaken by the authors under the auspices of the Organisation for Economic Cooperation and Development (OECD 1987). That earlier study concentrated on adults in higher education, comparing the levels and the conditions of adult participation across the same ten countries. We found then that adult students (defined as those aged twenty-five or over on entry to higher education) could in effect be taken as a proxy for non-traditional learners.

Although we concluded that the typical adult in higher education was 'more likely to be there because of previous educational advantages rather than disadvantages' (ibid. p. 37) their minority status in most systems, culturally as well as statistically, was key in identifying them as non-traditional. This minority status was accentuated by associated factors such as mode of study (frequently part-time) employment status and family circumstances.

There were significant differences in the levels of adult participation across the countries in the 1987 study and, while the main emphasis was on age of entry, account was also taken of social class, gender and ethnicity. For analytic purposes we developed a typology of countries along a continuum relating to the levels of adult participation in higher education.

- Those countries with relatively high levels of participation by adult learners and demonstrating a relatively high degree of flexibility in relation to entry criteria and study patterns; this category included Sweden and the United States.
- Those where there were significant, but lower, proportions of adult learners across the system as a whole, and where adult students were frequently located in open universities or dedicated centres of adult or continuing education within 'mainstream' institutions; this category included Australia, Canada, New Zealand and the UK.
- Those at the other end of the continuum with very low levels of adult participation in higher education (frequently less than 5 percent); this category included Austria, Germany, Ireland and Japan.

The present volume revisits policies and developments in the same ten countries just over a decade later, taking into account the greatly changed context of higher education. The objective of undertaking a follow-up study a little more than a decade later was twofold. First, we wanted to record progress towards participation by what had been called 'non-traditional students' in the 1980s in order to see to what extent the new wave of expansion in the 1990s had included students from non-traditional backgrounds and whether or not they were still under-represented. At the same time we were interested in seeing how the pattern of participation of 'traditional' students had been changing. We presumed that changes in both the socio-economic environment and the structure and delivery system of tertiary education would have an impact on the way students pursue their studies. We realised that the earlier exclusive focus on adults was too narrow and that we had to include other under-represented groups in order to understand the obstacles and challenges that non-traditional students are facing.

Second, we were aware that the exclusive focus on universities that we had chosen for the 1987 study was no longer appropriate given the far-reaching differentiation of the post-secondary education systems and the fact that, in most countries, the majority of under-represented groups were enrolled in non-university institutions and programmes rather than 'traditional' universities. Thus, the new study looked at universities, colleges and technical institutes as well as programmes that were delivered in conjunction with external partners.

The ten countries that were included in the two studies were all OECD members. Of these, five were (Western) European, belonging also to the EU, (Austria, Germany, Ireland, Sweden and the UK), three from the Pacific Rim (Australia, Japan and New Zealand) and two from North America (Canada and the United States). Classified according to their cultural rather than geographical dimension, six of the countries could be described as being of an Anglo-Saxon/American tradition, three belong to a (Northern and Central) continental European tradition, and Japan as a blend of its own cultural roots and traditions with some adapted features from Western countries.

We are fully aware of the limitations in this selection of countries. However, it did seem logical to focus again on the ten countries that had formed the main focus of the earlier analysis, in order to see whether (and how) progress has been made with respect to the inclusion of under-represented groups of learners and, more generally, to a system of tertiary education that is conducive to lifelong learning. Thus the emphasis is clearly on countries with highly developed higher education systems. With reluctance we decided we could not expand the original group to include to include case studies from Southern or Eastern Europe or those from the developing world.

In our view comparative analysis yields insights into the real nature of the changed systems underlying the policy rhetoric and barrage of statistical evidence. However, the value of comparative analysis depends to a considerable extent on the development and application of a common conceptual framework. This framework needs to be sufficiently sensitive not to mask real areas of difference, and flexible enough to allow the individual case studies to contribute in distinctive ways to a greater understanding of what are very complex phenomena. Like the 1987 OECD study, the present study is based on national case studies by authors from these countries, some of whom had previously been involved in the 1987 study. The authors met several times over 1997 and 1998 in order to discuss the common analytic framework, but it was understood that individual authors would have a choice of the particular emphasis of their study depending on the specific situations of their respective countries and their own personal perspectives. As coordinators, we were not disappointed in our hope that new insights would be generated by bringing together researchers from two different, although complementary backgrounds: higher education and adult education.

In most cases, the country studies were based almost entirely on secondary data, ranging from statistical and survey data to published research reports and general literature. In several cases, some primary data were used, mostly in the form of expert interviews. In only one case, Austria, the research team launched a major empirical study surveying some 8,000 students about their socio-economic situation and pattern of studying.

Not only have the numbers of students, staff, and institutions dramatically increased in these ten countries, there have also been numerous structural and organisational changes, including the diversification of higher education systems through the establishment of new types of institutions, programmes and courses of study. Probably more significant for the mission and the internal lives of higher education institutions, especially the universities, are other changes of a qualitative kind such as more flexible provision, new approaches to teaching and learning, and an increasing emphasis upon the evaluation and certification of learning. New forms of knowledge creation and dissemination, greater access to information sources, the use of new media and new channels of communication, the development of complex partnerships with both external providers and user groups, and the growing role of education markets are all factors that have a major impact on where, what, how and why tertiary/post-secondary students learn.

Two widely shared and interrelated assumptions are associated with these developments. First, with the participation rates in tertiary education in many countries approaching, or exceeding, 50 per cent of the school-leaving age group, it is often argued that issues of access and equity have essentially been solved, and that now there are opportunities for all who have the ability and the desire to pursue their education beyond secondary school. Second, and perhaps more contentiously, it is held that high participation levels mean that the role of higher education in selection and social reproduction is largely a feature of the past.

We do not agree with these assumptions. Rather, we believe that 'expansion has not been sufficient to reduce differences in rates of access of learners from different social and economic groups' (OECD 1999 p. 69) and that there is a need for special measures to be put into place, both in terms of public policies and institutional practice, that benefit especially under-represented groups.

Our conceptual framework can be characterised as a 'dual' lens. Firstly, at a general level, the country studies examine in some detail, and with different emphases, the interrelationship between competing interpretations of the concept of lifelong learning and the dramatically changing features of higher education. Alongside the schools, the work place, and the community, higher education represents just one element in any strategy for achieving the objective of lifelong *learning for all* (OECD 1996). Within this prescribed arena, however, the development of mass higher education while not synonymous with a lifelong learning system, is, in our view, a necessary precondition of its realisation.

The accelerating 'massification' refers largely to quantitative aspects – more students, more academic staff, more types of institutions, more programmes – but these quantitative changes have not necessarily been accompanied by a qualitative transformation of the academy itself (Barnett 1992, Duke 1992, Scott 1995). In other words, while there have been changes and innovation across the whole higher education sector, by and large the traditional institutions, especially the longer-established and more elite universities, have tried to accommodate growing numbers of students while preserving their traditional academic values, institutional structures and processes. More fundamental changes tend to be located mainly in the newer, more vocationally orientated institutions which, as most of the country studies in this volume confirm, continue to be ranked lower in terms of conventional indicators of prestige. We should of course not be surprised at this. As Halsey points out, institutional differentiation is socially controlled 'so that elite universities . . . remain the cultural possession of traditionally advantaged groups' (Halsey 1992 p. 15).

Our second conceptual lens turns attention to those who form the primary rationale of any educational system and corresponding analyses: the students. Who are the '*non-traditional*' students? What is the social composition of the groups that have fuelled the expansion of higher (tertiary) education? To what extent do they comprise sections of the population traditionally under-represented in higher education? Exploring different conceptions of 'non-traditional' students in different countries, and tracing changes over the last fifteen years or so, places a major question mark over the notion of a 'traditional' student within the present context of higher education. The evidence from many of the countries in this volume points to increasingly diverse patterns of work and study as many students combine their studies, whether by choice or force of circumstances, with employment.

The classic notion of the 'student' is also challenged by changes in the social, economic and technical environment, as we discuss in the next section. The broad context concerns the shift from an industrial to a post-industrial society, with significant implications for work, learning, and the combination of the two. At a more specific level are the changes emerging from the use of new technologies which are being increasingly used for electronic-based methods of learning. In the subsequent sections, we elaborate upon change in higher education viewed through our 'dual lens' of the notions of lifelong learning and non-traditional students respectively. In the final section we attempt to summarise our argument by outlining a model of change in higher education.

The context: the transformation of higher education as part of the transformation of society

The change from an industrial to a post-industrial age is, as has been observed (Scott 1995, 1997), more than just a change of the prevailing system of production that was based on a highly structured division of labour, undifferentiated mass production, a hierarchical social order and linear careers. The educational system of that period was structured accordingly: a mass school system, heavily stratified in the European countries, and a small higher education system that served the existing ruling order and produced the graduates for elite positions in society. Thus graduates from elite institutions normally became political and business leaders, and the bureaucrats and professionals needed for key roles in such a class-based society.

With the gradual transformation to a more differentiated socio-economic order, the function of higher education is also changing. In Peter Scott's view this development has fundamental implications for students in higher education:

> The graduates of the future will have experienced a new kind of higher education, and come from and go into a new kind of society. Both will be, or already are, radically different from the standard twentieth century models,

the meritocratish elite higher education that has emerged as a result of the
. . . expansion of the higher education system . . ., and the urban, industrial,
bureaucratic welfare state that so decisively shaped personal aspirations,
social expectations and economic patterns during the two post-1945 generations. Mass higher education and post-fordist society are less the linear suc-
cessors of these earlier forms than their dialectical challengers.

(Scott 1997 p. 44)

Whether or not such a post-modern characterisation of the emerging society
is valid, it is certainly the case that there is a changed relationship between
higher education and the labour markets for its graduates. In the new
economy, highly paid, securely tenured, and stable career jobs which were the
norm for graduates are rarely guaranteed, yet unemployment for graduates is
still relatively small compared to general unemployment rates; and post-
secondary education is increasingly seen as a precondition for any job.

In such a changed climate, the legitimacy of educational policy is determined increasingly by its utility for employment purposes and its ability to
yield explicitly financial benefits for both the economy and the individual. For
higher education, this means pressure towards a greater emphasis on productivity, measurable outputs, and concentration on increasingly market-driven
criteria for education and research. Among other effects this has led to the
rapid development of information and communication technologies (ICTs).

These technologies are transforming the workplace and markets in many
ways. Setting up new rules of participation in the labour market and, more
generally, the economic process (Rubenson and Schuetze, 2000), they are also
beginning to have an impact on education. Already, some higher education
institutions are using the ICTs, particularly the Internet, to expand their programmes geographically in order to reach new learners beyond their traditional catchment areas. While in the (recent) past ICTs have been mainly
used as supplements for traditional forms of educational provision and delivery, electronic learning is increasingly being considered a real alternative to
classroom and library based forms of learning (El-Khawas 1999). Recognising
the market potential of these new forms of learning, new private for-profit
institutions are now competing in a market in which higher education institutions used to have a virtual monopoly.

They identify an attractive 'niche' program that also is low-cost to provide,
design the program with convenience factors that attract adults, and then
package it in ways that achieve standardisation and high volume, all to
result in efficient, cost-effective, and profitable programmes.

(El-Khawas 1999 p. 14)

Such convenience factors that attract working adults include flexible schedules, easily reached locations, readily accessible and easy-to-digest programmes, links to sites that provide additional information and sources of

knowledge, and communication channels that permit interaction with resource persons and fellow learners. Although initially slow to adapt to these new media, as the country studies in this volume show, an increasing number of higher education institutions are now diversifying their programmes and offering part or all of them in electronic mode, permitting students to pursue their degree work from their computer at home or in the workplace. While the overwhelming majority enrolled in higher education still study in the traditional mode, it is highly probable that increasing numbers of students will follow the e-learning route, making them, at least for the time being, 'non-traditional' students in higher education. On the other hand, the strong emphasis being placed on the use of new technologies, the proposed 'marriage of "lifelong" and "virtual" as a response to the problem of resourcing mass higher education' (Bourgeois *et al.* 1999 p. 175) will most likely benefit primarily the already educated and the economically and socially advantaged, thereby excluding many other students in the former 'non-traditional' category.

This brings us back to the premises underlying our 'dual lens': namely, that the concepts of 'lifelong learning' and 'non-traditional' are problematic and contested and require further elaboration.

Lifelong learning: for all?

Policy documents from various countries, as well as reports from intergovernmental organisations, in particular the EU (EC 1995), OECD (1996), and UNESCO (1996), uniformly promote lifelong learning as the foundation for educational and training policy. Success in realising lifelong learning is seen as an important factor in promoting employment, economic development, democracy and social cohesion (OECD 1996). In tracing the changes which undoubtedly have taken place across higher education systems it is however

> difficult to distinguish between the intended outcomes of this flurry of policies directed at reform and innovation, their unintended consequences, and the impact of changes in the nature of the student body which result from broader social and economic forces.
>
> (Slowey in this volume)

In making sweeping claims for lifelong learning in terms of providing the solution to a range of economic and social problems, the concept has become something of a 'New Jerusalem' (Rubenson and Schuetze 2000). As always with such generalised frameworks, it is not quite clear what it means and how educational strategies can be implemented to transform the present system into one of lifelong learning.

> In contrast to other far reaching reforms or new initiatives in education, the lifelong learning mandate poses a particularly complex resource chal-

lenge because it poses so many parameters at once. It implies: quantitative expansion of learning opportunities to widen access to all; qualitative changes in the content of existing educational activities; qualitatively and quantitatively different learning activities and new settings; and changes in the timing of learning activities over a lifetime.

(OECD 1999 p. 8)

The case studies in this volume confirm that in many countries, in particular Australia, New Zealand, Sweden, and the UK, the rush of policy papers on lifelong learning in the mid-1990s was heavily influenced by the skills agenda. While this may form the dominant definition of lifelong learning, several of the contributors (for example, Boshier and Benseman) point to a broader – and older – understanding of the concept tracing back to the 'Faure' report (UNESCO 1972). At a superficial level, lifelong learning can be held to relate to 'a process of further learning and continuous self-education throughout [all peoples] lives', based on three attributes: lifelong, lifewide, and motivation to learn (Cropley 1981 p. 189). The emphasis on 'lifelong' means that it is no longer possible, as it was during the period of the 1970s and 1980s when the notions of 'recurrent education' and 'éducation permanente' were being promulgated, to concentrate only on post-compulsory education, especially adult and higher education (Schuetze and Istance 1987, Slowey 1996). Lifelong learning embraces more than adult education, even widely defined. The individual's formative years are of crucial importance for learning how to learn, as well as stimulating the motivation to engage in further learning. Therefore pre-primary and primary education are also core elements of the concept.

The fact that lifelong learning is also 'life-wide' recognises the fact that learning occurs not just in schools, colleges or universities but in many different settings. In such a system of 'lifewide' learning, all forms and kinds of education are treated as being part of a single learning progression that requires mechanisms for assessing and recognising skills and competencies, whether acquired through formal or non-formal learning (OECD 1996). New forms of evaluation are emerging which are independent of particular educational institutions. One influential example is the International Literacy Survey (OECD 1995, 1997), as we see from the Australian, Canadian, Irish and New Zealand contributions to this volume.

A third element of lifelong learning relates to the stimulation of individual motivation to engage in learning beyond compulsory schooling. Lifelong and lifewide learning depend on the individual's possession of the personal and cultural capital necessary for engaging in the process. This principle is commonly discussed in terms of fostering the motivation and capacity for learning-to-learn, which puts into focus the quality of a person's early educational experience, and his or her social capital and employment position or, respectively, the 'long arm of the family' and the 'long arm of the job' (Rubenson and Schuetze 2000, Schuller and Burns 1999).

It is interesting to see how this aspect is built into the policy interpretation of lifelong learning in Japan. Along with the need for the acquisition of new skills and knowledge to keep pace with economic and social change there is a focus which arises from what has been termed the 'maturation' of Japanese society.

> This maturation is reflected in the increasing demand for learning as a means of achieving richness of spirit and a sense of purpose in life. In this sense . . . learning for pleasure is one of the rationales for lifelong learning in Japan.
>
> (Yamamoto, Fujitsuka and Honda-Okitsu in this volume)

So what does lifelong learning mean for institutions of higher education? What does it mean for 'non-traditional students'? Is it the case that the 'breadth of the concept has made it a convenient slogan and its over-use has threatened to undermine its significance and impact'? (James and Beckett in this volume).

Lifelong learning and changing conceptions of non-traditional learners

Despite the fact that the notion of lifelong learning is not only vague but is subject to a variety of conflicting interpretations (see, for example, the special issue of the *International Journal of Lifelong Education* 2000), the on-going policy debate has brought a new dynamic to the discourse about the future mission of, and necessary reforms in, higher education. The focus of lifelong learning on both the learner and the process of learning calls for a reappraisal of such conceptual concepts as 'non-traditional' students and 'non-traditional' ways of learning. In this new context, lifelong learning means the provision of 'opportunities for higher learning and for learning throughout life, giving to learners an optimal range of choice and a flexibility of entry and exit points within the system' (UNESCO 1996). Thus, to accommodate the needs of lifelong learners it is now normally accepted that institutions have to become much more open, flexible and responsive to the different circumstances and motivations of the much more heterogeneous student body.

Before the development of mass higher education it was relatively easy to define the characteristics of 'non-traditional students'. In fact they were defined *negatively* to include all those who had not entered directly from secondary school, or were not from the dominant social groups, or were not studying in a conventional mode. 'Traditional' students were primarily male, white and able-bodied and came from the upper socio-economic class, which meant they had sufficient financial support to their studies in full-time mode without having to generate income from working during the academic term. All those not fitting these characteristics were 'non-traditional'. Although they were not always systematically excluded from access to higher education, they were – and remained – outsiders, even if enrolled. 'Non-traditional students' in this old system were clearly a minority: women, members of ethnic minorities, disabled persons, those without the standard academic access qualifications from secondary school. Overarching all these characteristics, it was clear that social class was the primary determining element across all these groups, including standard-age students.

As the1987 OECD study showed, in many countries the non-traditional group was also particularly associated with adults who with, or mostly without, the requisite entrance qualifications had proceeded directly from school to work and came to higher education at later stages in their lives. During the years of rapid growth and the extension of many higher education systems, adults entered in greater numbers, leading to talk about 'the greying of the campus' or the 'adultification' of higher education. While this did not reflect what was occurring in the majority of universities, these labels were accurate in some particular institutions, units and programmes where 'mature' or adult students were to be found in greater numbers (Davies 1995). Other 'non-traditional' groups also increased in numbers, women in particular, who now form the majority in higher education overall in most 'developed' or late-capitalist countries, although they are not equally distributed among institutions, types of programmes or academic level.

Largely as a result of the growth of the adult student group, the majority of whom are in employment, the proportion of students studying part-time has also increased, even if this growth is not always linear and is particularly sensitive to policy and employment trends; Canada is a case in point (see Schuetze in this volume.) This growth has occurred even where part-time students are not officially recognised as such. In Austria and Germany, for example, all students have full-time status, although as the two country studies in this volume clearly show, it is known that this is a 'fiction' as many combine their studies with other activities, in particular paid employment.

Thus, at beginning of the new century, does it still make sense to talk about 'non-traditional' students? If so, by what characteristics are they distinct from other, 'traditional' students? After the great expansion of the system, along with the wide range of differentiation and diversification of institutions and programmes and the much more heterogeneous composition of the student body, can we still talk about 'traditional' or 'typical' students? As the discussion above has shown, this is clearly problematic.

It seems therefore more appropriate to talk about 'under-represented groups', indicating sections of the population that are not fully included in a system of lifelong learning for all. However, defining what is meant by 'under-represented groups' presents its own problems. Such groups are not homogeneous but include rather disparate sub-groups, whose learning needs and background differ widely.

It is also increasingly difficult to talk about adults as under-represented. The 1987 OECD study distinguished between four categories of adults:

- students who enter or re-enter higher education as adults in order to pursue mainstream studies leading to a full first degree or diploma ('delayers', 'deferrers', or 'second chancers', i.e. those who are admitted on credentials gained via work experience or second-chance educational routes)
- adults who re-enter to update their professional knowledge, or seek to acquire additional qualifications, in order to change occupation or advance in their career ('refreshers', 'recyclers')
- those without previous experience in higher education, who enrol for professional purposes especially in courses of short duration
- adults, with or without previous experience in higher education, who enrol for courses with the explicit purpose of personal fulfillment ('personal developers').

Pechar and Wroblewski in their contribution for this volume develop a new categorisation of traditional and non-traditional students, based on an extensive survey of university students in Austria. Their distinction is based on three variables:

- the nature of entrance qualifications (conventional or alternative)
- the timing of participation (directly from school or at a later stage)
- the mode of study (defined not by administrative criteria but according to the 'time budget' which is available to the individual to be a 'student' after meeting other external commitments, in particular paid employment).

Using this categorisation, 'traditional' students are those with regular entry qualifications, namely a baccalaureate certificate from a grammar or upper secondary school, who enrol in college or university immediately after graduation from school and study full-time. In contrast, 'non-traditional' students are admitted with alternative access qualifications which have been acquired through a secondary route or a special admission procedure, or their entry is deferred, or, because of employment commitments, for all practical purposes they are studying on a part-time basis. The authors show how the latter pattern represents an increasing trend for both adult *and* younger students in Austria. The fact that for administrative and other purposes part-time study is not recognised formally at either an institutional or policy level provides a striking illustration of the gap between higher education policy and practice and the reality of student experience.

In their study on non-traditional students in the United States, Horn and Carroll (1996) distinguish six different factors that make students 'non-traditional'. They assume that enrolments in higher education delayed by a year or more after high school, and students who attend part-time, do not fit into the traditional student category, and would therefore be termed non-traditional. Rather than setting arbitrary cut-off ages for 'older' students, they use an 'older than typical age' criterion. Therefore, the definition of non-traditional students includes students who terminated their study for a period of time, enrolled on part-time basis, or otherwise took longer to proceed even if they did not delay their first entry into higher education. Other criteria are the financial and family status of students. Non-traditional students are assumed not to be supported financially by their parents, and therefore compelled to work in order to support themselves. Also, they tend to have family responsibilities and family-related financial constraints, such as having dependants (other than a spouse), or being a single parent.

Since many of these attributes are closely interdependent, they are combined to form a scale ranging from 'minimally non-traditional' through 'moderately non-traditional' to 'highly non-traditional'. As the report on the situation in the USA shows (see Agbo in this volume), the use of such categories is of interest as they show in detail some of the changes in the sociological basis of the higher education student population. However, since the clear majority of American undergraduates (about 70 per cent in 1992) are at least 'minimally non-traditional', and about 50 per cent were either in the moderately or highly non-traditional categories, this new majority does not fit the image of the marginal, under-represented group that is normally associated with the term non-traditional. When in the United States almost one-half of the students are older than the 'typical' age group, it is difficult to argue that this group of students is under-represented.

The German case study (Wolter in this volume) develops another categorisation based on three criteria associated with entry routes, modes of study and nature of programme attended which yields six categories:

- those who take a vocational route to the achievement of the *Abitur* (the 'second educational route')
- special admission examinations (the 'third educational route')
- students with the *Abitur* who undertake vocational training or work experience before moving on to higher education (the 'double qualification' route)
- students studying on a part-time or distance mode basis
- graduates who return to higher education for continuing professional development courses (often of short duration)
- older adults taking continuing education courses largely for personal development purposes.

In fact in the late 1990s only 4 per cent of all new entrants to higher education in Germany entered through the first two of the above 'alternative routes', indicating more symbolic than real significance.

Another approach to defining the non-traditional student is adopted in the chapters on Australia (James and Beckett) New Zealand (Benseman and Boshier) Sweden (Bron and Agélii) and the UK (Slowey). This makes a direct connection with the discourse of equal opportunities. In the case of Australia, for example, equity groups are defined as including people with a disability, indigenous groups, people of non-English speaking background and people from rural areas.

Whichever approach is taken, common disparities and imbalances point to the need to retain a focus on the continuing significant social stratification in higher education, issues to which we turn in our concluding section.

Developments and reality in ten countries: towards a framework of change in higher education

Overview

Drawing on the country case studies we can identify six criteria, or dimensions, which appear to be more or less conducive to the participation of nontraditional students and under-represented groups. In several of the countries that were included in this study, public policies have had a major impact on access and participation; in others, especially the Anglo-American countries, it has been primarily market mechanisms that have been influential in causing some breaches in the walls of higher education while simultaneously erecting a number of new barriers.

Governance and control

This dimension relates to the degree of institutional flexibility which exists in relation to the organisation of study, the curriculum, policies regarding the institutions' overall profile and emphasis, and their role in such matters as regional development, service to the community and, especially, to nontraditional students and under-represented groups. One important determinant of such options arises from the degree of institutional autonomy and the decentralisation of decision-making from central state bureaucracy.

The six Anglo-Saxon countries provide evidence of a wide variety of responses to new groups of learners. Institutional autonomy, especially of universities, is, of course, a more prominent feature in these countries than in the continental European countries and Japan. On the other hand, although in most countries considered here the new universities or other types of higher education institutions tend to have lower degrees of autonomy (the ex-polytechnics in Britain being an exception), they have frequently been established with the explicit brief of providing programmes and modes of delivery aimed at accommodating what are perceived to be the requirements of non-traditional students. Examples include the community colleges in the US and Canada, the new *Fachhochschulen* in Austria and Junior Colleges in Japan.

Institutional differentiation

Another indicator of the extent of 'openness' to non-traditional learners concerns the degree of differentiation of system of tertiary education. It could be argued that both vertical and horizontal differentiation, by permitting a greater functional division of labour within the overall system, allow individual institutions to concentrate on what they define as their core mission and clientele. In all countries covered by this study we are seeing a progressive differentiation, and hence greater specialisation, of institutions. This development has the effect that traditional research universities can – and in most cases do – choose to concentrate on their traditional 'core' missions of research and initial education of the 'best' students (by traditional academic standards) leaving the task of catering for non-traditional students to newer, more vocational- and practice-oriented institutions. Examples include the 'elite' universities in the US, Britain, New Zealand and Japan. In contrast, there is some evidence to suggest that universities in countries that are less vertically diversified, such as Sweden and Canada, place a greater emphasis on accommodating non-traditional students.

In other words, in countries where the post-secondary system is much differentiated, the majority of non-traditional students tend to be enrolled in non-university institutions in two year colleges rather than four year institutions, and in vocational programmes rather than in academic ones. While, in theory, more traditional institutions, in particular the universities, have also widened access to a certain extent, their gates largely remain closed to students who lack conventional entry qualifications or the necessary financial means, or who have substantial work or domestic commitments, or some combination of all these factors.

Flexible (open) admissions criteria

'Flexible' or 'open admission' for those without traditional entry qualifications is an important criterion of the openness of systems. The case studies indicate that most countries have placed some degree of emphasis on public and institutional policies aimed at widening access to non-traditional learners. Almost all are able to point to special entry routes for non-traditional students which grant admission either on the grounds of specific characteristics of learners (for example, their age and/or their work experience) or on the basis of specific entrance examinations or requirements. In this respect, Sweden has probably the longest track record of innovation.

In some countries, such as Germany, the opening-up of a second major access route, via the completion of vocational education and training, has been very successful, and has thus reduced the importance of other alternative routes for would-be students without the usual academic entry qualification. In spite of such developments however, arguably the most important route to tertiary education is still via the completion of upper secondary education. In fact, the proportion of young people completing high school and progressing to tertiary education has increased in the last decade.

Participation and mode of study

Even where admissions criteria are (relatively) open, the doors to higher education may still remain closed in practice to large sections of the population.

Many non-traditional learners are either in employment, engaged in domestic responsibilities, living at a distance from a tertiary institution, or otherwise prevented from attending traditional forms of higher education, which are still largely characterised by campus-based tuition and by services, facilities and schedules designed for young, full-time students. Thus the existence of modes of study that accommodate the particular needs of non-traditional learners are important for their actual participation (and the eventual completion of their programmes). Examples of such flexible modes of study include open or distance learning possibilities, modular courses, credit transfer, and part-time study.

Two other, more recent, instruments are widely heralded as having enormous potential for facilitating access and participation of non-traditional students and lifelong learners: information and telecommunication technologies (ICTs) and mechanisms for the assessment and recognition of prior learning (APL/RPL).

In the US, arguably the least regulated and most diversified of all higher education systems, examples of all possible modes and combinations can be found. In other countries (the UK is a case in point) there has been a clear development towards more flexible modes of study, in particular with respect to modularisation of the curriculum. On the whole however, these developments have been slow. In those systems that are relatively tightly regulated and controlled by the state, such as Germany and Austria, there is little variety between institutions and a high degree of uniformity, in spite of the federal structure of these countries and a tradition of regional variations and cultures in most other aspects.

While *part-time study* has generally been on the rise over the last decade (even if it seems to have hit a ceiling in some countries such as in Canada and Sweden), there are still some countries which do not recognise the existence of part-time students. Thus, Austria and Germany base their organization of post-secondary studies on the assumption that all students pursue their studies full-time, even when this is known to be a fiction.

Arguably the most important changes in the last decade of the twentieth century were associated with the advent and swift dissemination and utilisation of new *information and communication technologies* (ICTs), in particular the Internet, which have the potential of changing the modes of participation and learning in a major way. In the field of distance and open learning, while the US appears to be leading the trend, other countries such as Australia and Canada are quickly following suit. Many countries can point to examples where traditional universities, some of them public, have started to set up independent organisations for the development and marketing of web-based courses. ICTs have also had an impact on the emergence of a new private sector of higher education providers.

There is plenty of speculation, though as yet little hard data, about the implications of such developments on teaching and learning in 'mainstream' higher education. However, most of the county studies suggest that in the near future these technologies may be expected to have a major impact on the participation of non-traditional learners and, more generally, lifelong learning. In this way, they may well prove more effective than public policy or traditional market mechanisms in bringing about greater access to advanced learning opportunities of hitherto under-represented groups. Of course, ICTs have their own barriers; these may be different from the traditional ones but equally effective in excluding some groups. As the rhetoric of policy makers about their great potential increases, the need for research into the effects of these technologies on learning in general, and under-represented groups in particular, becomes ever more a priority.

Financial and other support

In different ways, the case studies address the role finance plays in the decision whether or not to study. The availability of funding in the form of student grants and loans, for which older students, learners studying in a part-time mode or at a distance, or those enrolled on short-term or vocational programmes are eligible, is therefore another important criterion. There are other support mechanisms as well that are of special importance for non-traditional learners: support for those living in rural areas and for the disabled and, in particular, childcare facilities for single parents are examples.

The issue of financial support of non-traditional students is very complex. In most countries alternative financial schemes exist beside the student financing systems proper for which non-traditional students might qualify. The main student financing systems tend to discriminate, however, against some groups of non-traditional students or certain modes of study. Examples are the age ceilings in countries such as Germany, where generally students above the age of thirty are no longer eligible for financial support. Part-time students who were ineligible in all countries some fifteen years ago now qualify in some countries and under certain conditions, for example in the US. On the whole, conditions of eligibility and of the terms of support remain blurred, inconsistent and, in most countries, suffer from a lack of transparency.

Continuing education opportunities

Not all non-traditional learners aim to study as part of a formal degree course, or towards a higher education qualification. In fact, lifelong learners are most frequently seeking shorter courses or non-credit programmes. The availability of such courses or programmes in tertiary institutions is thus another indicator of their commitment to playing a part in a broader system of lifelong learning. While many of the case studies point to significant developments in relation to the area of continuing professional development, the same could not be said about provision aimed at catering for the broader educational needs of the community at large. In Australia, Canada,

New Zealand, the UK, and the US for example, continuing professional education provided by university and other tertiary institutions is relatively well developed and increasingly based on market principles – in contrast to the situation fifteen years ago.

In comparison, continuing higher education (whether professional or general) in countries such as Austria, Germany and Sweden is relatively underdeveloped, partly due to the existence of what are perceived to be well functioning sectors of adult and continuing education which operate outside the university sector.

In general however, there does seem to be a trend for the provision of professional continuing education to have moved, compared with the situation fifteen years ago, from the periphery of the institutions more towards core units. While this may have to do with the need of the latter to bring in resources from alternative sources, it also reflects the faster turn-over of knowledge, especially in the technical and science-based fields, and the concomitant need for professionals to update their knowledge in a more systematic way. Even in the light of this development it is probably correct to say that, overall, tertiary education institutions have not substantially embraced continuing education as part of their mainstream mission.

A framework of change

Summing up this brief overview of developments, it is fair to say that there has been both progress and stagnation but that in spite of the increasing student numbers from formerly 'non-traditional students', participation is uneven. Although some predominant patterns can be observed, we are still hesitant to draw general conclusions from developments in the ten different countries included in this volume. On the other hand, we do think that the dual conceptual lens of lifelong learning and non-traditional students have proved useful in illuminating common patterns of change across these higher education systems.

Two aspects in particular appear to us to be of significance.

Increasing differentiation of higher education providers

The expansion and increasing marketisation of higher education have been accompanied by increasing institutional differentiation. However, as the case studies confirm, traditional hierarchies of esteem remain largely untouched. It might even be argued that elitist rankings have been reinforced.

The summary statistics provided by the contributors to this volume demonstrate that, in most countries, the expansion in student numbers has been disproportionately located in the new institutions of higher education established from the 1960s through to the 1990s. This pattern is particularly evident in the cases of Austria, Australia, Germany, the UK and Japan. In addition, the analyses of some countries highlight the way in which institutions which traditionally would not have been included within the category of higher education now account for a growing proportion of programmes defined as higher education provision. These include, for example, the 'dual' technical and further education (TAFE) higher education institutions in Australia, the institutes of technology (IoTs) in Ireland, some provision in the community colleges of the United States and Canada, and the colleges of further education (FE) in the UK.

Nature of the student body

As the students in tertiary education become increasingly heterogeneous, the old distinction between traditional and non-traditional student becomes less useful. What is required is a more sophisticated analysis located within the defining parameters set by social class/socio-economic status, and the nature of the tertiary education to which access is gained. This framework must take into consideration the differing needs, interests, and circumstances of students, comprehending a complex interaction of factors such as age, gender, ethnicity, disability, employment status and family situation. 'Although expansion has been advanced in several countries as a means to bring into tertiary education those who have been under-represented, prior patterns in the social and economic mix of students persist throughout the OECD area' (OECD 1999 p. 67). This is certainly the predominant pattern as far as the elite universities are concerned in our case-study countries. The task of dealing with new types of learners is, in effect, left to particular institutions such as open universities, to certain new institutions of higher education, or to specific units such as adult education departments and continuing education centres. These strategies allow the traditional universities to retain institutional hurdles which continue to prevent all but the conventionally qualified standard age entrants from participating.

We attempt to summarise these trends as a model of change in Figure 1.1. In this diagram universities are located within the context of a broader range of tertiary (post-secondary) institutions. The inverted pyramid represents a reverse *hierarchical ranking* in terms of common perceptions of prestige (with the most elite institutions at the bottom, the least prestigious at the top). It also, for some countries, reflects the relative rates of expansion of the various sectors, with the college/new institution sector growing most rapidly.

Importantly, all tertiary institutions need to be viewed within the broader context of lifelong learning opportunities offered by a myriad of providers, including private training agencies, employers, community organisations, adult education, and, as we emphasised earlier, the rapidly growing range of e-education available via the Internet.

There is also some evidence of blurring of boundaries between 'formal' and 'nonformal' learning. This is exemplified by developments such as work-based learning partnerships between employers and tertiary institutions, and opportunities for the accreditation and assessment of learning which takes place

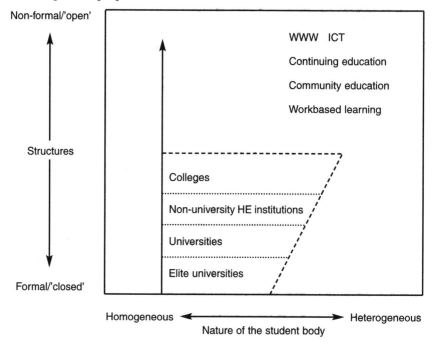

Figure 1.1 Higher education and lifelong learning: a framework of change

outside universities and colleges. It is interesting to note in passing that as the examples of institutions which are essentially quality assurance and validating bodies rather than educational providers grows in number, higher education could be reduced to a 'gate-keeping' function holding on to its (near) monopoly on the award of degrees and similar qualifications.

Along the horizontal axis of Figure 1 there is a continuum representing the nature of the student body. Rather than using the terms traditional and non-traditional – a distinction we have found to be blurred by recent developments – we find it more useful to address diversity on a *homogeneous–heterogeneous* scale. In different ways almost all tertiary institutions are increasingly dealing with a more diverse group of learners, whether they are highly qualified professionals returning for updating or 'second' chance students from under-represented groups. However, as the whole thrust of this argument has emphasised, the increasing numbers of new learners are concentrated in the new institutions.

Along the vertical axis there is a continuum representing the extent to which access to the provision or institution (or 'learning opportunity') is relatively 'open' or 'closed'. In this context, open or closed relates largely to the nature of the entry criteria. The case studies clearly demonstrate the continuing domination of conventional school leaving qualifications for entry to the higher status institutions. At the boundaries of the system there is, however, evidence of an increasing variety of access pathways including, for example, vocational routes to higher education and access programmes for adults.

Overall, our interpretation of the country studies points in the directions of change indicated by the arrow in Figure 1.1. The trends are indeed towards increasing diversity in the student body, towards increasing participation levels, and towards expansion of the range of tertiary learning opportunities.

However, when it comes to fundamental matters of equity we discern little evidence of change. In fact we would go further. It seems to us that rather than challenging existing social and economic inequalities, the increasing marketisation and differentiation of higher education actually works to allow the tertiary system to expand without questioning, let alone altering, existing hierarchies. It is true that the lifelong learning concept carries the potential for transformation in the relations between individual learners, higher education and the broader society; we are seeing ladders thrown over the walls of the academy – or at least some parts of the academy – allowing access for new learners and the exploration of new forms of knowledge. However, the analysis here indicates that progress is not only somewhat uneven but at an early stage, and it remains an open question whether or not lifelong learning seems likely to produce a more progressive, egalitarian outcome or not.

References

Barnett, R. (1992) *The Idea of Higher Education*, Buckingham: Society for Research into Higher Education/Open University Press.

Bourgeois, E., Duke, C., Guyot, J. L. and Merrill, B. (1999) *The Adult University*, Buckingham: Society for Research into Higher Education/Open University Press.

Cropley, A. J. (1981) 'Lifelong learning and systems of education: an overview', in A. J. Cropley, *Towards a System of Lifelong Education*, Oxford: Pergamon Press.

Davies, P. (ed.) (1995) *Adults in Higher Education: International Perspectives in Access and Participation*, London: Jessica Kingsley.

Duke, C. (1992) *The Learning University*, Buckingham: Society for Research into Higher Education/Open University Press.

EC (European Commission) (1995) *Teaching and Learning: Towards the Learning Society*, Luxembourg: Office for Official Publications of the European Union.

El-Khawas, E. (1999) 'The "new" competition: serving the learning society in an electronic age', *Higher Education Management* vol. 11 no. 2.

Halsey, A. H. (1992) 'An International Comparison of Access to Higher Education', in D. Phillips (ed.) *Lessons of Cross-National Comparison in Education*, Wallingford: Triangle Books.

Horn, L. J. and Carroll, C. D. (1996) *Nontraditional Undergraduates: Trends in Enrollment from 1986 to 1992 and Persistence and Attainment Among 1989–90 Beginning Postsecondary Students* (Report no. NCES 97–578), Washington, D.C.: NCES.

International Journal of Lifelong Education (2000) Special issue on lifelong learning, vol. 19 no. 1.

OECD (1987) *Adults in Higher Education*, Paris: OECD.

—— (1995) *Literacy, Economy and Society: Results from the First International Adult Literacy Survey*, Paris: OECD.

—— (1996) *Lifelong Learning for All*, Paris: OECD.

—— (1997) *Literacy Skills for the Knowledge Society*, Paris: OECD.

—— (1998) *Redefining Tertiary Education*, Paris: OECD.

—— (1999) *Education Policy Analysis*, Paris: OECD.

Rubenson, K. and Schuetze, H. G. (1995) 'Learning at and through the workplace: a review of participation and adult learning theory', in D. Hirsch and D. Wagner (eds) *What Makes Workers Learn? The Role of Incentives in Workplace Education and Training*, Cresskill, N.J.: Hampton.

—— (2000) 'Lifelong learning for the knowledge society: demand, supply and policy dilemmas', in K. Rubenson and H. G. Schuetze (eds) *Transition to the Knowledge Society: Policies and Strategies for Individual Participation and Learning*, Vancouver: UBC (Institute for European Studies).

Schuetze, H. G. and Istance, D. (1987) *Recurrent Education Revisited: Modes of Participation and Financing*, Stockholm: Almqvist and Wiksell.

Schuller, T. and Burns, A. (1999) 'Using "social capital" to compare performance in continuing education', in F. Coffield (ed.) *'Why's the Beer Always Stronger Up North?' Studies in Lifelong Learning in Europe*, Bristol: Economic and Social Research Council/Policy Press.

Scott, P. (1995) *The Meanings of Mass Higher Education*, Buckingham: Society for Research into Higher Education/Open University Press.

—— (1997) 'The postmodern university?' in A. Smith and F. Webster (eds) *The Postmodern University? Contested Visions of Higher Education in Society*, Buckingham: Society for Research into Higher Education/Open University Press.

Slowey, M. (1996) 'Universities and lifelong learning: issues in widening access', in T. Winter-Jensen (ed.) *Challenges to European Education: Cultural Values, National Identities and Global Responsibilities*, Frankfurt am Main: Peter Lang.

Trow, M. (1973) *Problems in the Transition from Elite to Mass Higher Education*, Berkeley: Carnegie Commission on Higher Education.

UNESCO (1972) *Learning to Be: The World of Education Today and Tomorrow* (the 'Faure' report), Paris: UNESCO.

—— (1996) *Learning: The Treasure Within* (The 'Delors' report), Paris: UNESCO.

Wagner, A. (1999) 'Lifelong learning in the university: a new imperative', in W. Z. Hirsch and L. E. Weber (eds) *Challenges Facing Higher Education at the Millennium*, New York: American Council on Education/Oryx Press.

Part II
Europe

2 Austria

The enduring myth of the full-time student: an exploration of the reality of participation patterns in Austrian universities

Hans Pechar and Angela Wroblewski

Background

For more than three decades, higher education systems in OECD countries have been in a permanent process of turmoil and restructuring. The expansion of the student population coupled with the dynamics of knowledge production have resulted in growing complexity and uncertainty.

One of the perceived problems confronting Austrian higher education is what is termed 'the long duration of studies'. On average, students take seven and a half years to complete their first degree. This has become an urgent issue for higher education policy but, as this chapter will demonstrate, this debate is often conducted in a superficial way. There are various reasons for the 'long duration of studies', including the widely neglected fact that many students are in employment. This chapter tries to make an unbiased contribution to objectivising the debate. First, some features of Austrian universities which contribute to the 'long duration' will be discussed. Second, the chapter will summarise a recent major empirical study which presents some evidence about the study conditions of different types of students. Third, we will draw policy conclusions which may have implications beyond the Austrian system.

The policy context

Austrian universities are a good example of what Clark (1983) describes as a state model of higher education:

- Universities are state agencies, owned by the federal government and governed by the ministry.[1]
- All university matters including admission of students, the curriculum, and quality control are heavily regulated by federal law.
- Academics are civil servants and are employed by the federal government; professors are appointed by the minister.

- Universities are almost entirely funded by the federal budget; no university is allowed to charge fees.

The basic characteristics of this state model of higher education have deep historical roots.[2] For centuries, the university was an elite institution which enrolled only a small proportion of the age group. For an elite institution the state model was quite appropriate, and problems developed in the course of the mass expansion of higher education that started in the 1960s.[3]

During the 1970s and 1980s Austria experienced an extraordinary increase of enrolments in post-secondary institutions. The total number of students rose from 52,000 in 1970 to 189,000 in 1990 (Table 2.1). This massive expansion was partly caused by demographic factors (high birth rates) and partly by growing participation rates (Table 2.2). The expansion was strongest in universities, where the number of students more than quadrupled between 1970 and 1990. At that time Austria had not diversified its higher education system, so universities had virtually a monopoly. However, the traditional university was not capable of handling this extensive massification, and it soon became evident that the quantitative expansion had to be accompanied by structural reforms.

For more than three decades, Austrian higher education has been in an almost permanent process of turmoil and change. In a first cycle of reforms during the 1960s and early 1970s, the nature of the state model was not

Table 2.1 Enrolment of Austrian students in universities and other types of post-secondary institutions, 1970/1–1995/6

	1970/1	1975/6	1980/1	1985/6	1990/1	1995/6
Universities	43,122	68,292	100,114	141,144	170,304	189,614
Universities of arts	1,457	3,052	3,744	4,372	4,683	4,359
Other post-secondary	7,432	13,073	12,678	12,082	13,844	16,699
Total	52,011	84,417	116,536	157,598	188,831	210,672

Source: BMWV.

Table 2.2 Changes in demography and participation rates, 1970–96

	Population aged 18 to 26	Students aged 18 to 26	Ratio of students to population of same age (%)
1970/1	796,704	32,281	4.1
1975/6	836,550	50,342	6.0
1980/1	919,337	74,055	8.1
1985/6	1,009,647	98,409	9.7
1990/1	930,593	107,745	11.6
1995/6	752,088	103,955	13.8

Source: BMWV.

challenged, in fact it could be argued that the federal government strengthened its power of guidance during that time. Developments over that period included:

- a reform of the study law, designed to make the curriculum more relevant for external stakeholders
- a reform of the organisational law, designed to make the university more democratic
- the introduction of a number of new post-secondary institutions with a more structured curriculum.[4]

The expansion of the 1960s and 1970s led to growing diversity and complexity in higher education:

- a diversity of students in terms of talent, expectations, and motivation
- a diversity of academics in terms of status, activities and interests
- a diversity of labour market demands which at the same time are rapidly changing
- a range of acts and regulations passed during that time which turned the university into a cumbersome and complex institution.

This increasingly complex mass higher education system became progressively more difficult to control from the political centre. During the 1980s there was growing dissatisfaction with the status quo among all actors including academics, students, politicians, and state bureaucrats. It became more and more evident that the higher education system, the universities in particular, did not appear to be adapting to the new realities of mass participation. Issues which were increasingly debated among policy makers were:

- Is a single-tier system still appropriate or should a more formal distinction between a first (undergraduate) and a second (graduate) cycle be introduced?
- Does the Humboldtian model still make sense? Is it feasible to include all students in research?
- Should universities have the right to admit and select their students? What are the implications of an open access policy, if enrolments are not linked to funding?
- What is the appropriate share of decision-making power between the government and the university?

Various indications of a crisis (e.g. an unsatisfactory teacher/student ratio, high drop-out rates, the long duration of studies) led to a change of paradigm in higher education policy. A consensus emerged that the state should cut down its regulation and grant more autonomy to universities. However, it remained highly controversial what conclusions should be drawn from this principle. Basically, there were two main paths to deregulation and decentralisation of Austrian higher education:

- On the one hand, a series of modifications to the traditional university sector were carried through, such as a second reform of university organisation, a new reform of the study law, the introduction of procedures for evaluation, and so on.[5]
- On the other hand, a completely new '*Fachhochschul*'-sector was established in 1993. The main rationale for this reform was to offer short-cycle alternatives to universities with strong links to the labour market. However, *Fachhochschulen* also differ from universities in terms of organisation and funding. They are not state agencies, but autonomous corporations and receive a 'lump sum' budget.

At the end of the 1990s, three post-secondary sectors can be distinguished, each with a different size, different patterns of institutional management, and different cultures of teaching and learning.

- The 'liberal types' of higher education comprise twelve universities and six universities of art and music. This sector has a total of 214,000 students (1995/6), which is almost 90 per cent of enrolment in post-secondary education. There is significant variance in the size of individual universities. At the University of Vienna, some 74,000 students are enrolled, at some special universities there are 2,000–3,000 students, while most colleges of art and music have only a few hundred students.
- The '*Fachhochschul*'- sector is still a small one (4,000 students in 1996/7) and will grow slowly. However, this new sector receives a lot of public attention as a model for higher education reform.
- 'School-like' institutions include colleges for teacher training, for social workers, and for paramedics. Enrolment here amounts to about 10 per cent of all post-secondary students. There are efforts to upgrade those institutions as part of higher education.

The differences between the various sectors can be defined according to four main features:

Reputation and formal recognition of degrees

There are differences between the liberal types of higher education and *Fachhochschulen* on the one hand, and the rest of the post-secondary institutions on the other hand. As regards the Austrian use of the term, the latter are not considered to be part of higher education ('*Hochschulsystem*').[6] This distinction is not just an 'old-fashioned' use of language but has an impact on administration and, more importantly, on the recognition of degrees.

Universities and *Fachhochschulen* are administered by the Ministry of Science and Research. The rest of post-secondary education is (together with the schools) administered in a more centralised fashion by the Ministry of Education. Domestic recognition of degrees varies significantly. Graduates from universities and *Fachhochschulen* (*Magister* or *Diplomingenieur*), but not from other post-secondary institutions, meet the entrance requirements for the top category of civil service (A-grade civil servants). Accordingly, there are different rules for transfer: '*Fachhochschul*'-graduates may start a doctor's programme, degrees at other post-secondary institutions are not recognised at universities.

Institutional autonomy

The liberal types of higher education and the school-like institutions of post-secondary education are state agencies, whereas the *Fachhochschulen* are independent. In a strict legal sense, *Fachhochschulen* are private institutions.[7] However, one cannot speak of a strictly private ownership. They are 'quasi-private' institutions where public bodies join the associations, or are shareholders of the companies which legally own the institutions. Nevertheless, there are huge differences between Fachhochschulen and all other types of post-secondary education with respect to legal regulation. Both liberal and school-like institutions are subject to tight regulation in terms of organisation, personnel and study courses.[8] Federal law for *Fachhochschulen*, on the other hand, provides a fairly open legal framework for the activities of the individual institutions.

Admission

There is 'open access' to universities since all citizens who hold a final certificate of the elite track of upper secondary education ('*Matura*') are entitled to enrol at any Austrian university and in any field of studies for as long as they wish to do so. There is no '*numerus clausus*' which would allow the rejection of students due to limited resources. *Fachhochschulen* and other post-secondary institutions, on the other hand, can only admit students on the basis of available study places, because their teaching culture requires that the number of students is linked to the number of teachers and other resources.

Culture of teaching and learning

Similar patterns to the above can be observed in other differences between liberal types of higher education on the one hand, and *Fachhochschulen* and other post-secondary institutions on the other. At universities, the liberal admission policy is reflected in a curriculum which is strongly shaped by the Humboldtian tradition. From the very first semester onwards students are assumed to be 'apprentice researchers', who are capable of conducting their studies in a completely independent way. It is up to them whether they attend lectures and seminars or not; the duties of academics are equally relaxed. A need for guidance and monitoring by the staff is not normally considered part of the system. Students are not supposed to be pupils who need help, but mature persons who should be able to learn independently. At *Fachhochschulen* and other post-secondary institutions, on the other hand, students are confronted with a rather 'school-like' curriculum. Both students and academics are supposed to meet more explicit obligations than at universities.

The long duration of university studies: or the domination of the concept of the full-time student

The differences between the three sectors of Austrian higher education result in a paradoxical situation. Universities, which are the institutions with the highest status and reputation, have the least control over their students. On the one hand, the open access policy at universities does not allow them to link student numbers to resources. In contrast to this, *Fachhochschulen* and academies select their students on the basis of available study places. Another aspect of the paradox is that the culture of teaching and learning at universities makes it difficult to define precise obligations. While studies in other types of higher education have a relatively structured and clear-cut shape, universities are characterised by an almost chaotic picture. Students come and go as they like, their progress is not monitored by their teachers, partly because it is impossible to do so (due to lack of information and control), partly because the the teachers do not consider it their task. Many of those enrolled are in fact students on paper only, but a precise distinction between active students and 'paper students' is impossible.

One aspect is of particular interest. Formally, Austria has only full-time students. In the non-university sectors of higher education the school-like type of curriculum indeed requires full-time study and presence during the day. At universities, however, there are no such requirements. Therefore many study part-time only, although they are officially labelled full-time students. Part-time studies can have many reasons, but the most frequent one is that many students are employed on a part-time or even full-time basis. Until the present study, empirical data about working students in Austria was scarce.

It is quite obvious at first sight that these features of universities, especially the 'hidden' part-time studies due to employment, are strongly related to one of the most debated issues in Austrian higher education policy: the long duration of university studies. It is bad enough that the drop-out rate is higher than 50 per cent; but those students who complete their studies on average take seven and a half years for their first degree. This situation is hardly satisfying and there are good reasons why the government and social partners are calling for a change. Industry in particular is seriously concerned about the fact that graduates spend too many of their most productive years at university and are 'too old' when they finally enter the labour market.

The reality is that there are many reasons why students take a long time to graduate. While delayed graduation may certainly be associated with a lack of motivation on the part of individual students, it may also be caused by structural factors beyond the students' control. Such factors may, for example, include teaching methods which are not geared to the needs of the students or significant shortages in laboratory facilities which lead to what is frequently referred to as an 'involuntary waiting time' for students. Unfortunately, the *laissez-faire* character of Austrian universities makes it extremely difficult to differentiate between the various reasons for the long duration of studies, or between the different types of 'long-term students'. As a result, the long duration of studies is mostly debated in a rather superficial way. Since little empirical evidence was available until recently, the discussion is dominated by strongly held, but unproven beliefs.

Obviously, the problem of the long duration of studies looks quite different if one takes into consideration that many students combine their studies with employment. Some supposed problems might be less dramatic than policy-makers would claim. Part-time students make only part-time use of university resources, so it is not clear that their studies are more expensive, even if they take more time to complete their courses. On the other hand, some problems which are not discussed at all become quite urgent. Do universities offer adequate conditions for students who need considerable flexibility in their schedules?

Why have these questions been neglected? One reason is the notion of the 'traditional student' which dominates the policy debate in Austria. Academics and policy-makers alike think of students as young persons who enrol at university immediately after the completion of secondary school and who study full-time. This is a normative view rather than an empirical one and it is known that an increasing number of students do not fit into it. Yet, from their statements and policy actions it appears that most decision-makers seem to think that non-traditional students should be an exception and that the majority of students should live up to the traditional idea of a student. Accordingly, the needs of non-traditional students are not taken very seriously. The aim of our empirical study, which will be summarised in the following section, was to confront this normative idea with some empirical insights concerning the lives, study conditions and needs of today's actual students.

Empirical findings

The starting point of the study to which we now mainly refer was the empirical evidence of the increasing number of students who do not correspond to the concept of 'traditional students'.[9] In Kellermann's terms (1991) 'traditional students' are those who enter university immediately after getting their final certificate of the elite track of upper secondary education, the so called *Matura* (or a year later in the case of men who complete their public or military service immediately after graduating from upper secondary school), and who have the opportunity to use their entire time budget for their studies. This means that they do not work during the course of their studies, with the exception of occasional jobs during vacation time. This concept of a student underlies Austrian higher education policy and is the basis for the discussion about the situation of non-traditional students. Several indicators in the official higher education statistics, however, suggesting an increasing number of working students or students with children, as well as a rising average age of students at enrolment or a rising average duration of studies, have been discussed in recent years.

Those involved in higher education policies had become aware of a rising number of non-traditional students, but until the study there was little reliable empirical information about the extent of non-traditional students or about their living and studying conditions. Furthermore, there is not just one group of non-traditional students but a highly heterogeneous group of students in which each subgroup is faced with different living and studying conditions. A large-scale survey was, therefore, conducted to inform the discussion with empirical findings about the extent and conditions of traditional and non-traditional students in Austria. Its aim was to collect empirical data about different factors which differentiate traditional and non-traditional students. In the course of the research project, different types of 'non-traditional students' were defined. These are distinguished by means of three dimensions:

- type of university entry ('regular', i.e. by means of *Matura*, or 'alternative', i.e. by means of a '*Studienberechtigungsprüfung*')[10]
- time of entry into the university system (immediately after the *Matura*, or delayed)
- intensity of study (full-time or part-time, depending on whether time for study was restricted by work or family-related responsibilities).

The main conclusion of the study is that, for policy purposes, it is simply not adequate to speak of of *students* in general. There are several distinct groups of students with different conditions of living and studying who are confronted with different problems during the various stages of their studies.

In the following discussions we present some of the results which indicate the extent of non-traditional students, as defined in terms of to the three dimensions mentioned above. We then concentrate in a more detailed way on the situation of students who are employed during the semester (working students), the biggest single group of non-traditional students.

Using the three dimensions of entry route, time of entry and intensity of studies, an interesting typology can be developed. We find, in fact that only 28 per cent of the students belong to the group of 'traditional' or 'regular' students (i.e. those entering via the regular entry route, directly from compulsory education/school and with few or no external commitments) which, up to now, has been the focus of higher education politics.

Key findings include:

Type of university entry

One out of two students entered university immediately after gaining their *Matura*, but at this point in time they have only a reduced time budget at their disposal. About 3 per cent of the students enter university later, and study full-time. However, most of the students with delayed entry have a reduced time budget, i.e. they study part-time.

About 4 per cent of the students have an alternative university entry. This is one of the smaller groups of non-traditional students, and for years a target group of higher education policy. Efforts to widen the access to higher education mostly address this special group of students.

Time of entry in the university system

One out of five students has a delayed university entry, and 61 per cent of these students have been in employment prior to enrolment. This is usually done for financial reasons (earning a living, trying to gain independence from one's parents). Another explanation for delayed entry which was mentioned quite often was the desire to obtain an alternative kind of education, or the wish to establish oneself in another profession. There is a slightly higher occurrence of women with a delayed university entry than of men (22 per cent of all female students but 16 per cent of male students).

Intensity of studies

Nevertheless, the most important factor the typology relates to is the amount of time available for study. We speak of a reduced time budget if some kind of employment is pursued during the course of the semester or, particularly for women, if there are duties resulting from child-care. Employment is definitely predominant, especially when there are children to be provided for; an additional income is required in most cases. Compared to men, women more frequently have a reduced time budget at their disposal.

Because of the importance of employment in defining 'non-traditional' students, the remainder of the discussion will concentrate on the situation of working students compared to non-working students.[11] The main questions are:

- How do the studying and living conditions of traditional and working students differ from each other?
- Are there particular problems confronting working students?
- Which measures could be taken in order to facilitate the compatibility of university-related and non-university-related (job or family-related) responsibilities?

Some socio-demographic characteristics

Altogether, the respondents comprise equal proportions of men and women. As we will see gender-specific differences emerge in regard to the student typology and the field of studies.

As mentioned above, about 28 per cent of all students correspond to the picture of 'traditional' students. Men belong slightly more often to the 'traditional' group (30 per cent) than women (25 per cent), but there are hardly any differences concerning the proportion of working students by gender (70 per cent of male and 69 per cent of female students are employed during the semester). These differences result from the fact that women more often have a delayed university entry. Further gender specific differences may be noticed with regard to the field of studies. The field of engineering is still male dominated, whereas women are more likely to be found in the humanities.

In terms of the field of study, there are also differences in terms of the presence of traditional and working students. The highest proportion of traditional students can be found in engineering, followed by law, where one out of three students has a traditional student history. In the humanities one can find the highest proportion of working students, including an above average number of students with a delayed or alternative university entry. The number of traditional and working students in the social and economic sciences corresponds to the average. In the social or economic sciences or engineering, about half of the students enrolled immediately after graduating from upper secondary school, but at the time of the survey they were only able to study with a reduced time budget. The proportion of students in the field of social/economic sciences who enter university later is clearly lower than the corresponding numbers found in the humanities. Engineering students only rarely have a delayed university entry or an alternative university entry.

The age *bracket* of the persons surveyed ranges between nineteen and seventy years, and the average age is twenty-four years (men: twenty-five years, women: twenty-four years). Correspondence to a specific student type changes significantly with age. While the youngest students correspond closest to the image of traditional students, the proportion of non-traditional

Table 2.3 Proportions of 'traditional' and working students by field of studies

	Traditional students (%)	Working students (%)	Other non-traditional students (%)*
Law	31.9	65.2	2.9
Social/economic sciences	25.4	71.8	2.8
Humanities	17.0	73.3	9.7
Engineering	35.7	64.3	0.0
Total	27.5	69.2	3.3

* students with alternative or delayed university entry.

Table 2.4 Traditional and working students by age

	Traditional students (%)	Working students (%)	Other non-traditional students (%)*
Less than 20 years	18.1	5.6	4.6
21–25 years	65.5	48.2	36.8
26–30 years	13.8	31.4	36.2
More than 31 years	2.6	14.8	22.4
Total	100.0	100.0	100.0
Average age	23.1 years	26.3 years	27.9 years

* students with alternative or delayed university entry.

students grows with age, since older students are clearly more likely to be employed. It is also obvious that not only does the status of students change over time (from traditional to working student) but also their living conditions and family background.

In most cases the necessity for employment occurs when students leave their parents' household and start living alone or with a partner (cf. BMWV 1999). Therefore the majority of the younger, traditional students still live with their parents or in a student hostel. Older students, who tend to live in their own apartment or house and are more likely to have their own family, have to earn a living on their own. Altogether, 10 per cent of the students already have children and live with them most of the time. Differences between traditional and non-traditional students become apparent in the different means of covering their living costs. Traditional students are mainly supported by their parents who pay most of their bills (81 per cent), or they receive a student grant (16 per cent). Working students earn most of their living from gainful employment, but many still receive financial support from their parents or are entitled to student assistance. Table 2.5 shows that about half of the working students earn the major part of their living themselves, whereas for the other half earned income is supplementary to parental support or student assistance.

Table 2.5 Traditional and working students by means of covering living costs

	Traditional students (%)	Working students (%)	Other non-traditional students (%)*
Employment	2.2	49.4	20.7
Partner	1.3	2.2	19.3
Parents	80.7	43.4	34.8
Student assistance	15.7	4.9	25.2
Total	100.0	100.0	100.0

* students with alternative or delayed university entry.

Table 2.6 Traditional and working students by social class

	Traditional students (%)	Working students (%)	Other non-traditional students (%)*
Working class	17.9	17.6	23.4
Lower middle class	23.8	25.4	25.5
Upper middle class	32.6	29.2	24.1
Upper class	25.7	27.8	26.9
Total	100.0	100.0	100.0

* students with alternative or delayed university entry.

In terms of the social status, more than half of the students come from the upper middle class or upper class.[12] Obvious class-specific differences emerge in relation to the typology of students developed in this study. While most students came from upper middle class and upper class backgrounds, a higher proportion of working and other non-traditional students came from working class and lower middle class backgrounds.

Nature and extent of employment of students

It has already been pointed out that the key factor distinguishing between traditional and non-traditional students is that of employment. 'Employment' can be defined in different ways. The range of possible definitions ranges from 'typical student jobs', which are used to provide additional finance for studies (e.g. temporary work in the restaurant business, messenger jobs, warehouse jobs, tutoring) through to permanent and registered full or part-time positions. In the following, every kind of employment during the semester, irrespective of the scale or kind of work, is taken into account, since it is the *reduction of the time budget* that is decisive for the typology developed here.

All in all, almost 16 per cent of the students work in a regular full-time job during the semester, 23 per cent have a part-time job (mostly salaried employees, officials, and clerks). Slightly more than a quarter (27.6 per cent) are intermittently employed during the semester (frequently on the basis of a work and service contract). Around 17.6 per cent of all the people questioned work only during holidays, and 15.7 per cent do not work at all. It has already been mentioned that the proportion of regularly full- or part-time employed students becomes significantly higher with increasing age. Students who already had a job prior to their studies, that is, students with a delayed university entry, are much likely to be employed on a regular basis.

To what extent can it be said that students are working for a living? Students with a full-time position work forty-one hours per week on average, those with a part-time job work seventeen hours, and those who are employed on a non-regular basis during the semester work eight hours per

Table 2.7 Extent of students' employment by age

	<21 years	*21–25 years*	*26–30 years*	*>30 years*	*Total*
Regular full-time employed	0.4	6.5	23.7	50.8	16.0
Regular part-time employed	13.8	23.8	27.1	18.1	23.1
Non-regularly employed					
during the semester	27.6	31.4	26.7	13.6	27.6
Holiday jobs	33.2	22.3	10.8	1.6	17.6
Not employed	25.0	16.0	11.7	15.9	15.7
Total	100.0	100.0	100.0	100.0	100.0

week. Intermittently employed students earn about ATS 3,500 per month, part-time workers have an average income of about ATS 6,200 and full-time workers get ATS 17,400 per month.[13]

Employed students mostly work in jobs that call for quite high qualifications. The so-called 'typical student jobs' are mentioned only rarely. Far more frequently students are in occupations such as banking, accounting, other office-related work, data processing, and jobs in the social or educational fields.

A study by the Labour Market Office (AMS 1997) shows that on entering the job market it is not only essential for a university graduate to possess professional skills; they must also be complemented by social skills. In particular, relevant work experience, which helps in acquiring both professional and social skills, is taken to be the key to a successful start of a career. At the same time, businesses pay increasing attention to the length of time students need for studies, as early graduation is taken as an indicator of goal orientation and efficiency. These requirements of the job market expose the students to a double dilemma, since on the one hand they are expected to complete their studies as soon as possible, but at the same time they are forced to work either because they need money or because the demands of the job market force them into employment.

Reasons for employment

Our survey shows that employment is based on practice-related as well as on financial motives. While in terms of financial motives there are hardly any differences between the students in each single field of studies, it is apparent, that practice-related motives also play quite a significant role for students of engineering and the social and economic sciences. The importance that the students attach to relevant practical experience is quite understandable. In order to improve their chances in a certain profession students of the social and economic sciences as well as the humanities are generally encouraged to acquire the relevant work experience as early as possible in the course of their studies. In contrast, graduates in a technical field of study are not expected to have as much work experience, but more importance is attached completing their studies in the shortest possible time.

Table 2.8 Importance of financial and practice-related motives by subject

	Financial motives[14]	Practice-related motives[15]
Law	2.37	3.21
Social/Economic Sciences	2.23	2.57
Humanities	2.19	2.88
Engineering	2.39	2.56
Total	2.28	2.75

Note: these results represent the average result derived from student answers, based on a scale on which 1 = 'totally agree' and 5 = 'do not agree at all'.

Employment-related advantages and problems

What are the advantages and problems connected to employment from the students' point of view? The primary *advantage* of employment lies in the acquisition of practical experience. About three-quarters of the students in economics, engineering and the humanities are able practically to apply the knowledge they acquired during the course of their studies; the same goes for half of the law students. Slightly more than half of the students who are employed state that their employment brings about advantages in their studies (e.g. because they work more goal-oriented and efficiently).

Among the *disadvantages* that arise with employment are a delay in university graduation and the difficulties in combining employment and study. Approximately one out of two students expect to delay the completion of their studies, while slightly more than a third have time-related problems in combining studies and a job. These problems multiply with increasing hours of employment.

The problem which was mentioned most frequently by working students is the reduced time budget in general. Organisational problems and time-related problems arising from course participation are named less frequently. More often they have to deal with problems related to the opening hours of libraries, dean's offices and institutes, though these affect not only working students but also traditional ones.

Whenever students have to work as well as study the question arises which one of these two areas has priority. For almost two-thirds of the working students, the priority lies with their studies, whereas for those who are employed full-time their job comes first. It is also apparent that working students who study in order to obtain a second degree or for their doctor's degree also attach more importance to their jobs.

Choice of subject and study motives

One of the main questions of this research study was whether, as defined by our typology, traditional and non-traditional students differ with regard to their choice of study as well as their study motives. In this context it could be hypothesised that different sources of advice and information are utilised.

These differences become apparent as traditional students ask for the advice of friends, acquaintances or vocational counsellors. They also obtain information through study or vocational guidance and the media, even though they state that they make the final decision on their own. Students with job experience on the other hand seem more inclined to arrive at a decision without using further sources of information.

What are the key motives which inform the choice of subject to study? The statement most people agreed with (70 per cent) was 'I attend university to broaden my horizon'. This rather general (and not directly employment-oriented) statement was made by students with delayed or alternative university entry at an above-average rate. On the other hand, students with immediate university entry are more likely to indicate employment-related reasons, in other words they expect better opportunities in the job market after completion of their studies. Traditional students primarily expect their studies to provide them with a basis for their future jobs, whereas beginners who already have job experience rather hope to develop additional employment-related knowledge and to broaden their horizons.

Problems at the beginning of studies

This study was based among other things on the hypothesis that traditional and non-traditional students (students who already had job experience when they started their studies) have to deal with different problems at the beginning of their studies. This thesis is confirmed by the data. Traditional students tend to have more problems than working students in learning how to manage their studies ('independent time management', 'management of studies'), whereas non-traditional students are more likely to have a lack of specialised knowledge in minor subjects. This applies especially to students with alternative university entry who struggle with the problem of having an insufficient basic knowledge in minor subjects.[16]

Compared to the educational situation they were used to before entering the university the self-management which is necessary at university frequently requires a process of readjustment from traditional students. Furthermore, the immediate transfer from the regular school system into the university system is often similar to a cross-over from one world into another. At the same time the social network of the fellow class-mates is lost, and in addition to that they miss the structured course of every-day life with its predefined assignments and appointments. The university system in contrast is characterised by a style of *laissez-faire*, where the students have to define their goals independently, as well as being responsible for achieving them.

It should also be pointed out that non-traditional students hardly ever complain about subject-related inadequacies. One explanation for this lies in the procedure of alternative university entry, since in the course of the

'*Studienberechtigungsprüfung*' these students have to demonstrate a certain basic knowledge of the field to be studied. In addition, students who have been employed prior to their studies will already have acquired the relevant basic knowledge in their jobs. Gaps in basic knowledge and the need to make up for them, mostly concern graduates of regular upper secondary schools who choose to study engineering or economics, and who show a lack of knowledge in basic subjects compared to graduates of secondary higher technical and vocational schools. These inadequacies can be made up for in the first few semesters, during which students often attend tutorial courses. These courses (which have to be paid for) are offered by private organisations, and the necessary basic knowledge is taught in a strongly school-like course system.

Students who have a reduced time budget at their disposal have to struggle with the problem of co-ordinating the time used for their studies with family-related and job-related responsibilities. Strikingly, it is more difficult to combine studies and childcare than studies and a job. While 71 per cent of the students with family-related responsibilities perceive this as a problem, only 52 per cent of the employed students find their work problematic.

Reconciliation of studies and employment

The majority of working students (78 per cent) are able to at least partly organise their working time themselves and thus reconcile the demands of their jobs and their studies. This flexibility in terms of job-related responsibilities enables and eases the combination of studies and job. An additional advantage is that at the larger universities in Vienna – especially at the beginning of studies – there is a sufficient range of parallel courses. That is why merely organisational questions such as course participation are not the primary problem of working students. It is more problematic – as already mentioned – to deal with the reduced time budget in general.

This becomes especially clear if one looks at the total time (in hours) invested in studying. As expected there is a connection between the extent of employment and the time budget available for studying. The students who are employed full-time spend about fifteen hours per week on their studies, partially employed students twenty-seven hours, and students who work on a non-regular basis during the course of the semester thirty-one hours. Traditional students spend thirty-four hours per week on average for their studies.

If we examine the amount of time given to both studies and job together, we find that students have on average a 'forty-hour week', regardless whether they are employed during the semester or not. However, students with full-time jobs represent a significant upward deviation, with an average working time of fifty-five hours per week,while students who do not work are slightly below average at thirty-four hours.

Regarding the principles on which students approach their studies it becomes clear that traditional students feel an extreme amount of pressure, and try to complete their studies as fast as possible. This pressure is created by the requirements which must be met in order to qualify for student assistance or family allowance, which have become increasingly strict over the last few years. Full-time employed students, on the other hand, appear to feel that they can study more slowly and without such pressure to graduate within a specific number of years.

Conclusions

What policy conclusions can be drawn from the present empirical research? If a majority of students depart from the traditional model, it becomes more and more problematic, as our findings suggests, to shape higher education policy and practice according to that norm. Policy-makers and academics have to accept that expansion has grave consequences for all aspects of higher education, including the demographic characteristics of the student population. What used to be a minority, an exception from the traditional type of student, as we have seen increasingly becomes the majority, a new type of 'regular student'. This requires a change of views at both the 'ideological' and conceptual levels of higher education policy and at the practical and organisational level in order to meet the needs of a new student clientele.

Beginning with the normative aspects of this policy issue. The most important precondition for any practical steps is that policy-makers and academics start to consider non-traditional students as a 'regular' clientele, with orientations, needs, biographies, and styles of study different from those they are used to, but nonetheless legitimate. The most controversial issue is whether one should consider a part-time (or even full-time) job as a normal part of student life which is not only tolerated but accepted by universities. The traditional argument against work of students during the semester is that any non-academic activity is in conflict with the 'vocation' of a student. Anything less than full-time devotion to academic subjects (at least for a few years) would not meet the requirements of serious study.

There can be no doubt that in many cases, especially for those who intend to follow an academic career, full-time study would be preferable to a combination of work and study. However, first, this is frequently just not possible and it makes no sense to complicate life for those who must take what might be seen as a 'second best' choice. Second, and more important, in the increasingly diversified world of mass higher education it is no longer true (if it ever was) that there is 'one best solution' for all students. The best option for one type of student might not be suitable for another type. There are many arguments why the combination of work and studies should not only be considered as a legitimate option, but in some instances even as preferable one:

- The most obvious point is that a job can be an enrichment because it adds practical experience to the theoretical knowledge which is acquired at university. This is especially true if students work in a job which is relevant to their field of study. In that case there may be a real synergy between work and study; the involvement in practical applications can improve the 'proceeds' of academic learning. The alternation of theoretical and practical phases can contribute to a deeper understanding.

- Only a minority of students are lucky enough to find a job which is relevant to their academic subject. But even those who work at simple or even low-skilled jobs gain experience which full-time students miss during their years at university. At a relatively early age such students have to cope with the organisational demands of working life. Whether in a big company or a small firm, it is an experience very different from the one they encounter in pedagogical institutions which in many respects are protected from the outside world. It might not always be a pleasant experience, but usually it helps students to adapt to the demands they are confronted with after leaving university. There are many complaints by employers that young graduates often lack the social skills which are necessary to fit into a business organisation. The older they are when they are confronted for the first time with such demands, the more difficult it is to acquire those skills. In that sense, working students have an advantage even if it is not reflected in their academic attainments.

- Regardless of additional qualifications, work experience provides students with a safety net if their ambitions for a professional career related to their university education fail. One inevitable consequence of the mass expansion of higher education is an increase in difficulties for graduates in the labour market. Many graduates will not find employment that suits their expectations and hopes. It makes a big difference whether students already have experiences in the labour market and in the world of business, or whether they only know the world of education. In the former case it is likely that their expectations will be adjusted more closely to their actual chances in the graduate market. In some cases that will imply a gradual 'cooling out' of unrealistic aspirations. As a consequence they will be more willing to accept job offers below the traditional profile of a graduate job.

- From the perspective of the employers, students are an extremely flexible segment of the labour force. In many cases, the request for atypical and non-standardised patterns of employment comes from both sides. Due to their age, for many the lack of family commitments, and the need to fit their work load into the time-frame of their studies, students usually have a higher tolerance for the stress of flexible jobs than most regular employees.

This is not to say that students should not have the opportunity to pursue studies full-time. It would be entirely desirable if students were not forced to work in order to earn a living. The combination of work and study should be a voluntary option (for gaining practical experience, for earning additional income beyond the subsistence level). In fact, this is true only for students from affluent middle-class families. Students who cannot rely on sufficient financial support from their parents are in a much more difficult situation. Only a minority of students are entitled to financial aid from the government. In Austria, about 10 per cent of the total enrolment receive grants to compensate for low family income. The money they receive hardly covers the cost of living. Without doubt it would be desirable to increase both the number of students receiving financial support and the amount of the grants.

However, it would be an illusion to hope that higher student grants could solve all problems and eliminate all financial incentives for students to work. Any aid system of necessity has to define the basic cost of living rather narrowly and many students are not satisfied with the standard of living allowed by such definitions. They prefer a life-style which requires financial means substantially exceeding the basic costs of living. For that reason a large number of students will work in order to earn additional income, even if student support is increased. As a consequence the higher education system must come to terms with the fact that the traditional full-time student is just one type of student alongside other ones.

We suggest two practical conclusions:

- The introduction of a formal part-time status. At present, all students are referred to as 'full-time-students' in Austrian statistics. At a symbolic level, this is a depreciation of part-time students. They are officially declared to be non-existent, or non-legitimate. The introduction of a formal part-time status would be a sign that the combination of studies and work is not only a private matter for the persons involved but also an issue for the university as an organisation. In addition, such a measure would substantially improve the validity of the Austrian higher education statistics.
- Organisational changes at universities. The biggest obstacles that working students complain about are time-related incompatibilities resulting from the fact that courses are tailored to full-time students. As long as the curriculum is geared to the perceived 'normal student biography', and as long as employment during the course of studies is taken to be each student's private concern, the universities will inevitably fail, despite the existing masses of non-traditional students, to draw any organisational conclusions where studies are concerned. As soon as the phenomenon of a mutual interaction of studies and employment is accepted such an attitude appears to be counterproductive. Not only is ignorance of the needs of working students annoying from the perspective of those concerned, but the resulting delay in studies is also a general problem for higher education policy. As soon as the existence of part-time students is recognised, it is only consistent to create opportunities for

students to study part-time (e.g. by means of stepping up the number of parallel courses, block teaching, use of IT, distance elements, extending opening hours for libraries).

Notes

1 Until recently, the government had a monopoly on the ownership of universities; it is only since 1999 that private universities have been permitted by law.
2 As in many parts of Europe, the corporative autonomy of the medieval universities was abolished in the course of the counter-reformation.
3 This is not to say that there were no problems in former times. For long periods Austrian universities were dogmatic religious institutions without academic eminence. In the first decades of this century anti-semitism spread among students and academics alike. However, problems of that kind were not linked to the nature of the state model of higher education.
4 For example the colleges for teacher training (*Pädagogische Akademien*), academies for social workers (*Sozialakademien*), and schools for paramedics (*Schulen für medizinisch-technischen Dienst*). In the Austrian context, those schools are not regarded as part of the higher education system.
5 In 1993 a new organizational act (UOG 1993) was passed, which strengthened the managerial level at universities and shifted some decision-making power from the state to the institutions. The UOG 1993 is still in the process of implementation and very controversial (cf. Pechar and Pellert 1997). It is not yet clear to what extent its full implementation will result in an effective deregulation of higher education.
6 In countries with large mass higher education systems (e.g. USA, Japan) those institutions would undoubtedly be included.
7 Since post-secondary education, by constitutional law, is the responsibility of the federal government, only federal institutions are considered as public. According to that rule, e.g. the college for teacher training, which is maintained by the City of Vienna, is regarded as a 'private' institution.
8 As mentioned, the regulatory framework of universities is in a process of transition, but universities are still subject to tighter regulation than *Fachhochschulen*.
9 The main part of the study was a written survey. The written interviews were conducted in May and June 1997 and included 8,000 students of the Social and Economic Sciences, Law, Engineering, and the Humanities, who were randomly chosen from the student list. These fields were chosen because the indicators in the official statistics point out that they feature very high proportions of non-traditional students. About 36 per cent of the distributed forms were returned. A total of 2,599 questionnaires were used for the evaluation. In addition to the student survey, several guided interviews were conducted to take account of a variety of opinions. Altogether fifteen interviews were conducted with representatives of the political parties, the federal ministry of science, the '*Arbeitsmarktservice Austria*' (Austrian Public Employment Service), the '*Arbeiterkammer*' (representative body of employees) and the '*Industriellenvereinigung*' (representative body of industry) as well as with members of the various universities and student representatives (cf. Pechar and Wroblewski 1998).

10 With the exception of art universities, the matriculation standard is a requirement in order to be admitted to study as a regular student. Matriculation standard is usually attained by means of *Matura*. The '*Studienberechtigungsprüfung*' is an exam that provides people without *Matura* with an alternative way to be admitted to university. A prerequisite for this exam is that the person who takes it is older than twenty-two years and has already completed some kind of professional training.

11 For further information on the situation of other groups of non-traditional students see Pechar and Wroblewski 1998.

12 The variable 'social class' is constructed on the basis of the education and job-status of both parents.

13 Up to a monthly income of ATS 3,740 there will be no loss of student assistance or legal claim to family allowance.

14 The index 'financial motives' consists of the following items: 'I'm employed in order to earn a living', 'I'd like to be able to afford certain things', 'I'd like to earn my own money, to be independent'.

15 The index 'practice-related motives' includes the following items: 'I'd like to establish contacts that will be important for my future career', 'I'd like to gain practical job experience', 'I'd like to apply practically the knowledge I gained through my studies'.

16 Bacher *et al.* (1994) arrived at a similar result.

References

AMS (Public Employment Service Austria) (1997) *Unternehmensbefragung – Beschäftigungschancen für HochschulabsolventInnen*, Vienna: AMS.

Bacher, M., Blumberger, W., Grausgruber, A. and Weilguni, R. (1994) *Studium ohne Matura: Motivation. Probleme. Studienverläufe*, Linz: AK Oberösterreich.

BMWV (Federal Ministry of Science and Transport) (Hrsg.) (1999) *Materialien zur sozialen Lage der Studierenden 1998*, Vienna: BMWV.

BMWV (Federal Ministry of Science and Transport) (1999) *Hochschulbericht 1999*, Vienna: BMWV.

Clark, B. (1983) *The Higher Education System. Academic Organization in Cross-National Perspective*, Berkeley, Los Angeles: University of California Press.

Pechar, H. and Pellert, A. (1997) 'Managing change: organisational reform in Austrian universities', *Higher Education Policy* no. 11 (1998).

Pechar, H. and Wroblewski, A. (1998) *Non-traditional students in Österreich: Studienbedingungen bei Nebenerwerbstätigkeit, verspätetem Übertritt und alternativem Hochschulzugang*, Vienna: IFF.

3 Germany

Non-traditional students in German higher education: situation, profiles, policies and perspectives

Andrä Wolter

In Germany, as in most other modern industrial societies, the overall process of expansion of higher education has led to a different, more heterogeneous composition of students in terms of social and family background, gender, age, life-style, motivation for studying, future vocational perspectives and other characteristics. As outlined in Chapter 1 (Schuetze and Slowey) of this volume, the definition of 'non-traditional students' has substantially changed with this transformation of higher education to a mass system. In this introduction, the meaning of 'traditional' students is explored in the German context. This leads on to a definition of the main features of 'non-traditional' students. In the following sections, an overview is given of the higher education system in Germany in general. It will be shown that the question of access is central in the German system to any discussion of traditional and, by contrast and extension, non-traditional students. But it is also clear that the rigid organisation of studies and especially the almost complete lack of distance-learning and part-time provision constitute barriers to all those who want to study in a more flexible manner. As will be shown, there has been little policy concern, debate, or action in Germany concerning specific measures in favour of 'non-traditional' students.

Introduction: traditional and non-traditional students in Germany

A 'traditional' or 'regular' student in German higher education would normally attend an academic stream upper secondary school (*Gymnasium*; we shall use the British term 'grammar school' as an equivalent here) for a certain number of years, graduate with an *Abitur* (baccalaureate) certificate, which gives him or her the quasi-automatic right to enrol at a university or any other institution of higher education, and then move directly on to higher education (in the case of male students interrupted only by national service). The student would study in full-time mode and attend lectures, seminars and laboratories on campus, graduate in principle after eight or ten semesters (in reality, more), depending on the field of study, and then move on to a (full-time) job. Only exceptionally would some of the graduates return to university for continuing higher education, usually only for short courses during their working life.

This model of a traditional student reflects some specific features in the organisation of the German education system, in particular the highly structured secondary school system in which the grammar school plays a particular role as it is the only school type that awards the *Abitur*, the general entrance entitlement for higher education. It shows further the prevalence of full-time and classroom-based organisation of studies in higher education, as well as the traditional division of roles between higher education and a well-established separate system of adult and continuing education outside higher education which delivers the bulk of professional and general continuing education.

Students who do not take this traditional route or who study in a non-traditional mode are, by definition, non-traditional students. However, for the sake of a closer analysis it is useful to differentiate between six distinct types of non-traditional students:

1   Those leaving school without an *Abitur* who, after completing vocational training as an apprentice and gaining some practical work experience, attend an alternative upper secondary school (*Abendgymnasium, Kolleg*). Such schools, established specifically for this target group, offer full-time or part-time courses leading also to an *Abitur* certificate (which normally takes three years to complete). This route is known as the second educational route (*zweiter Bildungsweg*).

2   Those without an *Abitur* who are admitted by way of a special admission exam at university level. This route which is further discussed below is often referred to as the third educational route (*'dritter Bildungsweg'*).

3   Those students who have an *Abitur* but do not transfer directly from secondary school to higher education. They first complete a phase of vocational training and sometimes gain work experience before moving on to higher education. This is the route of a 'double qualification' (*Doppelqualifizierung*).

4   Those students who are admitted because they have one of the required access qualifications but who do not study in the traditional full-time, on-site mode but in a different mode such as distance-learning or part-time courses.

5   Those who already hold a degree but who re-enter higher education to further their education, either pursuing an advanced degree, a special advanced qualification in their professional field, or some other shorter non-degree programmes. These students are continuing their earlier education, mostly for professional or job-specific reasons.

6   Those people, known as senior students, who enrol after their retirement, mostly for personal interests or self-realisation.

Compared with the classification of the 1987 OECD report on adults in higher education (see Schuetze and Slowey in this volume), the first and the second group consist of 'second chancers', the difference between them being the access route. The first group is 'traditional' in so far as students possess the *Abitur* and 'non-traditional' in so far as they gain it after a period of vocational training and work experience. In contrast, the second group – those without the *Abitur* – pursue an alternative access route. The third group – school leavers who have an *Abitur*, but take a circuitous route to higher education – corresponds to the 'deferrers' in the OECD typology. The fifth group are 'returners'. The fourth group consists of students – mostly 'traditional' in terms of access – who prefer a more flexible form of studying, mainly due to their living conditions, life-styles, work and social commitments. Because there are very few provisions for part-time or distance studies in Germany, this group is small although growing. Senior students, or what we might call 'very late second chancers' under the OECD classification, have hitherto not generally been considered as 'non-traditional' students because they are perceived as studying 'simply' for reasons of personal fulfilment and interest. However, regarded from a lifelong learning perspective, this group reflects changing biographies, life-cycles and the changed role age plays in modern societies, in other words some of the very elements on which the model of lifelong learning is supposed to be built.

Higher education in Germany

Before looking at non-traditional students and their circumstances, it is necessary to outline briefly the German system of secondary and tertiary education (for more details see KMK 1997, Peisert and Framhein 1994, Kehm 1998). Five distinctive features are important to an understanding of the German system of secondary and tertiary education and the institutional construction of access to higher education.

Basic educational structures

Important to an understanding of the working of the German system of education is the fact that Germany is a federal state and that the right to regulate education is almost exclusively the right and responsibility of the sixteen *Länder*. This makes for some interesting variety in the school sector, even if there is some degree of conformity which is largely due to the work of an inter-state co-ordination body (the Council of Ministers of Education: *Kultusminster-Konferenz*); this body discusses educational policy and practice with the aim of securing a basic level of comparability and student mobility. Although this principle of *Länder* autonomy applies also to higher education, there is somewhat more uniformity at this level due to the fact that the federal level of government has a small but important number of responsibilities of its own. Besides an active role in the financing of research, student financial assistance and construction and major equipment, the federal parliament has the right to regulate the 'framework' of higher education. The Higher Education Framework Law (*Hochschulrahmengesetz*) sets forth the principal structures, mechanisms and procedures of higher education, including the general rules of admission. While this results in much conformity across the country, there are some (minor) fields where the *Länder* are free to experiment and to set up their own structures and procedures.

A second basic factor which has a great impact on access to higher education is the fact that secondary education in Germany is not organised as a comprehensive system. Rather, upon completion of primary school, which lasts normally four years, parents choose between various educational tracks and different types of schools. The main route to higher education, in particular to universities, is through the grammar school which awards the *Abitur* certificate upon completion of the 13th form and the passing of a special exam. The other two main types of secondary school are the main school (*Hauptschule*), at lower level (ending with either grade 9 or 10), and the middle school (*Realschule*), at middle level (ending with grade 10). At the age of fourteen, about 25 per cent of all pupils attend main schools, 27 per cent middle schools, 32 per cent grammar schools, and 16 per cent other school types. The grammar school usually comprises grades 5 to 13 (in some East German *Länder* to grade 12).

Germany has a well established system of vocational education apart from higher education. Pupils who attend and graduate from the lower secondary schools (*Hauptschule* or *Realschule*) normally transfer into institutions of vocational training to follow a course which usually takes three years. Vocational education is offered in two main ways: first, as an apprenticeship under the so-called dual system which combines part-time vocational school with practical on-the-job-training at the place of work or, second, in attending full-time vocational school (*Berufsfachschule*).[1] Vocational education in one of these forms leads to either a journeyperson's certificate or a certificate of vocational proficiency. While neither certificate entitles the holder to go on to higher education, they open access to upper secondary vocational schools (*Fachoberschule*), the completion of which gives access to non-university higher education, i.e. the *Fachhochschule*.

Recently, the pursuit of vocational education, especially apprenticeship training, has also become very attractive to those who successfully complete the *Gymnasium* and hold an *Abitur*. Currently, about 40 per cent of all school leavers with *Abitur* transfer to one of the institutions of vocational education before or as an alternative to studying.

As mentioned already, a binary system of higher education has been established with, on the one hand, the universities and a number of university-like colleges (such as teacher-training colleges, art academies, theological colleges), and, on the other, *Fachhochschulen* which are more work-related providing programmes of shorter duration (three to four years). Presently about 30 per cent of new entrants in higher education and about a quarter of all students are enrolled at one of the *Fachhochschulen*.

Finally, and very important is the traditional German concept of higher education, according to the classical (Humboldt's) idea of a university, which stresses primarily research and academic teaching, both of which are seen as complementary. Unlike universities in North America, universities in Germany are traditionally not seen as service institutions for society. Therefore, activities such as applied research and continuing education (which were at the heart of the American land grant universities and their Canadian counterparts) are not seen as central to the mission of a university and as a consequence the status of these activities within the academic community is relatively low.

Access to higher education

Access to higher education is granted to all holders of an *Abitur* certificate, and vocational qualifications can lead to access to the *Fachhochschulen*. Institutions of higher education have no selection rights of their own and are obliged to admit any *Abitur* holder. There are a few exceptions to this general principle: art and sports academies require additional evidence of talent and aptitude. More importantly, for some heavily over-subscribed fields of study – such as medicine and dentistry – restrictions are imposed on the number of applicants who are admitted (the so-called *numerus clausus*). In principle, admissions for these fields are centrally allocated for all universities; however on a pilot basis, institutions in some of the *Länder* can also admit a certain contingent of students on the basis of personal interviews. Currently, a lively debate is going on the efficiency of the centrally controlled admission procedure for *numerus clausus* fields of study, with a growing number of experts arguing in favour of making the selection and admission procedures the sole responsibility of the higher education institutions themselves.

In addition to these two main access routes, every *Land* – except Bavaria – has opened a third educational route, a small door for adults with vocational training and work experience but without the *Abitur* or formal vocational qualifications at an advanced level. The forms of this access route vary considerably from *Land* to *Land*. Three main types of admission procedures exist:

- admission via an entry examination
- conditional admission (*Probestudium*), which allows applicants with relevant professional experience to register without any kind of entrance exam for a maximum of four semesters; during this time they must prove their ability to study on the basis of study progress or special exams
- admission after an interview or a consultation.

To be eligible for these admission procedures, applicants must be of a minimum age – often twenty-four years – and must have vocational qualifications and several years of work experience. Some *Länder* have special arrangements – open admission or trial studies – for people with excellent vocational qualifications (for master craftsmen or technicians, for example).

The prevailing mode of unified and standardised, full-time and on-site course of study indicates a general deficit in institutional flexibility concerning the organisation of studies and teaching. This is, apart from the issue of access requirements and admission procedures, the main obstacle for non-traditional students in German higher education. With a few exceptions, especially in the *Fachhochschulen*, it is fair to say that the higher education system is not very conducive to the particular needs and demands of students with a non-traditional biography and that there has been hardly any institutional response to the demands of non-traditional students.

The organization of studies

During the last two decades, the differentiation and the specialisation of the academic programmes offered in German higher education has increased substantially. The most important institutional and curricular differentiation in German higher education is that between studies in the university sector and studies in the *Fachhochschulen*. The traditional academic professions and subjects leading to a professional degree (such as medicine and law) are taught exclusively at university level. Universities also offer advanced studies for research training, as they have the exclusive right to award advanced degrees, especially doctoral degrees. Studies primarily oriented towards the acquisition of professional, especially engineering, skills in response to the requirements of the employment system are the responsibility of the *Fachhochschulen*.

In contrast to undergraduate education in North America, especially in liberal education or the liberal arts, the initial phase of studies does not have a general educational character. Students enter directly in subject-specific or discipline-based programmes. Courses of study are normally not modulized and there is no system of credit awards for individual courses that could be accumulated and transferred to a different programme or to another institution. Nor is there a vertical differentiation between undergraduate and graduate studies with corresponding degrees (Bachelor's and Master's).[2] This structural organisation makes for great inflexibility: for one thing, students can only exit their programmes with an advanced degree (in most fields of study equivalent to a Master's level), after a final exam that comprises the entire syllabus that has been covered over the duration of studies. Moreover, they cannot easily change their programmes without losing all or most of their course credit and having to start in the new field practically from scratch.

Some changes have been made over the last few years in order to reduce the high drop-out rate and the long duration of studies. Innovations in the organisation of studies include the establishment of a sequential structure of studies with two successive examinations and a stronger modularization with a credit point system. However, so far such reforms are no more than pilot projects, and the majority of courses of study in German higher education are organised in the traditional way.

As mentioned already, distance or part-time studies have so far played a minor role and this, as is well known from other studies, is the greatest obstacle for non-traditional students, especially working adults who combine education and work. With few exceptions, study programmes in initial higher education are designed to be full-time, scheduled at times when students with jobs are working to earn their living.

Distance learning is not yet very common and very few institutions offer their programmes or individual courses at a distance, although this may change with the rapid emergence and sophistication of new media, software for independent learning and interactive information and communication technologies. So far, the most important provider of distance studies is the *Fernuniversität* (Distance University, DU) located in Hagen in the Ruhr district, which offers a wide range of programmes in initial and continuing higher education. Unlike the Open University in the UK, after which the Distance University has been modelled, the DU is not open at all when it comes to admission to degree studies; the same entrance qualifications are required as in other universities. Only a very few other institutions offer distance studies at university level; one example is Dresden University of Technology, which is involved in distance studies in the field of engineering. At the level of *Fachhochschulen* there are several private institutions (e.g. the *AKAD-Fernfachhochschule*), and recently some networks of several *Fachhochschulen*, which provide distance courses in a small number of subjects, mainly in engineering and business studies.

As mentioned before, there are hardly any institutionalised part-time studies in German higher education, with the exception of distance studies and some non-degree bearing courses in continuing higher education. This is so despite the fact that the predominant classical pattern of full-time students who devote their time and efforts exclusively to their studies has decreased during the last twenty years.[3]

Patterns of participation

The most important change in German higher education during the last four decades has been the incessant expansion of student enrolment and the growth of the whole higher education system in terms of the number of institutions, staff and buildings and the extent of funding. This process of mass expansion has influenced the development of higher education in Germany far more than any reform. There were several reforms following the 1960s, yet none of them significantly changed the traditional core of the German university. The increase in social demand for higher education that led to fast-rising enrolment has continued without interruption until the present time, even if the rate of increase has somewhat levelled off. Since unification in 1990 the same process has occurred in East Germany. Some figures may illustrate this fact.

From the beginning of the 1950s, the ratio of school leavers with an *Abitur*, related to the age cohort, grew rapidly from 4.5 per cent in 1952 (West Germany) to 37 per cent in 1993 (West Germany) and 37 per cent in 1997 for all Germany.[4] Despite the fact that the transition rates between school and higher education have decreased over the last two decades, the majority of pupils who leave the school system with a study entitlement have enrolled in higher education. The number of new students, as a percentage of the age group, increased from 4 per cent in 1950 (West Germany) to 35 per cent in 1993 for West Germany and 31 per cent in 1997 for all Germany. In East Germany the proportion was between 12 and 14 per cent during the 1970s and 1980s. In 1950 the total number of students enrolled was 130,000 whereas it was 1.7 million at the end of the 1990s. While this growth may look very impressive, it must be noted that it stems not only from increased enrolment but also from the fact that the average period of study for the first degree has risen from four to more than six years, which is a serious concern for policy makers.

At present 78 per cent of all new entrants in higher education have passed the *Abitur*-examination, 4 per cent have taken the second or third educational route and another 11 per cent have attended the *Fachoberschule*.[5] However, these figures vary considerably between the university sector and the non-university sector. In the university sector the proportion of grammar-school leavers with *Abitur* is about 92 per cent, which underlines the central importance of the *Abitur* for access to the universities. In the *Fachhochschulen* 54 per cent of all new entrants have the *Abitur* while a third of all new entrants have received their study entitlement from the a upper secondary vocational school (*Fachoberschule*). This proportion has changed somewhat during the last decade as studying at a *Fachhochschule* has become more attractive for grammar school leavers who appreciate the close connections between the *Fachhochschulen* and industry and business. The proportion of students coming from the second or third educational route mentioned above is approximately 3 per cent in the university and about 5 per cent in the non-university sector.

Student finance and support

Because the great majority of adult and other non-traditional students are entering higher education via the main access routes – *Abitur* or special vocational qualifications for access to *Fachhochschulen* – they are not given a special status nor any particular support. Individual institutions sometimes have preferential clauses for student housing for married students, but student housing is scarce and there are few dormitories with larger apartments that could house a couple or a family. Day-care facilities for children of older students are equally scarce. On the whole, non-traditional students are considered to be regular students of the traditional kind, and treated as such in every respect.

There are however exceptions which work against non-traditional students. Thus, for example with respect to financial support, regulations concerning eligibility for the federal student loan system (*Bundesausbildungsförderungsgesetz*, or *Bafög*) discriminate against older students. Students who start their programme after the age of thirty are normally not eligible, with the exception however of those who have taken a special entrance exam or who have just completed their *Abitur* via the 'second educational route' and are enrolling in a university or *Fachhochschule* immediately after completion. Thus, while older students coming via alternative routes to higher education are not excluded, the system certainly does not make it easy for them.

Another example that shows the rigidities of the German system concerns the eligibility of students for unemployment insurance. As a full-time student (and almost all students are, as noted already, considered full time) an unemployed person is ineligible for benefits as he or she has to be available for work which, it is argued, they are not when studying. While this regulation may have its legitimate rationale, it is another barrier in the road to a system of lifelong learning. These examples show that especially older adults who work for a living, or who are unemployed and wish to study with the objective of increasing their chances to find a job, face considerable barriers.

The profile of non-traditional students in German higher education

In the course of expansion, the patterns of participation and the social composition of students have changed significantly. For example, the proportion of women among new entrants in higher education increased from 27 per cent in 1960 to 49 per cent in 1997. In fact, since 1995 the majority of new entrants in universities have been women. However, participation varies widely according to the subject, and the proportion declines as the level of qualification rises.

The number of students without *Abitur* has increased as well, but only in the *Fachhochschul* sector, to which, as noted already, access is open to applicants with other school and vocational qualifications. In the university sector the proportion of students without *Abitur* has constantly been extremely low.

The average age of the new entrants has increased from twenty to twenty-two years during the last few years. However, this increase in the average entrance age is not the result of opening up the university, but of the extension of the average completion time necessary for the *Abitur* or, alternatively, the alternative qualifications via the vocational route, and the longer average time span between attainment of the *Abitur* and enrolment in higher education.

The proportion of students with a working class background rose from 4 per cent in 1953 to 14 per cent in 1997 with a peak of 16 per cent in 1982, but this proportion is still well below the proportion of working class people in the German population. Most students of this group choose the vocational route to higher education; the proportion of students with a blue-collar origin is higher in the *Fachhochschul* sector than in the university sector (25 to 13 per cent in 1997).

Looking closer at the six groups of non-traditional students defined earlier (p. 49), the following details may illustrate the present situation (BMBF 1999, Lewin *et al.* 1998, Schnitzer *et al.* 1998).

Group One: the second educational route (Abitur *after vocational training*) The ratio of new entrants with a study entitlement obtained in one of the institutions of the second educational route (*Abendgymnasium, Kolleg*), related to all new entrants in higher education, is presently 3.2 per cent (university: 2.6 per cent; *Fachhochschule*: 4.4 per cent). The majority of students entering higher education from the second educational route is 60 per cent male and female students are under-represented with only 40 per cent. This under-representation of women is a result of their extremely low number in the *Fachhochschul* sector.

This access route was established to cater for two particular target groups first, workers and craftsmen, interested in social upward mobility through higher education and, second, people with a working-class background who had been less likely to attend a normal grammar school. However, it has not fulfilled the expectations of either group, even if the proportion of students with a working class family background is higher on this than on any other route to higher education (30 per cent compared with 11 per cent in the group of grammar school leavers).

Group Two: the third educational route (via special university entrance exam) The proportion of new entrants with a study entitlement obtained by a special entrance exam is also very small, namely 0.6 per cent of all new entrants to higher education (university: 0.5 per cent; *Fachhochschule*: 0.9 per cent). This fact clearly demonstrates the marginal role of this access route in German higher education, although there are considerable differences among the sixteen German *Länder*. For example, in the *Land* of Lower Saxony (Niedersachsen), which has been a leader in the establishment of this access route, the proportion has varied between 2 and 4 per cent during the last twenty-five years, which means that on average between 600 and 800 applicants annually are admitted via this route. However except for the *Länder* of Berlin and North Rhine-Westphalia where numbers are slightly higher, the number of students who annually enter higher education via this path has been lower than 100 in most *Länder*.

During the last two decades the proportion of women who have entered higher education via this route has risen from about 50 per cent to approximately 65 per cent. The proportion of students from working-class families that has been admitted via this educational route (about 30–35 per cent) is double that in the total student population in German higher education. Hence, access to higher education via this route is significantly more open for social groups with a lower socio-economic status than is access to higher education in general. In contrast to students with *Abitur*, the motivation to study of such students with vocational training and work experience is characterised by a strong non-materialistic component which focuses on such values as personal development, self-realisation, searching for a new identity or realising individual aspirations. Thus, this group consists of highly qualified and intrinsically motivated people who have made a clear personal decision to transfer from previous work to higher education and to get a new profession which is more in accordance with their aspirations (Schulenberg *et al.* 1986, Wolter and Reibstein 1991, Isserstedt 1994, Wolter 1994).

Group Three: double qualification (vocational training after the Abitur *and before entering higher education)*   About 15 to 20 per cent of all new entrants in higher education with the traditional *Abitur* have had a phase of vocational training between their graduation from grammar school and the beginning of their studies (university: 12–17 per cent; *Fachhochschule*: 20–27 per cent). Of course, the total proportion of all new entrants with vocational training and work experience including those with vocational training before gaining the study entitlement is higher than that. Approximately one-third of all new students have undertaken vocational training before they transfer to higher education, either before or after obtaining their study entitlement (18–20 per cent in the university sector, 60–70 per cent in the *Fachhochschul* sector).

The proportion varies not only with the type of higher education, but also with the subject. In the university sector about 30 per cent of all new entrants in economics, about 27 per cent in architecture and civil engineering and 25 per cent in social sciences and education have undertaken vocational training, whereas only 10–12 per cent have done so in law or medicine. In the *Fachhochschul* sector the proportion of students with vocational qualifications is considerably higher in all fields; about 70 per cent in economics, 65 per cent in engineering and 60 per cent in social work have acquired work experience before entering higher education. This double qualification route is in accordance with the occupation-related mission of the *Fachhochschulen*. University students often want to enhance their qualifications in order to improve their future chances on the labour market, making the double qualification route primarily an insurance strategy for graduates against the risk of unemployment.

Group Four: distance and part-time students   Approximately 70,000 students are enrolled in distance learning, of whom more than half, 44,000, are at the Distance University in Hagen. Compared with the total number of students in Germany – 1.83 million in 1997 – this is a very small number indeed. As noted already, the lack of institutional provision outside the Distance University can be regarded as the main reason for this extremely low level of participation. Although some new providers of distance studies have been established during the last few years, the range of subjects offered is very small. The promotion and extension of distance (and part-time) studies may be one of the most important projects for both public higher education and institutional policy in the years to come.

During the last ten years the number of students who carry out their studies in the traditional mode of full-time studying has been steadily declining. Correspondingly, there has been an increasing number of students who study *de facto* part-time, despite the fact, mentioned above, that there are no formal part-time courses (apart from distance studies). According to a recent study on the social circumstances of German students (Schnitzer *et al.* 1998 p. 491ff.) four types of students can be distinguished (the study defines every student who invests less than twenty-five hours a week in studying as a *de facto* part-time student):

- full-time students with a low level of work commitment
- full-time students with a high level of work commitment (and a high level of additional stress by the time spent on work)
- part-time students with a low level of work commitment
- part-time students with a high level of work commitment (and a high level of additional stress caused by the time spent on work).

The size of the latter two groups grew from 11 per cent (in 1988) to 19 per cent (in 1997). The traditional mode of studying has decreased in size, but it is still the predominant type. The proportion of *de facto* part-time students varies with the subject, the phase of studying and, of course, with the social, economic and family circumstances of students. It is higher (up to 33 per cent) in humanities (such as education, social science, psychology) and lower (less than 15 per cent) in sciences, engineering, law and medicine. The main reasons for the emergence of *de facto* part-time students may be seen, first, in the growing necessity for many students to earn their living and, second, in the attempt to balance out different social activities, of which studying is one.

Group Five: continuing higher education There is not much reliable statistical information available about participation in continuing higher education, that is, non-degree studies. This is due to two factors. First, continuing higher education provision is extremely fragmented as there are a large number of public and private providers, including professional associations, companies, academies or other special continuing education organisations, which sometimes operate in conjunction with higher education institutions and often use academic staff for the delivery of their programmes. Second, many continuing higher education activities inside the university are organised as individual courses, seminars or workshops for which a formal enrolment at the university is not required. Therefore, the status of participants in continuing higher education varies between programmes and institutions.

Only between 5 and 10 per cent of all provision of continuing higher education was offered by universities or other higher education institutions (BLK 1990, Lullies and Berning 1990, Kuwan *et al.* 1996). Although two-thirds of staff members were involved in continuing higher education activities, around half of these taught courses which were offered by providers outside the university, thereby supplementing their income from non-university sources (Holtkamp and Kazemzadeh 1989).

However, higher education institutions have extended their provision for continuing education during the last decade, especially by offering two types of longer term courses. The first consists of so-called contact courses of study (*Kontaktstudiengänge*), sometimes also called continuing education courses of study (*Weiterbildende Studiengänge*). These are designed primarily for people who already have an academic degree and some work experience in their profession and who require additional qualifications in new fields of knowledge, sometimes but not always related to their original field of study. The second type consists of additional, supplementary or extension courses of study (*Zusatz-, Ergänzungs- und Aufbaustudiengänge*) which are designed to broaden existing qualifications through more specialised knowledge or skills. The majority of participants in these courses are students who have just obtained their first degree and are seeking an additional qualification to improve their future chances on the labour market.

In spite of the increasing emergence of such programmes – there are now over 1,200 such programmes offered in German universities and *Fachhochschulen* – their overall importance is still relatively low; the ratio of students enrolled in such continuing higher education programmes, related to all students, is about 1 per cent.

Group Six: senior students   Currently, about 25 000 senior students – most of them around the age fifty-five or older and already retired – are enrolled at higher education institutions. About 6,000 are enrolled as full-time students in standard courses in the same way as other students, in order to get a normal degree. Seniors also enrol in special non-degree programmes designed specifically for older students. In 1997 forty-two universities offered such programmes to about 12,500 participants. As an alternative, about 6,500 older people studied under a special status as so-called auditors or 'guest students' to participate in regular programmes.

Women comprise 60 per cent of the senior students. Their previous education levels are normally very high; most senior students hold an *Abitur* certificate and many a first academic degree. The subject preferences and thematic interests centre on humanities and arts. As one would expect, seniors' motives to study are non-employment-related and very individualistic in nature, including intellectual curiosity and the training of mental abilities, a search for social contacts and communication, self-realisation and personal development. It can be safely predicted that the number of older students will grow rapidly as a result of an ageing society, changes in life styles and the rise of educational attainment and income.

Public and institutional policies

Although there has been, over the last ten years, a lively policy debate about the necessary reforms in German higher education, including calls in favour of opening up further access for non-traditional students, it has been observed that traditional institutions, in particular universities, have changed neither far enough nor fast enough to respond to the needs of non traditional learners (Hackl *et. al.* 1997). The main finding of the 1987 OECD study of adults in higher education regarding the situation in Germany would also apply to 'non-traditional' students in 1999:

> Germany, which has one of the lowest proportions of mature entrants in higher education, may serve as an example of a system that appears to have done very little to make higher education more accessible to mature applicants.
>
> (OECD 1987 p. 47)

What is the reason for this relative neglect of non-traditional students and non-traditional modes of studying? And why is this topic not of high priority on the higher education policy agenda in Germany? There seem to be several answers, some of them resulting from a lack of vision, flexibility and innovation grounded in traditional views about society and the function of higher education. Non-traditional students are not of central policy interest in Germany for four principal reasons.

First, during the last several decades the higher education system in Germany has turned – in terms of statistics – from elite to mass higher education, but without making the necessary reforms in the organisation of studies and of institutional structures and processes that would allow for more openness of access and flexibility (OECD 1997). However, because of this great expansion in participation, there is a widespread impression that there is no need to open any additional access routes to higher education. Higher education is seen by many actors and observers to be in deep crisis as the massive expansion, which was not accompanied by corresponding financial resources, has resulted in serious overcrowding and understaffing (Wolter 1995). Under such circumstances it is arguably difficult to implement any new programmes to open up access to higher education for new student groups, because it is feared that such measures would make the overcrowding of higher education even more critical.

Second, the concept of widening access to higher education for applicants without the *Abitur* is very controversial in Germany. One of the main objections to this concept is based on the issue of the ability or aptitude to study (*Studierfähigkeit*) which is usually identified as identical to the knowledge that is required for, and certified by, the traditional *Abitur*. The historically evolved social meaning of the German *Abitur* consists of more than just a formal study entitlement. The *Abitur* is linked to a particular pre-academic syllabus and, furthermore, with particular notions about a cultivated, well-educated personality. There is a widespread assumption that students without the *Abitur* do not have sufficient the ability to study and, therefore, a strategy of open – or at least more open – access to higher education would overcrowd the universities with a large number of unqualified students. This assumption is widely held, particularly in the universities, which are very reserved about opening up higher education for new target groups. This is so in spite of ample empirical evidence which shows that students without the *Abitur* carry out and finish their studies as successfully as other students – and sometimes even more successfully (Schulenberg *et al.* 1986, Wolter 1997). However, the traditional myth of the German *Abitur* – and the presumption that *Studierfähigkeit* can be acquired only through the *Abitur* – is strong and remains one of the most important obstacles for the recognition of work-based learning as being functionally equivalent to formal qualifications for higher education.

Third, these reservations about the concept of opening up access to higher education are reinforced by the recent developments in the labour market for graduates in Germany. Mass higher education is thought to have led to an ever-increasing mismatch between higher education and employment. The trend towards a 'highly educated and a highly qualified society' is assumed to result in an 'overeducated' and 'overqualified' academic workforce on the one hand and a lack of workers and craftsmen on the other. Indeed, graduate unemployment has risen significantly during the last ten years, even if the proportion of graduates who are unemployed (currently 4 per cent) is much lower than the average rate of unemployment (about 10 per cent). Currently, approximately 200,000 graduates are unemployed in Germany, mainly in the areas of engineering, humanities and teacher-training; the two latter fields are the traditional choice of non-traditional students. This number is about the same as the annual output of graduates.

Fourth, one of the main objectives for the introduction of special admission procedures designed for applicants without the *Abitur* has been concern for the viability of the German system of vocational education and training and an attempt to increase its attractiveness. Because more and more pupils in German upper secondary education prefer the grammar-school track to the vocational track, and because the demand for vocational training had dropped during the early 1990s, many policy makers and representatives of industry and business were concerned about an increasing mismatch between the social demand for education and the needs and requirements of the labour market. Therefore, the establishment of special access to higher education for people with vocational training was seen as a suitable measure to enhance the status and reputation of such training, which had come to be seen by many young people as a dead-end route. The possibility of transferring directly from vocational to higher education was regarded as one of the main criteria for enhancing such equivalence and making it more attractive for young people to choose the vocational route. In reality, the number of applicants for vocational training places is currently higher than the number of apprenticeships available. As a result of this shift, political interest in the topic of equivalence diminished immediately, as did the interest in further opening access to higher education for young people with vocational qualifications.

Conclusions: lifelong learning and non-traditional students in German higher education

The 'massification' of higher education has taken place mainly as a result of two mechanisms: first, the widening of the traditional route via an expansion of academic-track upper secondary education leading to the main academic entry qualification, the *Abitur* and, second, the establishment of a new type of institution of a non-university type, the *Fachhochschulen*, which provide access for students with vocational qualifications who do not hold the *Abitur*. Students who would formerly have been seen as 'non-traditional' have gained access primarily by one of these two routes. To be sure, some alternative access and admission procedures for students with vocational training and work experience were established, but their quantitative effects have turned out to be very modest. Apart from these special access routes, no special arrangements have been made to support these groups and some of the rigidities in the organisation of studies and in the financial support system are working against them.

Although discussed in Germany and embraced by policy makers in principle, the idea of lifelong learning challenges some traditional beliefs: that higher education institutions are primarily designed for educating people during their youth; that the most important qualifications for successful studying are acquired through grammar school education; that higher education should be organised according to a model of research-based academic learning; and that open access and recognition of other than academic knowledge amount to a perversion of the traditional idea of academic education.

The very concept of lifelong learning implies that learning and education take place not only in schools, universities and other institutions of formal learning but also in many other informal and non-formal situations and contexts outside the education system (Dohmen 1996, Alesi *et al.* 1999, Rubenson and Schuetze 2000). This implies that the position of the grammar school as the central and only legitimate preparatory institution will need to change, and other learning places and routes to higher education must be recognised as alternative and equally legitimate.

Such a paradigm shift will have many consequences. For example, new assessment procedures are needed for the recognition and certification of experiential – informal and non-formal – learning, and in particular, of work experience and learning through working, a departure from the tradition of strictly separating general (or 'liberal') education (*Allgemeinbildung*) from vocational education and training (*berufliche Bildung*). Also, the traditional organisation of studies requires some far-reaching changes, especially with a view to more flexibility and new methods of instruction and learning that make possible learning that is independent of place, time and other restrictions.

Some empirical studies estimate the proportion of people in the German working population who are seriously interested in opening access to higher education at approximately 10 per cent (Schwiedrzik and Mucke 1996). However, the pressure for a more flexible organisation of higher education does not only arise from the changing social demand. Probably more important are the changing requirements and needs of the labour market and the employment system.

In an increasing number of jobs the links between qualification and the allocation of occupational roles have become more flexible and uncertain. This is true in terms of the subjects as well as distinct levels of education or qualification. It is necessary to consider the interdependencies between the changing conditions of work, qualification and education. These changes in the occupational structure arise not only from the expansion of higher education, but also from changes in the social and economic structures in modern societies which foster the process of upgrading the qualification structure. They are part of the overall transformation from an industrial to a post-industrial society and from a Fordist to a knowledge-based economy. This continuous process towards a knowledge-based economy and, more generally, a knowledge society seems to be the most important force behind the necessity for an open door policy in German higher education.

Notes

1 These exist in different forms, some providing complete vocational training (three years) and some only a basic vocational education (one or two years) which serves as a preparation for training in the dual system.
2 The Federal Higher Education Framework Law has recently been changed to make a re-structuring of programmes along these lines possible.
3 The lack of part-time studies has been recognised in German higher education policy, and some German *Länder* recently changed their higher education laws in order to promote the introduction of part-time studies.
4 In the 1970s and 1980s the proportion of young people with study entitlement was lower in East (between 12 and 15 per cent) than in West Germany (from 15 to more than 30 per cent).
5 All statistical data are from 1997.

References

Alesi, B., Kehm, B. M. and Lischka, I. (1999) *Lebenslanges Lernen und Hochschulen in Deutschland – Literaturbericht und annotierte Bibliographie (1990–1999) zur Entwicklung und aktuellen Situation*, Wittenberg: Institut für Hochschulforschung Wittenberg an der Martin-Luther Universität Halle-Wittenberg.

BLK (1990) *Weiterbildung im Hochschulbereich*, Bonn: Bund-Länder-Kommission für Bildungsplanung und Forschungsfoerderung.

BMBF (1999) *Grund- und Strukturdaten 1998/99*, Bonn: Bundesministerium für Bildung und Forschung.

Davies, P. (ed.) (1995) *Adults in Higher Education: International Perspectives on Access and Participation*, London: Jessica Kingsley.

Dohmen, G. (1996) *Lifelong Learning: Guidelines for a Modern Education Policy*, Bonn: Bundesministerium für Bildung, Wissenschaft, Forschung und Technologie.

Duke, C. (1999) 'Lifelong learning: implications for the university of the 21st century', *Higher Education Management* vol. 11 no. 1.

Hackl, E., Istance, D., Schuetze, H., Slowey, M. and Wolter, A. (1997) 'Higher education and lifelong learning', in S. Hill and B. Merrill (eds) *Access, Equity, Participation and Organisational Change*, Warwick/Louvain: European Society for Research on the Education of Adults.

Holtkamp, R. and Kazemzadeh, F. (1989) *Das Engagement der Hochschulen in der Weiterbildung*, Hannover: Hochschul-Informations-System.

Isserstedt, W. (1994) *Studieren ohne schulische Hochschulzugangsberechtigung – Ergebnisse einer Befragung von Zulassungsbewerbern*, Hannover: Hochschul-Informations-System.

Kehm, B. (1998) *Higher Education in Germany: Developments, Problems and Future Perspectives*, Wittenberg: Institute for Higher Education Research.

KMK (1997) *The Education System in the Federal Republic of Germany*, Bonn: Council of Ministers of Education and Cultural Affairs.

Kuwan, H. (1999) *Berichtssystem Weiterbildung VII*, Bonn: Bundesministerium für Bildung und Forschung.

Kuwan, H., Gnahs, D. *et al.* (1996) *Berichtssystem Weiterbildung VI. Integrierter Gesamtbericht zur Weiterbildungssituation in Deutschland*, Bonn: Bundesministerium für Bildung, Wissenschaft, Forschung und Technologie.

Lewin, K., Heublein, U., Ostertag, M. and Sommer, D. (1998) *HIS-Ergebnisspiegel 1997*, Hannover: Hochschul-Informations-System.

Lullies, S. and Berning, E. (1990) *Länderbericht der Bundesrepublik Deutschland zur OECD-Studie über wissenschaftliche Weiterbildung*, Munich: Bayerisches Staatsinstitut für Hochschulforschung und Hochschulplanung.

OECD (1987) *Adults in Higher Education*, Paris: OECD.

—— (1996) *Lifelong Learning for All*, Paris: OECD.

—— (1997) *Thematic Review of the First Years of Tertiary Education: Germany*, Paris: OECD.

Peisert, H. and Framhein, G. (1994) *Higher Education in Germany*, Bonn: Federal Ministry of Education and Science.

Rubenson, K. and Schuetze, H. G. (eds) (2000) *Transition to the Knowledge Society:*

Policies and Strategies for Individual Participation and Learning, Vancouver: UBC (Institute for European Studies).

Schnitzer, K., Isserstedt, W., Muessig-Trapp, P. and Schreiber, J. (1998) *Das soziale Bild der Studentenschaft in der Bundesrepublik Deutschland*, Bonn: Bundesministerium für Bildung und Forschung.

Schulenberg, W., Scholz, W. D., Wolter, A., Fülgraff, B., Mees, U. and Maydell, J. (1986) *Beruf und Studium – Studienerfahrungen und Studienerfolg von Berufstätigen ohne Reifezeugnis*, Bonn: Bundesministerium für Bildung und Wissenschaft.

Schwiedrzik, B. and Mucke, K. (1996) 'Hochschulzugang Berufserfahrener ohne Abitur – Ein Beitrag zur Diskussion der Gleichwertigkeit beruflicher und allgemeiner Bildung', in Bundesinstitut für Berufsbildung (ed.) *Forschungsergebnisse 1995*, Berlin: BIBB.

Teichler, U. (1999) 'Lifelong learning as challenge for higher education: the state of knowledge and future research tasks', *Higher Education Management* vol. 11 no. 1.

UNESCO (1998) *World Declaration on Higher Education for the 21st Century*, Paris: UNESCO.

Wolter, A. (1990) 'Die symbolische Macht hüherer Bildung', in N. Kluge, W. D. Scholz and A. Wolter (eds) *Vom Lehrling zum Akademiker – Neue Wege des Hochschulzugangs für Berufserfahrene*, Oldenburg: Universität Oldenburg.

—— (1994) *Hochschulzugang im Umbruch? Die bildungspolitische Entwicklung des Hochschulzugangs für Berufstätige*, Oldenburg: Universität Oldenburg.

—— (1995) *Die Entwicklung der Studiennachfrage in der Bundesrepublik Deutschland*, Hannover: Institut für Entwicklungsplanung und Strukturforschung.

—— (1997) 'Hochschulzugang aus dem Beruf – Forschungsstand und bildungspolitische Perspektiven', in K. Mucke and B. Schwiedrzik (eds) *Studieren ohne Abitur*, Bielefeld: Bertelsmann Verlag.

Wolter, A. and Reibstein, E. (1991) 'Studierfähig durch Beruf und Weiterbildung? Eine empirische Studie anhand der Bildungs- und Berufsbiographien von Erwachsenen', in A. Wolter (ed.) *Die Oeffnung des Hochschulzugangs für Berufstätige*, Oldenburg: Universität Oldenburg.

4 Ireland

Adult learners and non-traditional students in Irish higher education

Tom Collins

While the concept of the non-traditional student refers to a wide range of students typically under-represented in higher education due to structural barriers of class, gender, ethnic group or age, this paper will focus primarily on mature student participation. While there is much in the literature on higher education in Ireland concerning differential participation, it has been slow to manifest itself as a major concern in Irish higher education policy. A sustained drive to the mass expansion of third level education in Ireland over the past two decades, leading to a situation in which one in every two school leavers now progresses to third level education, has tended until recently to obviate concerns with differential participation rates or with the under-representation of some groups in third level.

This chapter, therefore, will explore the emerging nature of higher education in Ireland with particular reference to the structure of participation in higher education, specifically the participation of adults. The chapter is structured in three sections. The first looks at the changing policy and socio-economic context of adult education in Ireland. The second looks at the participation of adults in higher education and the likely future trends in the area. The final section explores the future directions which universities and higher education institutions must take if a commitment to democratising knowledge is to be realised.

The context

Ireland is a small, open economy. It produces 1 per cent of European Union GDP. Its labour market has traditionally been closely integrated with that of the UK, giving it the character more of a regional than a national economy.

For most decades of the twentieth century, national discourse has focused on the economic ills of the country, attempting to explain the persistent failure of the country to achieve economic take-off. As recently as 1989 for instance, Professor Joe Lee of University College Cork concluded that:

> no other country, east or west, north or south, for which remotely reli-
> able evidence exists, has recorded so slow a rate of growth of national

income in the twentieth century. . . . It is difficult to avoid the conclusion that Irish economic performance has been the least impressive in Western Europe, perhaps in all of Europe, in the twentieth century.

(Lee 1989)

In recent years, however, all of this has changed. The OECD has for instance recently referred to Ireland's current economic performance as 'stunning'. Ireland's economic performance on all indicators through the 1990's has been certainly remarkable. Only once since 1994 has GNP growth been less that 7 per cent; in 1999, for the first time in Ireland's per capita GNP exceeded that of the EU average. Government indebtedness as percentage of GDP dropped from over 90 per cent in 1993 to just over 50 per cent in 1998. Unemployment has fallen from a high of 17 per cent in the late 1980s to just over 4 per cent currently.

Policy context

A major public debate took place in Ireland in the early 1990s about the education system. This debate focused on the National Education Convention, the ensuing White Paper on Education, *Charting our Education Future* (DES 1995), and subsequent legislation. This is the contextual framework within which educational planning in Ireland is currently pursued. Education policy-making is in addition increasingly influenced by the policy concerns of the European Union as well as by National issues. In this regard, the European Commission White Paper, *Teaching and Learning: Towards the Learning Society* (EC 1995) is an important policy reference point also.

The Government White Paper identifies the State's key concerns in relation to education policy as 'the promotion of quality, equality, pluralism, partnership and accountability' (DES 1995 p. 3). Spelling out the philosophical basis of Irish Education in more detail, the White Paper argues that a key consideration is:

The articulation, nationally, of a statement of broad educational aims, which focus on nurturing the holistic development of the individual and promoting the social and economic welfare of society, including the provision and renewal of the skills and competencies necessary for the development of our economy and society.

(DES 1995 p. 4)

Trends in education numbers

From 1965 onwards, there was a dramatic increase in the numbers attending second level education in Ireland. From this point, attendance at second level school was more common than non-attendance. A downturn in second level numbers is currently being experienced, linked closely to demographic patterns in the population.

The number of primary level attendances can also be linked closely to the demographic structure of the country. Numbers attending primary level peaked in the mid 1980s, a direct result of the high under-fourteen population at that time. This in turn led to the high second level figures in the early to mid-1990s. Future projections suggest quite a dramatic reduction in the numbers attending primary schools – falling from the peak of about 570,000 in 1985 to about 370,000 in 2015. Clearly these changing numbers in primary and secondary level will have implications for the numbers of traditional applicants for third level places.

Numbers attending third level have increased dramatically since the mid-1980s. The increase in third level can be linked to two factors – the changing demographic structure (similar to primary and secondary level) and the higher proportion of entries to third level.

Increased levels of participation in higher education have been one of the most important changes in education in the industrialised world in recent decades. Although in Ireland the mass expansion in higher education occurred a little later than elsewhere – reflecting the unique post-war demography of Ireland in Western Europe – between 1970 and 1990, the country experienced one of the fastest growing enrolment rates in Western Europe. While the expansion has spread across the two sides of the binary divide – universities and institutes of technology – the growth has been particularly high in the non-university higher education sector.

Currently, Ireland has more third-level entry places than almost any other country in relation to its population: about 9.4 per thousand of the population as against between 5 and 7 per thousand elsewhere. About 50 per cent of the annual cohort of school leavers progress onto third level.

Increasing absolute numbers and increasing proportions of higher education entrants obscure the persistence of significant inequalities in access to higher education. Clancy (1995) and Clancy and Wall (2000), in a number of profiles of higher education entrants in Ireland from the early 1980s, draw particular attention to the persistence of such inequalities. By comparing the distribution of respondents' fathers' socio-economic group with the national distribution of the population under fifteen years from the 1986 census, a participation ratio is calculated based on the extent to which each social group is proportionately represented, under-represented or over-represented among third level entrants.

This analysis reveals very large disparities among social groups, with entrants from the higher professional groups accounting for more than 10 per cent of the total intake, although they represent little more than 4 per cent of the national population. In contrast, entrants from the unskilled manual workers group accounted for just 3 per cent of all higher education entrants, though accounting for more than 8 per cent of the population. In general, all of the five lower socio-economic groups are under-represented amongst new entrants, most notably those with manual backgrounds. Conversely, those from the upper socio-economic groups (particularly if farmers are excluded from the discussion because of the diversity within that sector) are heavily over-represented among new entrants.

None the less, there has been some decline in inequality over time. While unskilled manual workers, for instance, who obtained only 37 per cent of the places which their proportion in the population would warrant, are still seriously under-represented in higher education, there has been significant improvement. Their participation ratio increased from 0.13 in 1980 to 0.16 in 1986 and to 0.37 in 1992. Conversely, the participation ratio of higher professionals declined from 3.37 in 1980 to 3.00 in 1986 and to 2.47 in 1992.

Social selectivity in higher education as a whole is complemented by further selectivity by sector and by field of study. The five socio-economic groups which were significantly under-represented in higher education as a whole had their highest representation on the technical side of the binary divide. Those from semi-skilled and unskilled backgrounds accounted for less than 4 per cent of entrants to university in 1992, while accounting for 14 per cent of the national target population (Clancy 1995 p. 63). The same pattern broadly persists with regard to fields of study, wherein the higher status disciplines disproportionately attract students from the higher status social groups while the lower income groups are disproportionately represented in the lower status disciplines and faculties.

Lynch and O'Riordan (1999), in a series of intensive interviews with low income, working class students at both second and third level, and also with teachers and community activists, explored the processes of social selectivity and reproduction in higher education access and participation. They found economic barriers to be the main obstacles to equality of opportunity. These obstacles manifested themselves in a number of ways:

- costs of sending and maintaining a student in college
- differential access to the private education market, as in intensive, one-to-one coaching and extra-curricular activities
- the need to work
- inadequate maintenance support.

Social and cultural barriers also emerged as significant obstacles. The issues which emerged here included:

- a perception that working-class ways of thinking and being were devalued in the school curricula
- a sense amongst the students that education generally, and particularly higher education, was remote, alien and frighteningly unfamiliar
- a belief amongst the teachers in the study that 'working class people do not dream of educational success for their kids as they did not have success in education' (Lynch and O'Riordan 1999 p. 108)

- a belief amongst community activists that educational institutions were inflexible and unresponsive to the needs of working class students; the community activists in the study also tended to believe that middle-class teachers were either lacking in understanding of working class students or lacking commitment to their education: 'it is a bit of a self-fulfilling prophecy, the expectation for working class students is lower' (ibid. p. 115).

With regard to gender differences, Lynch and O'Riordan found that the main gender specific barrier identified by the women interviewees was lack of adequate childcare. There was also a belief amongst some interviewees that the peer group culture among working-class men was more hostile to prolonged participation in education than that among women.

All the universities and institutes of technology now employ access officers who have the task of widening the base of higher education participation. Their role, however, appears to be largely confined to developing innovative but ultimately peripheral entry programmes for students from lower-income, working-class schools who would otherwise not gain entry. Many officers have also put in place a range of specific financial and educational supports to such students during their higher education programme. Notwithstanding the desirability of such initiatives, it is unlikely that they herald a fundamental interrogation of the institutional and cultural constructs of higher education institutions which underpin their overriding tendency towards the reproduction of the social order.

Adult education

Most commentators in Ireland – perhaps less so outside it – point to a well educated youthful population as the underpinning foundation of the dramatic economic turnaround referred to above. The expansion of mass second-level education in the 1960s, was underscored by the then prime minister's assertion that it was not that Ireland was too poor to embark on such an investment programme, but that it was too poor not to. The expansion in second-level education, followed in the 1970s and 1980s by mass third-level education, is currently, according to this view, yielding its reward.

It is now, therefore, a propitious time in Ireland to argue the case for more investment in education. There has rarely been greater unanimity on the point that such spending is an investment rather than a cost.

It is largely this analysis, combined with concerns about emerging labour shortages both in the short-term and, even more severely, in the longer term that has forced policy makers, especially labour market strategists, to look to new sources of well educated labour market entrants other than school/college leavers. For the first time therefore, adult education is being looked at to play its part in feeding the Celtic tiger. In 1998 the government published the green paper on adult education: *Adult Education in an Era of Lifelong Learning*. After a wide ranging consultation process on the green paper, the government published the country's first white paper on adult education, *Learning for Life*, in July 2000.

While both papers make a strong case for adult education in the context of its contribution to social inclusion, to active participative citizenship and to enhanced personal well-being, the green paper in particular is at its most forceful in making the case for adult education on the grounds of national competitiveness. It shows that the number of school leavers will drop from a current figure of about 70,000 annually to about 48,000 in 2012. It also draws attention to the fact that 80 per cent of those currently in the workforce in Ireland will still be there in 2010. The case therefore for looking within the current workforce to meet new skills needs, and for looking to new labour pools other than school leavers in the adult population, is self-evident. Instrumental, labour-market considerations are then the foundation of the conversion of Irish education policy towards lifelong learning. In this sense, it probably shares similar origins to the mass literacy movement of the mid-nineteenth century in Europe and America. This mass movement was largely based upon the requirements of an expanding infrastructure for a literate workforce. In the sense then that education policy has always tended to reflect economic priorities, Adult Education policy in Ireland is part of a general and long-running pattern.

Education levels of Irish adults

As mass second level education did not develop in Ireland until the late 1960s, it is not surprising that the education levels of Irish adults, particularly of those aged forty-five or over, compare unfavourably with those of other OECD countries.

As Table 4.1 shows, only 30 per cent of the fifty-five to sixty-four age cohort in Ireland have completed second level education, compared with an OECD average of 42 per cent. The table, however, also shows educational levels improve significantly among the younger age cohorts though, even here, Ireland continues to compare unfavourably with most other OECD countries. Only seven of the twenty-seven countries looked at have a lower level of secondary completion than Ireland amongst those aged twenty-five to thirty-four.

Concerns with national competitiveness mean that policy makers are also recognising that, despite improved levels of completion amongst current school leavers, wide country differentials will persist unless those who have left school are also attended to. As Figure 4.1 (page 74) shows, even at 1995 completion rates, the Irish adult population will still lag behind most other OECD countries in 2015, in the absence of targeted interventions.

Valuable insights into the nature and extent of participation in Adult Education and training may be gleaned from the OECD study, *Literacy Skills for the Knowledge Society: Further Results from the International Adult Literacy*

Table 4.1 Percentage of the population completing at least upper secondary education in two age cohorts

	Population presently aged 55–64	Population presently aged 25–34
Australia	46	62
Austria	53	82
Belgium	31	70
Canada	56	85
Denmark	50	74
Finland	40	83
France	38	74
Germany	71	86
Greece	22	66
Hungary	28	80
Ireland	30	66
Italy	17	52
Japan	—	—
Korea	25	88
Luxembourg	20	32
Mexico	—	—
Netherlands	47	72
New Zealand	49	65
Norway	62	91
Poland	47	88
Portugal	9	32
Spain	11	50
Sweden	53	87
Switzerland	71	87
Turkey	7	23
United Kingdom	60	87
United States	77	87
Country mean	42	72

Source: OECD (1998).

Note: Different measures are used to calculate the percentages for the different cohorts, so within cohort country data are most appropriate for comparisons across the age groups.

Survey (1997) which, while primarily focused on literacy, also produced general data on participation in Adult Education and training for Ireland and for other OECD countries.

The main findings of this study in regard to Ireland are as follows:

- 29.5 per cent of all respondents (28.5 per cent males and 30.5 per cent females) had participated in Adult Education or training in the previous 12 months.
- Of this, 42.5 per cent was self-financed, 27.3 per cent was employer funded, 19.6 per cent was State funded, and the remainder was funded by trade unions or other agencies or provided free.

- 29.5 per cent was provided in a publicly funded third level college, 18.5 per cent in a second level school, 12.8 per cent in a private college, 12.2 per cent at work, and 8.5 per cent in a training centre.
- 31.4 per cent of participants were employed, 14.8 per cent were unemployed, 10.9 per cent were in the home, and 3.3 per cent were retired.
- 47.5 per cent of participants were in the 16–24 year age group, whereas only 9.1 per cent were aged between fifty-five and sixty-four.

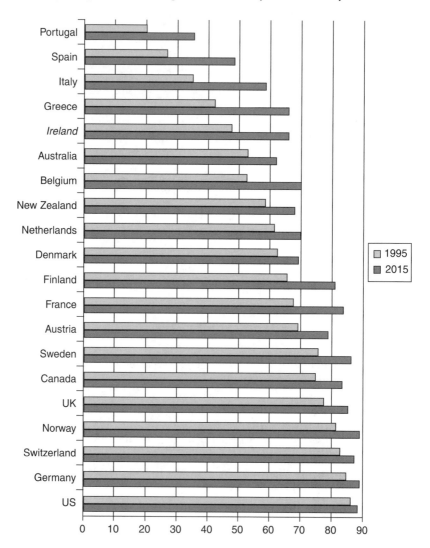

Figure 4.1 Projected growth in the educational levels of the adult population: percentage of the population aged twenty-five to sixty-four having completed upper secondary education assuming 1995 youth qualification rates

- 55.3 per cent of participants were graded at Literacy levels 4/5 (the highest), compared with 10.5 per cent and 22.5 per cent respectively at Literacy Levels 1 and 2.
- Participation was strongly linked to prior educational attainment, with 54.2 per cent of college graduates having taken part in Adult Education and training in the previous twelve months compared with only 8.5 per cent and 17.7 per cent of respondents with primary or junior cycle qualifications.

Perhaps the most telling finding in this study was that which showed that 25 per cent of Irish adults aged over twenty-five were at Literacy Level 1, a further 32 per cent at Level 2, and only 6 per cent at Literacy Level 5.

It is considerations such as these which predispose Adult Education policy makers in Ireland towards an emphasis on second chance basic education rather than on second chance higher education. The recently published white paper, therefore, proposes a 'Back to Education Initiative' consisting of a continuum of programmes from foundation level literacy up to complete second level provision. While progression to third level is also provided for, the greater share of public expenditure on Adult Education in the future will be directed towards more basic provision.

Adults in higher education

Unlike other western countries, particularly America and Great Britain, the expansion in higher education in Ireland has drawn little on mature students. The growing political support for Adult Education in Ireland is now serving to turn attention to the participation of adults in higher education even if this is not, as stated above, the main focus of concern. From 1970, the political drive for the expansion of higher education in Ireland has been almost totally directed towards the provision of full-time places in universities and institutes of technology for school leavers. Concern with the needs of mature students first emerged in official publications in 1995 with the Interim Report of the Technical Working Group of the Higher Education Authority's Steering Committee on the Future Development of Higher Education.

Considering the recency of the phenomenon then, it is not surprising that adults form a small percentage of higher education entrants in Ireland. Data in the 1997 OECD Report *Education at a Glance: Policy Analysis* showed that on average 19.3 per cent of entrants to universities in OECD countries were aged twenty-six or over. The comparative figure for Ireland was 2 per cent. For the non-university sector, the OECD average was 36.8 per cent, while for Ireland the figure was 1.1 per cent. Ireland's adult participation rates are significantly lower than those for all other OECD countries for which data are available.

While the participation rates of adults in higher education in Ireland are low by international standards, there is also evidence to show that participation rates for older students (forty-five and above) and for socially disadvantaged groups are particularly low. As shown above, socially disadvantaged groups, regardless of age are generally poorly represented in Irish higher education, with particularly stark differences in entry rates between the two highest socio-economic groups and the two lowest.

While this general pattern is echoed in the structure of mature student participation, it does not transfer identically. Those from unskilled manual backgrounds for instance are more than twice as likely to be found in the mature student population than among the student population overall, while higher professionals are between two and three times less likely to occur in the mature student population than in the overall population of college entrants. The groups which are most likely to be over-represented in the mature student population however are salaried employees – many of whom are likely to be in part-time study – employers and managers and lower professionals.

Of the generic barriers to mature student participation in higher education, structural barriers of class, age and, to a lesser extent, gender are clearly critical. The issue of class has been dealt with above. With regard to age, over 50 per cent of all mature students in Ireland are under thirty years of age and 85 per cent are under forty. With regard to gender, there are more men than women in higher education (50.8 per cent as opposed to 49.2 per cent). Men account for almost 60 per cent of part-time students but there is gender parity in the full-time student population (Lynch 1999).

There is growing attention in the literature and in policy-making in Ireland to the institutional barriers to mature student participation. These include:

- rigid, or obscure, entry requirements to third level
- inadequate development of access courses, particularly in science and higher-status disciplines and faculties
- the persistence of the universities with traditional pedagogical and assessment procedures, according little validation to prior learning or experience
- poorly developed systems of credit transfer, credit accumulation or course modularisation
- inadequate funding of mature students, particularly in areas such as child care, books and (in the case of part-time students) fees.

A questionnaire survey of 119 adult students in four Irish higher education institutions conducted by the author in 1999 as part of a wider European study suggests that mature students in Ireland are:[1]

- typically aged between twenty-five and thirty-four, with the over forty-fives accounting for less than one quarter of all mature students

- more likely to be female than male: two thirds to one third
- likely to be married or living with a partner
- slightly more likely to have no children than to have children
- slightly more likely to be working than not working or engaged in home duties
- more likely to cite interest in the subject area and intellectual enrichment rather than career advancement as their reason for their return to education
- more likely to list factors of finance, family commitments and time as major barriers to returning, with issues of work commitments and self-confidence being also important
- unlikely to be able to utilise prior work experience or prior experiential learning in gaining admission
- unlikely to be satisfied with the level of student involvement in the learning programme
- likely to rely on other students or sources other than those strictly within academic circles as the main source of feedback on performance.

In their study of mature students in University College Dublin, Inglis and Murphy point to the fact that while mature students generally hold positive views about academic staff, they experience high levels of frustration and rejection in gaining admission to university and high levels of anxiety throughout their university life. While many of their respondents enjoyed the learning and the pursuit of knowledge, and welcomed the contact with other people in college, they also felt isolated by the age difference, one of them, for instance, feeling 'she had stuck out like a sore thumb last year' (Inglis and Murphy 1999 p. 37). Many were dissatisfied with the College library and creche facilities and only half were satisfied with the teaching methods used by staff in the College.

Two recent major contributions to higher education policy – the *Report of the Commission on the Points System* (CPS 1999) and the *Report of the Review Committee on Post-Secondary Education and Training Places* (HEA 1999) set explicit and ambitious targets in this regard. The Points Commission looks to increase the rate of mature student participation to 15 per cent by the year 2005 and 25 per cent by the year 2015. Additionally it calls for the establishment of a co-ordinated system of assessment of mature student applicants by Autumn 2002 and for a review of the definition of 'part-time' courses. It also considers that people who did not enter third level education on leaving school should have access to the same financial support as school leavers, if they wish to enter third level education in later life, whether on a full-time or a part-time basis. It takes the view that 'the State has a responsibility to provide third level places for adults who did not have access to third level when they left school as well as having responsibility for providing third level places for school leavers' (CPS 1999 p. 115).

The Review Committee noted that the:

high proportion in the age cohort under review who do not have upper secondary education is striking. Many people in this age group would have chosen to participate in third level education if they had the opportunity. It seems clear that the Leaving Certificate is still the critical gateway for further and higher education and training. The means by which adult learners can either access the Leaving Certificate, or have alternative qualifications recognised for access, needs to be addressed.

(CPS p. 59)

The Committee went on to recommend an 'additional stock' of up to 10,000 places for mature students, of which at least 80 per cent should be part-time.

The recently published white paper on adult education, referred to above, includes a range of incentives and proposals to enhance mature student participation in higher education. These proposals include, *inter alia*,

- the adoption of a target of 15 per cent for mature student representation in higher education by 2005
- the establishment of a targeted higher education mature student fund to enable third level institutions to make innovative strategic shifts towards adult-friendly policies
- the extension of free third level fees to part-time students in particular social categories.[1]

In the light of these proposals and developments, the question arises as to whether Ireland is about to solve the challenge of democratising higher education. This issue is looked at in the next section.

Democratising higher education

Irish higher education institutions generally, particularly the universities, have aimed to guarantee standards by restrictive entry arrangements. A competitive points system, based on second level examination results, has both restricted access to higher education generally and to the high status faculties and disciplines in particular. The entry of non-traditional students into the system, therefore, has been discretionary, rather than entitlement based. Mature students on undergraduate programmes in particular frequently feel not just inadequate in using a 'back door' entry but also unworthy to be there at all on having gained entry. The rituals surrounding the entry of non-traditional students may even serve to reinforce the legitimacy of existing entry criteria by extracting a psychological and emotional payback from those students who do not meet these criteria. In this process, the institution is likely to undervalue the 'common sense' and experiential knowledge which the mature student brings to the academy. In this situation, the non-traditional applicant enters a relationship of unequal exchange in which the power of the institution – even where mitigated by more benign procedures – goes largely unchallenged.

The task of democratising knowledge is surely more fundamental than simply opening a few sidegates in a largely unbreached wall. Indeed, one could suggest that it is precisely the opening of such sidegates which has enabled the wall to continue unbreached. The fundamental assumptions of higher education regarding the nature of knowledge, its construction and its acquisition have remained largely untroubled by increasing participation rates of adults and other non-traditional students. Rather, they may indeed have been reinforced by them.

Wagner (1999) identifies some of the main attributes of the university of the future. These include:

- a relationship between higher education and learners which extends over a lifetime
- new ways of thinking about standards and qualifications
- expanded partnerships and links, within and across sectors and levels
- new approaches to securing and using resources.

Assuming that the changes anticipated by Wagner do in fact occur, the concern is that they can occur without a fundamental reassessment of the nature of higher education and accordingly may have little impact on democratising higher education. This is so because the changes to which Wagner alludes are concerned more with the delivery of knowledge rather than with its construction or validation.

The differentiation and globalisation of knowledge delivery systems will inevitably compel higher education institutions to respond to market forces in their delivery systems. Distance education and on-line courses in particular are forcing a cultural shift in higher education institutions from one of deflecting demand to generating demand. Like many other services, universities and other third level institutions are encountering the vagaries of a free and global market. While recognising the potential for cultural imperialism in those developments, they are also inevitably going to force higher education institutions to look to pools of students which they had heretofore ignored or only marginally engaged with.

An Adult Education critique, however, while welcoming the increased opportunities likely to arise from such developments, would also concern itself with qualitative aspects of such increased opportunities. In particular, it would concern itself with the interaction between the commonsense knowledge of day-to-day life and the prevailing 'magisterial' view of knowledge in the academy. Murphy and Fleming describe the interrelationship between these two types of knowledge as a conflict 'between what we might call "common" or subjective knowledge and "college" or objective academic knowledge (and between) two different approaches to learning, the experiential learning approach ... and the academic approach to learning' (Murphy and Fleming 2000 p. 86).

Much of the 'really useful' adult learning activity in Ireland, in recent years, has happened outside the tutelage and the remit of the academy. The growth of community based women's education, driven by the participants in co-learning contexts, could be seen to have had a dramatic impact on the personal lives of the participants, on the life chances of their children and on the broader political landscape of the country as a whole. Despite this, the learning attained within this context goes largely unobserved and unacknowledged in conventional academic circles. Little effort has been made to construct meaningful relationships between the academy and the community education sector. The individualised, competitive entry and assessment processes within higher education are uniquely inappropriate to the communal, mutually supportive and co-operative ethos of the community education sector. Indeed, the selective, privatised recruitment criteria of higher education institutions can progressively weaken the capacity of the community education sector to create its own knowledge.

Apart from such structural and institutional barriers to mature student participation some authors have called attention to barriers concerning personal confidence and self-esteem (Lynch 1999, Merrill 1999). The fear of second-chance failure characterises the initial experience of many mature students in the early stages of their third level career. This is so despite the fact that there is growing evidence that mature students perform better in college than the general student body. Confirmation of such a pattern would have profound implications for third level recruitment policies in that it would challenge the dominant assumption that standards are best assured by restrictive entry rather than by sanctioned exit.

Community-based women's groups are just one area where 'really useful' learning is occurring outside academia. The area of complementary therapies is a second such area, significant perhaps because it is developing as a challenge to mainstream medicine, traditionally among the highest-status and most restrictive of university faculties.

Ireland is one of many countries which has experienced significant growth in complementary therapies in recent years. Like community education, this growth has occurred more in spite of formal systems than through them. In its relationship with the formal systems it shares many of the attributes of community education. This is particularly true of its focus on holistic learning, on learning as construction rather than instruction, in its concern with good health rather than disease control and in its view of the 'patient' as a self-directed, self-healing system. In having been largely – though not entirely – ignored by the conventional university-based medical schools, the complementary therapies have pioneered ground breaking approaches to health outside of the walls of academia, in much the same way as community education has done to notions of learning and knowledge.

The challenge of the adult learning critique to universities is to move them from a position in which the student is the target of a knowledge delivery system to one in which the student is actively engaged in constructing knowledge through reflective practice; from one which removes the learner from a real world situation to one which relies on the real world situation as the learning agenda; from a concern with access to one of emancipation; and from one which organises knowledge in linear, closed discipline areas to one which recognises the multi-disciplinary, open and systemic nature of knowledge.

It is excessively simplistic, therefore, to reduce the task of higher education reform to more flexible systems of entry and dissemination. To confine the discussion to this level is to ignore the challenge of a meaningful democratisation of knowledge. This challenge requires a more fundamental reassessment of the very paradigm upon which higher education is based. Viewed in this way, the challenge is not only to democratise higher education in the interest of those not in it, but to do so in the interest also of those who are.

Notes

This study was undertaken as part of a wider European study of non-traditional students in higher education in six countries: UK, Germany, Spain, Sweden, Belgium and Ireland (European Union: TSER Project SOE2–CT97–2021).

1 Free fees already apply to full-time third-level students on undergraduate programmes.

References

Clancy, P. (1995) *Access to College: Patterns of Continuity and Change*, Dublin: Higher Education Authority.

—— (1998) *Who Goes to College*, Dublin: Higher Education Authority.

Clancy, P. and Wall, J. (2000) *Social Background of Higher Education Entrants*, Dublin: Higher Education Authority.

CPS (Commission on the Points System) (1999) *Report of the Commission on the Points System*, Dublin: Stationery Office.

DES (Department of Education and Science) (1995) *Charting Our Education Future: White Paper on Education*, Dublin: Stationery Office.

—— (1998) *Green Paper on Adult Education: Adult Education in an Era of Lifelong Learning*, Dublin: Stationery Office.

—— (1999) *Ready to Learn: White Paper on Early Childhood Education*, Dublin: Stationery Office.

—— (2000) *Learning for Life; White Paper on Adult Education*, Dublin: Stationery Office.

EC (European Commission) (1995) *White Paper, Teaching and Learning: Towards the Learning Society*, Brussels/Luxembourg: Office for Official Publications of the European Commission.

HEA (Higher Education Authority) (1995) *Interim Report of the Steering Committee's Technical Working Group*, Dublin: Stationery Office.

—— (1999) *Report of the Review Committee on Post-Secondary Education and Training Places*, Dublin: Stationery Office.

Inglis, T. and Murphy, M. (1999) *No Room for Adults: A Study of Mature Students in University College Dublin*, Social Science Research Centre and Adult Education Office, Dublin: UCD.

Lee, J. J. (1989) *Ireland 1912–1985: Politics and Society*, Cambridge: Cambridge University Press.

Lynch, K. (1999) *Equality in Education*, Dublin: Gill and Macmillan.

Lynch, K. and O'Riordan, C. (1999) 'Inequality in higher education: a study of social class barriers', in K. Lynch (ed.) *Equality in Education*, Dublin: Gill and Macmillan.

Merrill, B. (1999) 'The adult learner – developments and research in the United Kingdom: contextualising access in the UK', in T. Fleming, T. Collins and J. Coolahan (eds) *Higher Education: The Challenge of Lifelong Learning*, Centre for Educational Policy Studies, Maynooth: NUI.

Murphy, M. and Fleming, T. (2000) 'Between common and college knowledge: exploring the boundaries between adult and higher education', *Studies in Continuing Education* vol. 22 no. 1.

OECD (1997a) *Literacy Skills for the Knowledge Society: Further Results from the International Adult Literacy Survey*, Paris: OECD.

—— (1997b) *Education at a Glance*, Paris: OECD.

—— (1998) *Education at a Glance*, Paris: OECD.

Smyth, A. (1999) 'Introduction', in C. McHugh, *A Study of Feminist Education as an Empowerment Strategy for Community Based Women's Groups in Ireland*, Dublin: WERRC.

Wagner, A. (1999) 'Lifelong learning and higher education: the international context', in T. Fleming, T. Collins and J. Coolahan (eds) *Higher Education: The Challenge of Lifelong Learning*, Centre for Educational Policy Studies, Maynooth: NUI.

5 Sweden

Non-traditional students in higher education in Sweden: from recurrent education to lifelong learning

Agnieszka Bron and Karin Agélii

Introduction

Since the 1950s the Swedish higher education system has been characterised by important changes which have contributed to the opening up of opportunities to different categories of students, who might be called non-traditional. Not only the number of students, but also the proportion of mature students increased dramatically. As far as non-traditional students are concerned, it was the reform of higher education from 1977 onwards which had the biggest impact on their access to higher education, coupled with the introduction of the student loan system in the late 1960s.

The pattern of formal and linear progress directly from school, which had previously been dominant, changed to a more recurrent style. It is very common for young people to postpone their higher education after they leave school and instead to find a job and gain wider life experience first. It is also common for students to interrupt their studies and to continue later. In this chapter we want to show how it was possible to change the traditional patterns of participation to such an extent that the traditional student now is in the minority. It is young, full-time, direct school entrants who are in effect non-traditional. Sweden is unique in this respect compared to most other OECD countries, and as such is a particularly interesting case study.

In this chapter we start with the national system of higher education, followed by an exploration of the concept of non-traditional students and their participation. We then present institutional policy and practices, and analyse policy changes over the last fifteen years, focusing in particular on changes in the labour market and their impact on students' demands and patterns. We end with conclusions for policy, practice and research.

The national system of higher education in Sweden

Admission routes

Since 1993 the secondary school system has been organised in sixteen different three-year national programmes sharing the same general core curriculum. All programmes confer basic eligibility for further studies at university level. To gain admission to higher education, students have to satisfy not only basic eligibility requirements but also specific course requirements. Basic eligibility is determined by the government and applies to all higher education institutions, while course requirements are linked to a particular group of programmes, such as those for graduate engineers. Basic requirements are formal grades from upper-secondary education or provable knowledge in Swedish and English that is equivalent to the three-year secondary school programmes in Sweden. Examples of specific requirements are formal grades and provable knowledge equivalent to a secondary school diploma in certain fields. Other examples of specific requirements may be in the form of previous higher education courses or relevant work experience. Two of the secondary school programmes – natural science and social science – are especially focused towards university entrance, thus offering the richest range of specific course requirements. The other programmes have more of a vocational character, which narrows the scope of accessible courses and programmes into higher education.

It is always however possible for graduates of these secondary vocational programmes to undertake any required additional subjects through municipal adult education (*Komvux*). Municipal adult education thus provides an important 'second chance' education to adults at both basic and secondary levels. Secondary schooling for adults has the same syllabi as for young people and, as of 1 July 1994, they share the same curricula, but the two are not identical. On the adult orientated programme the students themselves determine the number and combination of subjects to be taken and the rate of progress to be achieved. Courses are organised on both full-time and part-time bases. In 1996 the average age among adult students was approximately twenty-seven, with about 35 per cent being older than twenty-five and about 56 per cent being women. The most common reason for study at *Komvux* was to become eligible for higher education (SCB 1996).

Another interesting form of adult education in Sweden is the Folk High School (FHS), residential institutions of liberal adult education that attract some hundred thousand enrolments every year. It is possible to prepare for admission to higher education through FHS courses.

Other ways to gain access to higher education include a national university aptitude test. This was introduced in 1977 to increase the opportunities for applicants without a secondary school diploma, specifically those with a FHS certificate and those from the '25:4' scheme. The latter programme was introduced in 1977 and provided a general entitlement of access to higher education to applicants who were at least twenty-five years of age and had a minimum of four years of work experience. Importantly, however, specific requirements remained in place thus limiting in practice the options for mature students. However, since 1992, the aptitude test has been opened to everyone. A good score can result in extra credits, whether for applicants with a traditional educational background (grades from secondary education including *Komvux*) or for students with non-traditional qualifications (25:4

scheme or FHS certificate). The test takes place twice a year and a small fee is charged. Each year, more than 100,000 people take the national university aptitude test, which remains valid for five years. Some 40 per cent of those admitted to higher education gain admission on the basis of their performance in the test. The National Agency for Higher Education (NAHE) is responsible for administration and co-ordination of the test.[1] Though the main responsibility for applications and access regulations lies within each individual institution, there are some central guiding regulations governing the rate of access for students with different qualifications. These regulations provide that at least one-third of the places on single courses or programmes should be distributed to applicants from the aptitude test quota, and half of these places should be distributed to applicants with work experience (the former 25:4 quota).

Structure of the system

The Swedish higher education system is relatively uniform and coherent in its structure. In practice it comprises all types of post-secondary education. There is, however, a considerable degree of flexibility for the individual institutions in terms of content and organisation of the courses and educational programmes. In 1996 there were about seventy public institutions of higher education in Sweden and a very small number of private institutions.

A distinction can be made between five main types of higher education institutions (HSV/Brandell 1998).

- Universities provide education in almost all academic fields. Fifty per cent of the students study at one of about twelve universities (university colleges can apply to become universities and so this number is growing).
- Specialised colleges of higher education provide education and research within a specific field, for example technology. Around 12 per cent of the students study at these institutions which include some longer, high-status professional programmes such as medicine.
- Small and medium-sized university colleges provide education within a diversified spectrum including a number of shorter professional programmes. Most of them run only undergraduate studies. About 30 per cent of all students study at a small or medium-sized university college. Their dominant fields of study are technology and teacher training.
- Institutions for the medical and paramedical professions (for example laboratory assistants, physiotherapists and nurses) form the fourth category of higher education establishment. This institutional group contains around 7 per cent of the student population.
- Other types of institution make up a very small category mainly consisting of institutions of theology, which are non-state run, and the independent university colleges of art and design in Stockholm.[2]

Within these different types of institutions of higher education (HE), students can choose amongst a vast variety of shorter single-subject courses or longer programmes. Single-subject courses are a traditional way of acquiring higher education in Sweden, as in the German university system. They are seen as more academic courses, and are called 'free' courses as students can choose those which best fit their interests. In this way they can build their own curriculum. Programmes more directly geared towards the labour market are characterised by fixed curricula which students have to take over two, four or five years. Institutions often offer some of their courses as either full- or part-time. Most of them also provide programmes leading to a specific profession, for example teaching, psychology or medicine. There are around forty different professional programmes of different lengths leading to a professional degree. These programmes have a centrally (state) determined curriculum while the locally determined courses and programmes have local curricula.

The following general degrees at the undergraduate level are specified in the Degree Ordinance (*Högskoleförordningen*) of 1993:

- A Higher Education Diploma (*Högskoleexamen*) is awarded after studies amounting to no less than eighty credits (two years of full-time study). The diploma is not a full academic degree; in other words, it does not prepare students for graduate studies. Artistic subjects and journalism are examples of an HE Diploma.
- A Bachelor of Art, Science or Law (*Kandidatexamen*) is awarded after studies amounting to no less than 120 credits (three years of full-time studies) with sixty credits in one subject and including ten credits for a thesis. This degree gives an opportunity to continue education with Ph.D. studies.
- A Master's degree (*Magisterexamen*). This degree was introduced by departments at universities several years ago. It can be awarded on the basis of 160 credits (four years of studies) with eighty credits in one subject and twenty credits for one or two theses. However, this degree is not necessary for Ph.D. studies and it is not offered at all university departments.

Research training leads to a Ph.D. degree. It takes a minimum of four years to complete doctoral studies (usually with eighty credits of courses and eighty credits for the thesis).

Resource allocation for HE differs for undergraduate and graduate studies. Allocation of funds for graduate students is based on the number of professors and successful graduates of Ph.D. programmes. The size of state grants for the undergraduate level is based on the number of students registered and the number of study credits they achieve. The financial aid system for individual undergraduate students is also linked to the credit system. Students must complete a certain number of credits per year (usually thirty credits) to get loans and grants for their studies. Undergraduate students have the right to a maximum study loan (including the grant) for twelve semesters. For the time being, the maximum loan (together with the grant) amounts to around 7,000 Swedish kronor per month, of which 2,000 kronor is a grant and the rest has to be paid back when the studies are finished. Students are usually not eligible for the loan or the grant if they are over forty-five years of age. The amount of the grant and loan is reduced and/or the opportunity to benefit from the financial aid system is taken away when a student earns money by working in addition to studying.[3]

Since 1979, there has been a *numerus clausus* policy in higher education, restricting admission to certain high-demand disciplines. Though the total number of students was permitted to increase by 75 per cent between 1985 and 1995 and though the system continues to expand, many applicants still have to be turned away. The National Agency for Higher Education (NAHE) decides on the standard course requirements and monitors how institutions apply their admission rules.

Participation of non-traditional students

The concept of 'non-traditional' students in Sweden is problematic. The expression has been used in different historical, political, geographical and academic settings to refer to different groups. However, taking into account previous research (including that of the authors), commissioned work and evaluations carried out by state agencies and authorities, we would argue that the main categories of student likely to be considered as non-traditional in Sweden today include:

- *Mature students* This term relates to students who start their studies for the first time at the age of twenty-five or later, including those who gain access through work experience and the aptitude test (and former 25:4 applicants) (Abrahamsson 1986, Abrahamsson and Rubensson 1981, Dahllöf 1983, Bron and Agélii 1997, Kim 1980, 1998, HSV/Brandell 1998). Before 1977, there were no national statistics on the age of students at entry to higher education, so it is difficult to trace trends in the percentage of students entering higher education at twenty-five years of age or over.
- *Younger students* Since it is rare in Sweden for teenagers to enter higher education directly from secondary school, the number of young students aged between nineteen and twenty-one is low. Defining the concept of non-traditional students as equivalent to minority student groups, it could, in contrast to the situation in many other countries, be argued that young students (nineteen to twenty-one) are non-traditional in Sweden (Kim 1998, Lönnheden 1999).
- *Working-class students* Students coming from non-academic, working-class families with a father who is a blue-collar worker (Eriksson &

Jonsson 1993), or who are blue-collar themselves (Bron-Wojciechowska 1989), are under-represented in Swedish higher education.

- *Part-time students*   Such students are defined as those taking less than fourteen credits in six months. One out of five students studies part-time (HSV/Brandell 1998).

- *Students with non-Swedish ethnic backgrounds*   These groups are considered minorities and are thus defined as non-traditional (Bron and Agélii 1997, Gerani 1998).

- *Students with a Folk High School (FHS) certificate*   Those who gain access through residential FHS form a very small group (Bron and Agélii 1997).

- *Other groups*   Students falling into this category are returning students, that is students who return to HE after a break of at least 1.5 years (HSV/Brandell 1998), students with children who perceive their roles and life-situations differently from other students (HSV/Brandell & Höög 1998); and disabled students.

One feature of the Swedish higher education system is that it is difficult to distinguish statistically between non-degree and degree students since there are no special programmes for students aiming towards a Bachelor's degree.[4] In other words, students explicitly working towards a Bachelor's degree in a specific subject and students who are studying without this explicit aim can take the same courses. It might well be that a non-degree student has been studying for a longer time and gathered more credits in different subjects than a student who has reached a Bachelor's degree in a single subject. What differentiates the two is that the latter has completed a final thesis paper, and thus obtained the formal academic education certificate.

National statistics specifying the participation rate and conditions for different student groups are limited in Sweden. The NAHE co-operates with Statistics Sweden (SCB) and is in charge of gathering, analysing and presenting national data and information about the higher education system to parliament, the government, various higher education institutions and the public. However, neither the NAHE nor the individual higher education institutions and departments provide official statistics illustrating, for example, the number of disabled students, employed/working students, students' access routes and students' ethnic backgrounds. The imprecise definition of the concept of the 'non-traditional' student alongside the 'statistical problem' makes meaningful comparisons with other nations very difficult.

In an attempt to compensate for the lack of relevant statistics, we present some unpublished figures and data including both national statistics from 1995 and statistics from a student survey carried out by the NAHE in 1996. The latter survey was sent out to 3,000 students who were fairly representative for the total student population in Sweden.[5]

Since the number of places in HE is restricted, the opportunity for students to get into higher education depends on the number of places available and the number of applicants. In 1996, there were a total of 113,000 applicants to higher education and only 44,000 (less than 40 per cent) were admitted to single-subject courses or programmes (SCB 1997).

During the 1980s, the total number of registered students (full-time and part-time) remained around 150,000; however, this changed in the 1990s when there was a large increase in student numbers. By 1997, the total number of students was approximately 264,000, with plans for continuing expansion.

The increase in student numbers has mainly taken place in the single-subject courses within the regional university colleges. As a consequence of special and intense recruitment policies there has also been an increase in participation in specialised technological colleges of higher education. The number of students at the larger universities in fact decreased over 1995–6 (HSV/Brandell and Petri 1996). As in many other countries, regional universities and colleges play an increasing part in attracting mature students from the local area. These institutions are also getting increasing financial support from the state through the allocation of places, not least because of the emphasis they place on collaborative links with local industry and the public sector.

Nearly 50 per cent of the students in Swedish undergraduate education are aged twenty-five years or older, and over 25 per cent are over thirty. There are more women (56 per cent) than men among Swedish higher education students. Women are a majority in all age groups, but most of the women are to be found in the youngest (under twenty-one) and the oldest (over 30) cohorts. Female domination is particularly strong in the forty-year-old and older cohorts.

The number of students entering higher education at the age of twenty-five or above has been of special interest when considering the issue of non-traditional participation. Some of the earlier research and commissioned work (e.g. Kim 1980, Abrahamsson 1986) has focused on the situation of, and the access regulations for, entrants over twenty-five years of age. This age-related concern is coupled with the 25:4 scheme which was introduced in 1977.

In recent years, since policy efforts now focus on lowering the age of entry of students, the number of entrants who are twenty-five and older has decreased. This can be supported by examining the rates of student participation in 1985 and 1995, that is, the quotient for the student participation rate (the per centage of the Swedish population aged eighteen to sixty that was involved in higher education in those years). In this ten-year period, the largest increase in participation took place among the youngest age cohort. The participation rate more than doubled in the nineteen to twenty-one age range for both men and women, while the increase in participation was small for those aged around thirty. After this age, the increase was higher among women than among men (HSV/Brandell 1998).

Swedish higher education however continues to be highly segregated by sex. Typically men have a strong predominance in the fields of maths and science, engineering and technology while women dominate in the field of healthcare. In terms of age and subject of study, the age ratio in the field of life health is 'well balanced', whereas the fields of maths/science, engineering and technology have the lowest proportion of students who are thirty or older.

The social background of students is a factor that has been studied and followed with interest by Swedish politicians and researchers (see Ericsson and Jonsson 1993). In practice, the term 'social background' refers to the socio-economic background of the father of the student. The NAHE states that students from different background groups differ in terms of age, field of study and institution attended and presents the following data about students from three different social groups.

- *Group 1*   Children of parents who have an academic education or who are 'higher employees' (civil servants). Thirty per cent of all students belong to Group 1. A high proportion of these students study at universities and specialised HE institutions. They are under-represented among older students (over thirty), and have as many women as men.
- *Group 2*   Children of 'other types' of employee, entrepreneurs, the self-employed and farmers. Fifty per cent of all students in Sweden, no matter their age cohort or the type of HE institution attended, belong to this group. It is, however, made up of more women than men.
- *Group 3*   Children of blue-collar workers. Twenty per cent of students belong to this group. Sixty per cent of them are women and they are a majority among students over thirty years of age (HSV/Brandell 1998).

We will now look at the NAHE 'Students in Sweden' (StudS) survey for data concerning the financial circumstances of the students (finance and work), students with children, their marital status and the students' types of residence.

Finance and work

In 1964, a study loan was introduced, giving all students the right to a loan that included an educational benefit in the form of a grant as well as a larger part that had to be paid back. In 1965, a law was introduced permitting employed people to get educational leave to acquire higher education (*studieledighetslagen*). Today, approximately 80 per cent of the students in Sweden benefit from the special economic aid system for students. Of these students, 60 per cent take both loans and grants and 20 per cent take only grants. The rest of the students (20 per cent) manage their finances by working, getting economic support from their parents and/or spouses, and so on. The StudS survey material indicates that 33 per cent of students (part-time and full-time) in Sweden undertake some kind of work besides their studies and 10 per cent work full-time (HSV forthcoming).

Students with children

The StudS survey indicates that more than 22 per cent of the female students and 13 per cent of the male students have children under eighteen years of age. Seventy per cent of the female students aged thirty to thirty-nine have children under eighteen and 3 per cent of all students are single parents with children living at home (HSV forthcoming). Students, especially women with small children, find it very hard to combine their role as parents with their role and duties as students and 33 per cent of the students with children (double the proportion found among students without children) perceive their economic situation as hard (HSV forthcoming, HSV/Brandell and Höög 1998).

Marital status and type of residence

The StudS survey also shows a higher proportion of male than female students to be unmarried/single. Approximately 46 per cent of female students are married or living with a partner, compared with 30 per cent of men. The survey also reveals that Swedish students live to a large extent in rented apartments; fewer than 5 per cent of the students live in special student rooms. Male students (16 per cent) are more likely than female students (11 per cent) to live with their parents (HSV forthcoming).

To summarise, we can say that in Sweden there are limited official national statistics specifying the participation rate and conditions for groups that might be considered non-traditional. Nevertheless, the following facts are of interest:

- Sweden has a growing HE sector. The number of students has increased mainly in the small and medium-sized HE institutions, and the increase has been larger among younger students than among older ones.
- The age pattern of Swedish students is, nevertheless, high in comparison to other nations. Nearly 50 per cent of the undergraduate students in Sweden are aged twenty-five or older and more than 25 per cent are over thirty.
- There are more women (56 per cent) than men among undergraduate students. Women are a majority in all age groups.

Institutional policy/practice towards non-traditional students

The Swedish higher education system is centralised, but it also has a high degree of autonomy. The overall plans for funds and their allocation, the number of student places and recruitment strategies, as well as degrees and examination procedures, are decided centrally by the state. Each faculty and department within the system, however, is decentralised and it can make individual decisions within a given framework. In other words, such bodies have a fairly free hand in deciding not only how to implement the state policy, but also how to carry out innovations and new practices. Access opportunities are decided centrally as far as programmes are concerned, but remain decentralised as far as single courses are concerned.

Generally the whole higher education system is flexible to such an extent that it allows individual students to remain in, to drop-out and to come back to it, but also to choose and change different combinations of disciplines.

Alternative routes to HE already exist on the central level. We have already mentioned the national aptitude test, *Komvux* competencies, FHS certificates, and the 25:4 scheme. In addition, there are programmes run in collaboration with higher education institutions which continuously target the government's employment policy. A recent example of such an activity is the so-called '*Aspirantutbildning för invandrar-akademiker*', which is a one-year training programme aiming to facilitate entry to the labour market, mainly for unemployed immigrants with foreign academic qualifications. Few of the Swedish universities were commissioned to offer such a programme during 1995–7. Another current example is the so-called *NT-SVUX* activities which offer economically favourable conditions for adults with a minimum of five years work experience when they begin to study certain programmes within the field of science and applied science. To be eligible for this programme, students have to be between the ages of twenty-eight and forty-eight. Currently around 9,000 students are taking part in *NT-SVUX*.

These examples show state intervention in higher education by the tailoring of special programmes for target groups. There is, however, another dimension as far as co-operation between higher education and the labour market is concerned. Public–private partnership is a growing field in Sweden and there is great interest from higher education policy-makers to establish such co-operation. We can talk about the following fields or spheres:

- co-operation between higher education institutions and the outside world on research; externally commissioned education
- co-operation between universities and the outside world on education and the future work of students
- co-operation between higher education and industry (mostly on research)
- co-operation between higher education and the outside world in connection with research and development projects
- direct contact between universities and the outside world in the dissemination of research information.

Adult students are particularly represented in the growing area of what is termed 'external education'. Three main categories of external education can be identified. First, there is a growing field of commissioned training and education. This includes 5 per cent of all revenues for undergraduate studies, and about 2 per cent of the total revenues for all higher education institutions (HSV/Rapport 1999). Three higher education institutions have been very successful with commissioned education: a middle-sized institution in Karlskrona/Ronneby (with 17 per cent of revenues), Linköping University and Stockholm School of Education (both with 10 per cent of revenues). Traditionally, the courses were directed to the public sector, chiefly the care and teaching professions, but private sector work is growing slightly. These courses are commissioned for working personnel who lack higher education.

The second field in external education is continuing education. Higher education institutions co-operate both with the private (e.g. technology) as well as the public sector (e.g. teacher training) by, for example, offering open seminars.

The third sector is distance learning. Developments in information and communication technology are providing new opportunities for distance education. Several higher education institutions put together consortia, like the National Distance Consortium in 1993, to co-operate in distance education. Until June 1998, as many as 6,000 students participated. The Swedish Distance College (a consortium of several colleges, Educational Radio and one Adult Education Association) had 500 full-time student places in 1999. Many municipalities have developed Learning Centres to help distance students at the local level. Since 1999, fifty-seven of these centres have been working in a network: the Network Group for IT-based Education. Thus, distance education is an expanding field in higher education in Sweden.

Swedish higher education institutions do not yet recognise prior learning for academic credit, but prior work and life experiences are counted towards one of the access routes. Each applicant may apply through different quotas. One of the quotas consists of number of places reserved for those who took the aptitude test. Transferring credits is rather difficult, as there are no standardised curricula for single courses in the country, so the only possibility is to recognise and transfer credits on an individual basis.

There is no system of part-time instruction of the type that exists in some other countries. Part-time students are there, of course, but they study alongside full-time students. Scheduling is an important issue for non-traditional students. However, few courses are organised in the evenings, as most of the students, single mothers for example, prefer to study during the daytime, since they can leave their children in a municipal or private day-care centre.[6] Another reason for not having many evening courses is the system for allocation of funds, which rewards institutions (with financial remuneration to departments) more for full-time students who take a greater number of credits a year and therefore graduate more quickly.

Higher education is free of charge in Sweden and, as we have mentioned, all students are entitled to study loans for twelve semesters. Introduced in the 1960s, this system of loans contributed to the expansion of higher education and to adult students' interest in returning to education. Unfortunately, there are insufficient services for non-traditional students in the form of counselling and information. Each department has a student counsellor, but he or she serves all the students, including mature students.

Analysis of policy changes over the last fifteen years

Though the focus of this review is on the last fifteen years, we believe that, since the cornerstone of higher education policy in Sweden is the 1977 reform, we have to go somewhat further back in time. This reform opened access to the universities to adult students and especially those who did not have an entrance prerequisite or qualification of a traditional kind. The increasing enrolment of adults started, however, long before then and can be traced to the late fifties (see Dahllöf 1983). Kjell Härnqvist in 1956 undertook commissioned studies based on the premise that there was a large unused intellectual capacity (*begåvningsreserven*) in Sweden that ought to be better utilised. It was thought that a way of making this possible would be to facilitate the access of underprivileged groups to higher education.

Through the reform of 1977, Swedish higher education was made into one unified system. Moreover, the reform introduced, all over the country, new higher education colleges on a regional level to open opportunities to people living there. The 1977 reform changed access routes to higher education as well as regulating a new general admissions system which adjusted previous practice.

Another aim of the 1977 reform was to develop the curriculum in such a way that it would better meet the needs of a particular growing category of students: mature students with work experience. Two categories of courses were introduced: professionally-oriented study programmes and single-subject courses, frequently connected with the labour market and the preparation of students for employment. Short-duration programmes of two years were also introduced, allowing students to gain a certificate quickly in preparation for employment (Higher Education Diploma). Likewise, part-time opportunities were developed which gave mature students increased opportunities to participate. The open admission system was however changed into a *numerus clausus* system, with the limitations on places decided by the government, starting first with the programmes and later on with the single-subject courses (see Kim 1980). In addition, as already mentioned, admission to higher education has been completely restricted since 1979.

The educational changes in Sweden from the late 1950s to the beginning of the 1990s focused on two central objectives:

- to give everybody the opportunity to be able to continue education after compulsory schooling, by equalising access possibilities
- to lessen the gap between theoretical and practical programmes at secondary school and in higher education (by integrating, under the same roof, practical/vocational and theoretical/academic programmes).

Follow-up studies and evaluation suggest that the 1977 reform was certainly positive in bringing more adults into the system. Abrahamsson called this phenomenon the 'adultification' of Swedish higher education.

Abrahamsson clarified, however, that 'adultification' did not imply the extensive participation of so-called underprivileged adults with a restricted educational background:

> rather, a number of adults tend to be educationally well-equipped as far as both qualified professional experiences and prior schooling are concerned. This is very significant as far as degree-programmes are concerned (where only 5 per cent of newly enrolled students embark on the so called 25:4 scheme)
>
> (Abrahamsson 1986 p. 6)

There are also other research and commissioned studies showing that there was little change in regard to the social composition of the students. A survey by Eriksson and Jonsson (1993) confirmed that inequality and selection, because of social background, starts very early on in educational careers – at higher primary/lower secondary level – and continues in Swedish higher education institutions.

It also turned out that the 1977 reform had a negative impact on the recruitment of younger students and the statistics indicated that direct inflow from secondary school diminished. According to Tuijnman, difficulties were encountered in recruiting young students to natural sciences and mathematics. These difficulties can be explained from various perspectives. First, there was a demographic reason: the size of the age cohort which could have entered higher education directly after secondary school diminished. Second, the organisation of undergraduate programmes in these areas of higher education was perceived as being similar to that in secondary school and was, therefore, not very attractive to young people. Third, there was a lack of adequate economic and social incentives to undertake university studies, especially at the postgraduate level (Tuijnman 1990).

The low proportion of students aged nineteen to twenty-one in higher education has been (and still is) a major worry for educational policy makers in Sweden. Thus, one aim in the latest major reform of Swedish higher education, which took place in 1993, was to bring in more young students. The main aim, however, was to *decentralise* responsibility for higher education. The 1993 reform, therefore, attempted to:

- open doors to younger students by increasing places and including students with three-year secondary school certificates in the aptitude test quota
- change the vocational orientation of the curricula towards a more 'traditional theoretical' character by creating more single-subject courses, closing down vocationally-oriented programmes and reintroducing the Master's degree on the undergraduate level.

Moreover, the changes in policy gave importance to the following issues:

- allocation of research funds to regional colleges, giving them rights to run postgraduate education and allocate professorial chairs there
- decentralisation of decision-making in higher education as far as admissions, finances, curricula and organisation of study are concerned; undergraduate studies are thus now financed by the state on the basis of credits earned by students and not, as previously, based only on the places allocated
- evaluation of the quality of teaching and higher education institutions functioning both on a local and national level.

In 1992–3, the secondary school sector was also undergoing a reform which gave more chances for vocationally-oriented students to go on eventually to higher education either directly or by complementing their secondary education at adult education institutes. As the statistics given earlier (pp. 87–90) showed, the entry-age as well as the average age of the students has been successively decreasing. The labour market situation however became more positive in the late 1990s, reopening possibilities for young people to get employment after secondary school. The low and restricted number of places in higher education during the 1980s might have created a pool of adults who (within the framework of the Adult Education Initiative and the expansion of higher education) now see an increased chance of gaining access to higher education. The number of mature students might, therefore, reach another peak during the first decade of the new millennium.

Changing economies/labour markets and their impact on student demand and career patterns

As in other countries, interest in participation in higher education, among both non-traditional and traditional students, depends to a large extent on the labour market situation. The pressure to gain access to higher education increases when the prospects of getting jobs are low. From the beginning of the 1990s, the pressure to get a place in higher education (*numerus clausus*) was high because of growing unemployment. This was matched by the concern of policy makers to get more young people into the system. In the late 1990s, however, the labour situation improved and there again appeared to be a decline, especially among younger people, in entry to higher education.

Moreover, the pattern of expectation in relation to education has changed because of a long-lasting tradition of 'adultification' of higher education. Thus, to start higher education a few years after leaving secondary school is not the exception but the rule in the minds of many young people. At the start of the twenty-first century, the most typical pattern for Swedish students is to continue their education *after* some years of work and life experience. Not following a linear pattern (education, job, retirement) but, instead, a recursive one (participating in recurrent education) now has a long tradition in Sweden.

Another feature of the higher education system in 2000 is a discrepancy between students' demands for special disciplines and the places available. The state policy allocates more funds to the natural sciences and technology, both in undergraduate and graduate studies, than to the humanities and social sciences. However, the demand for places is just the opposite, in other words there are more students who are interested in the humanities and social sciences. Demand is also related to age and gender. Younger men predominate in technology and natural sciences, while both young and mature women choose humanities and social sciences as well as vocationally-oriented programmes in the field of healthcare. Teacher training is no longer a popular educational career even if there are good employment prospects (although often accompanied by lower salaries).

The state policy of allocating funds to the regional university colleges tends not to be consistent with younger students' demands, as they tend to choose old, traditional universities in big cities. In this way, applicants from Stockholm, Malmoe and Gothenburg have to compete with applicants from the whole country. However, regionalisation of resources and the creation of labour markets on the local level is a key political goal for the Swedish government and the allocation of funds to university colleges gives mature students the possibility to continue their higher education at their place of residence.

Another interesting phenomenon is a prolongation of study towards MA/MSc degrees. This is connected not only with Swedish and European demands for better educated employees, but also with European mobility and the desire to acquire employment abroad. Students who think about mobility participate more than others in the EU exchange programmes such as *Socrates* and *Erasmus*. However, mature students with family obligations usually have more difficulty in studying abroad.

The issue of economic aid to individual students has been continuously debated and investigated. Issues currently under discussion include:

- a reduction in the study loan and/or the removal of the opportunity to benefit from the financial aid system when students earn over a certain level
- students with children and the abolition of supplementary grants
- the political suggestion of allowing the unemployed to retain their unemployment subsidy when studying in higher education
- special and liberal economic aid for students choosing the fields of science and technology.

Conclusions for policy, practice, and research

Sweden offers an interesting comparison with other countries on the access of non-traditional students to higher education. Even if the concept of 'non-traditional student' is not well established in the higher education literature and research in Sweden, mature students with life and work experience have been the focus of educational reforms for the last forty years. Giving access to mature students profoundly changed the composition of the Swedish higher education population and had an impact on the younger generation's view of universities and colleges. Through this, the idea of lifelong learning has become a reality not only to politicians but, most of all, to Swedes themselves. Sweden is, thus, a country in which the policy towards non-traditional students is very advanced. However, today, interests have shifted towards the problem of younger students, instead of deliberate action towards both groups. Often, higher education policy is far removed from students' and professors' demands and preferences; one example is the policy of allocating more funds to technology and natural sciences, and creating more graduate places in these disciplines.

Another issue is the difficulty in recognising foreign students' prior learning. As a result, many are required to 'complete' their secondary education, in Sweden before being accepted into higher education, regardless of existing qualifications they may have from their home countries. A basic year at the university, as we have for technology students, could be a solution. This, however, is a matter of priorities and finances, as well as attitudes towards immigrants. It calls for flexibility and recognition of the prior, experiential learning of all mature students.

The 'adultified' higher education system and the expanding system of higher education has, of course, implications for individual students' perceptions of, and achievement in, higher education. This remains a major field of interest in our own ongoing meso- and micro-related research. For example, research undertaken at Stockholm University indicates that students appreciate studying in mixed-age groups. Younger students, as well as teachers, appreciate the experience of the mature students and their courage to ask questions and express themselves, as this deepens the discussion in a positive way (Bron and Agélii 1997). The ongoing expansion of higher education entails a greater number of students in higher education without the economic means for institutional departments to increase the number of staff. An interesting point in the StudS student survey (HSV forthcoming) is the students' sense that they get hardly any help or feedback from lecturers. This experience is especially strong among students in the field of technology. Therefore, we assume that there is a need in the future to turn interest (political and scientific) towards the interaction between students and teachers, focusing on the methods and quality of teaching as well as the depth and quality of the students' knowledge.

Generally, in the last ten years there has been little interest in research into higher education. Sweden, with a good reputation for the collection and maintenance of statistics, falls down in regard to higher education. One of the biggest problems in undertaking research, especially comparative research on non-traditional students of higher education in Sweden, is access to relevant data. Even though the Swedish record concerning non-traditional students and their involvement in lifelong learning and higher education is very positive, there are still many aspects in policy and practice which require both more in-depth research and change.

Notes

This chapter is part of a TESR EU-Project on Adult Access Policies: SOE2–0797–2021.

1 An interactive demonstration test is available at the Agency's Website (http://www.hsv.se) on the Internet.
2 All other art and music institutions were linked to the nearest universitites after the 1977 reform except the institutions in Stockholm, which remained independent.
3 Nevertheless, students can work and be paid to some extent and still be able to get the state support. This is because the loan can only be taken away during the effective time of study, i.e. ten months a year.
4 Some of the professional programmes might however include a Bachelor's degree in a specific subject.
5 The survey was carried out as a part in the Agency's ongoing inquiry called Studenterna i Sverige (The Students in Sweden), StudS for short. StudS aims to offer decision makers, researchers and other interested parties, a broad analysis of today's studentship in a macro as well as a micro perspective. Karin Agélii took part in this inquiry in 1997/98 by administrating, conducting and analysing in-depth interviews with students.
6 All students in Sweden are entitled to day-care if they have children.

References

Abrahamsson, K. (1986) *Adult Participation in Swedish Higher Education*, Stockholm: Almqvist and Wiksell.

Abrahamsson, K. and Rubensson, K. (1981) 'Higher education and the "lost generation": some comments on adult students, knowledge, ideas and educational design in Swedish post-secondary education', paper presented at the IMHE workshop on *Meeting the Demands of the Adult Population: A Challenge for Management*, CERI/OECD, Paris May 1981.

Bron, A. and Agélii, K. (1997) 'Mature students' access to Stockholm University', in *Access, Equity, Participation and Organisational Change*, ESREA/Department of Continuing Education, University of Warwick.

Bron-Wojciechowska, A. (1989) *Workers and Post-Secondary Education. A Cross-Polity Perspective*, Uppsala: Acta Universitatis Upsaliensis/Almqvist and Wiksell.

—— (1994) 'Non-traditional students access into academy: changes in higher education policy in Europe and Sweden', *Erwachsenenbildung in Österreich* no. 4.

Dahllöf, U. (1977) *Reforming Higher Education and External Studies in Sweden and Australia*, Uppsala: Acta Universitatis Upsaliensis/Almqvist and Wiksell.

—— (1983) 'An educational magpie: a case study about student flow analysis and target groups for higher education reform in Sweden', paper for the UBUC conference, Dalarö, Sweden.

Eriksson, R. and Jonsson, J. O. (1993) *Ursprung och utbildning – social snedrekrytering till högre studier*, Stockholm: Utbildningsdepartementet, SOU: 85.

Gerani, F. (1998) *Sällan sedd, aldrig hörd. Kvinnor med invandrarbakgrund på Stockholms universitet. En analys av några kvinnors berättelser*, BA thesis, Department of Education, Stockholm University.

Högskoleförordningen bil.3 (1993) Examensordning (Degree Ordinance).

HSV (forthcoming) A preliminary draft of a forthcoming final StudS-report (*StudS slutrapport, nr.7*), Stockholm: Högskoleverket.

HSV/Brandell, L. (1998) *Nittiotalets studenter bakgrund och studiemönster, StudS arbetsrapport nr.2*, Stockholm: Högskoleverket.

HSV/Brandell, L. and Petri, C. (1996) *Studenterna höstterminen 1995 – några basdata, StudS arbetsrapport nr. 1*, Stockholm: Högskoleverket.

HSV/Brandell, S. and Höög, H. (1998) *Med studenternas egna ord. Svaren på två öppna frågor i en enkät hösten 1996 till studenter i Sverige StudS arbetsrapport nr.3*, Stockholm: Högskoleverket.

HSV/Rapport (1999) 'Högskolans updragsutbildning – ett regeringsuppdrag', *Rapport 1999*: 14.

Kim, L. (1980) 'New rules for admission to higher education in Sweden', *Current Sweden*, Stockholm: Svenska Institutet no. 252.

—— (1998) *Val och urval till högre utbildning: en studie baserad på erfarenheterna av 1977 års tillträdesreform*, Uppsala: Acta Universitatis Upsaliensis.

Lönnheden, C. (1999) *Student på olika villkor*, MA thesis no. 25, Department of Education, Stockholm University.

SCB Statistics Sweden (1996) *Fickhandboken*, Örebo: SCB Publikationstjänsten.

—— (1997) *Statistiskt meddeland*, U 46 SM 9701.

Ståhle, B. (1996) 'Universiteten och forskarna: från stagnation till förnyelse. Universitetsforskare, forskarutbildning och forskarrekrytering i Norden', *Nord 1996*.

Tuijnman, A. (1990) 'Dilemmas of open admission policy: quality and efficiency in Swedish higher education', *Higher Education* no. 20.

6 The United Kingdom

Redefining the non-traditional student: equity and lifelong learning in British higher education, 1985–2000

Maria Slowey

> The principle of equality of opportunity to participate in higher education is now well founded, but the means for achieving this remain flawed.
>
> (Smith and Webster 1997 p. 110)

Introduction

At the start of the twenty-first century, one of the defining features of higher education policy in Britain lies in the extent to which it is located within a rhetoric broadly associated with lifelong learning. At one level, many of the features associated with the current emphasis on lifelong learning in the higher education context can be traced back to what Johnstone (1999) has termed 'the standing reform agenda' of Western higher education systems. For the better part of half a century this agenda has included an emphasis on matters such as the need for more attention to students, especially at the undergraduate level; the enhancement of teaching performance; the development of closer partnerships with employers and other external agencies; the securement of allegiance by staff to institutional missions; and the expansion of interdisciplinary teaching and research.

It may well be the case that the lifelong learning agenda which (re)emerged in Britain in the 1990s, as elsewhere across OECD member states, contained within it familiar elements which had previously sought to influence policy under a number of different guises, and this focus had, of course, long been central to the broader arena of adult education from the time of the 'Faure' report (UNESCO 1972). What was dramatically different however was the *scale* and *shape* of the higher education system at which policy was now being targeted. In terms of scale, as we will see in this chapter, with the abolition of the binary divide between universities and polytechnics in 1992 the number of institutions with the title 'university' almost doubled. More importantly however, in relation to matters of access and participation, the number of students doubled. With this expansion came increasing diversification in relation to types of institutions and students as well as forms of provision (including the use of information and communications technology) and the nature of the curriculum (increasingly applied and vocationally orientated.)

The strength of perception of increasing differentiation in the system is graphically demonstrated by the results of a survey of academic staff carried out for the National Committee of Inquiry into Higher Education (NCIHE 1997). Traditionally – with the exception of a small number of universities enjoying particular prestige – there was a widespread view that British universities were regarded as broadly equal in terms of status. The emphasis in the elite UK system was on common admission criteria and common outcomes so that a 'degree' was expected to be of the same standard regardless of the institution attended (Trow 1989, 1993). By the mid-1990s however, this perception had changed to the extent that an overwhelming 94 per cent of academic staff surveyed perceived universities as being ranked unequally (NICHE 1997, Appendix, Report 3, p. 107).

This differentiation of institutions was matched by increasing diversity of the student body. As will be elaborated later in this chapter, the concept of 'non-traditional' student in Britain was closely associated with mature students whose age and life-style contrasted to the image of the 'traditional' student as being young, full-time and directly entering higher education from school. Or, as a comparative study of adults in Belgian and English universities describes the stereotype of the latter group 'young, much preoccupied with sport and sex and clad in a college scarf and sweater' (Bourgeois et al. 1999, p. 2).

However, taking the mid-1990s as a benchmark, the numbers of mature students or adult learners (defined as those aged twenty-one or over on entry to higher education) had grown to such an extent that, across the system as a whole, they had come to constitute around half of all new entrants to higher education. In this context, the obvious question arises as to whether it makes any sense to continue to regard adult students as being in any way 'non-traditional'.

Of course the bald statistics conceal a great deal, even more so in an increasingly differentiated system. Any meaningful analysis needs to move beyond a simple classification based on age to take into account the key factors of social class, gender, previous educational experience, ethnicity, family circumstances and employment situation. Knowing what we do about the composition of the student body and the nature of the higher education to which they are gaining access, there is in fact every reason to question the assumption that problems of equity have been resolved by expansion of the system.

The lifelong learning agenda in its recent guise is largely dominated by an economic and skills focus. However, it does allow for different and often competing interpretations. One interpretation of lifelong learning in higher education moves beyond the 'standing agenda' to address in an explicit way matters of access and inclusion. It therefore seems timely to revisit a number of the key issues addressed in the OECD study of some fifteen years earlier which sets the context for this volume. Delving further into the reality behind some of the 'headline' indicators of change in higher education in the

UK over this period gives rise to three questions which underpin the discussion in this chapter.

1   With the move to a mass system of higher education, to what extent does the concept of a 'non-traditional' student still have value for analytic purposes?
2   Can it be assumed that the issues previously associated with adult participation in higher education have now largely been subsumed under the rubric of lifelong learning?
3   Crucially, how far can the expansion of higher education be said to have actually contributed to increasing equality of opportunity?

It is important also to note that the period in question was one of significant political change in the nature of the nation state, which carried implications for the development of differential educational policies. The United Kingdom (comprising England, Scotland, Wales and Northern Ireland) in common with other OECD members was subject to simultaneous, complexly interlocking, pressures towards *globalisation* at one level and *regionalisation* at another. The structure of educational provision had for long differed in certain important respects between the different parts of the UK, in particular in relation to the nature of the secondary school leaving qualifications and the tradition of the four-year honours degree in Scotland. (It was, and continues to be, widely held that there are major differences in relation to the value placed on general education between the different parts of the UK, although the extent to which this owes more to ideology than reality is much debated; see for example, Field and Schuller (1996), Patterson (1997), Bryce and Humes (1999).) Relevant for purposes of our discussion is that significant moves towards further devolution took place at the end of the twentieth century with the establishment of the Scottish Parliament and Welsh and Northern Ireland Assemblies.

    The remainder of this chapter is organised in six parts. Our starting point lies in the 1980s, and the significant policy emphasis which came to be placed on adult learners. The second section provides an overview of what proved to be a period of remarkable change and policy development in higher education. In the third we look in particular at the use (and abuse) of the concept of lifelong learning. The fourth part outlines some of the interventions and innovations which have flowed from policies aimed largely at encouraging higher education to become more 'flexible' in response to different student (for which also read 'client') needs. We then revisit the concept of the non-traditional student in part five, concluding with some reflections for the future.

Adults in higher education: the 1980s and 1990s policy proxy for non-traditional students?

The UK was one of the countries which participated in the OECD comparative study *Adult Participation in Higher Education* undertaken in the mid-1980s (See Schuetze and Slowey in this volume). In the UK study commissioned by the Department of Education and Science (as a contribution to this exercise) a number of factors were identified as pointing to adult participation in higher education as a topic of increasing interest for policy (Slowey 1987, 1988).

With three significant exceptions there had been little evidence in the previous decades of interest by policy makers or by universities in students who were not direct school leavers. These exceptions included:

- the establishment of the Open University in 1969 which represented a major step in the expansion of opportunities for adult learners
- the extra-mural centres and departments of adult continuing education which for long had provided courses for large numbers of adults, including an increasing number of innovative programmes aimed at preparing mature students (in particular women returners) for entry to higher education via alternative access routes (Kelly 1992, Jarvis 1992, Fieldhouse 1996)
- an extensive range of part-time and evening degree courses mainly provided by polytechnics, by university adult education centres and by specialist institutions such as Birkbeck College of the University of London (Bell and Tight 1993).

In the late 1970s and early 1980s however a number of now-familiar factors combined to change this relative neglect of the matter of adult participation in higher education. At one level, analyses of demographic trends projecting a substantial decline in the numbers of young people coming through from schools fuelled concerns about skill shortages in certain areas and about recruitment to higher education. Human capital theories had also become highly influential amongst policy makers and politicians. Unfavourable comparisons were made with competitor countries, including many OECD member states, which appeared to show significantly greater levels of participation in higher education than in the UK. Human capital theories also sparked a renewed emphasis on the continuous need for updating and retraining the work force, focusing attention on the extent to which university systems, structures and staff were in fact geared up to meeting the projected demand from employers and the professions. Additionally, for institutions, continuing professional/vocational education also was being viewed as a potential source of new revenue – increasingly important as a result of the stringent efficiency savings imposed by the radical right-wing Conservative Government elected in 1979.

Over and above all these factors, and interacting with them in complex ways, was the issue of equality of opportunity in relation to participation in higher education. The participation rate in higher education in the UK was viewed by most commentators as being extremely low with, in 1979, around 87 per cent of the relevant school leaving cohort failing to progress to higher education. The figures varied across the UK with, for example, those for Scotland tending to be marginally better than for England – a pattern which has been maintained with Scottish figures for participation in post-compulsory education being, on average, consistently around 10 per cent higher than for England (ASCETT 1997). Crucially, despite the existence of a student grant system which at the time appeared relatively generous by international standards, the social class composition remained unrepresentative of the population at large, women students were in a minority, and the limited information available on participation by those from ethnic minority groups raised questions about the existence of indirect, if not direct, discrimination.

High profile initiatives supported the development of 'second chance' and 'access' routes for adults along with an emphasis on flexible degree courses aimed at meeting the perceived needs of such students. In England in particular, the academically orientated entry qualification route of A (Advanced) Levels was increasingly viewed as presenting a major barrier to increasing participation. As a result, an emphasis was placed on the development of alternative pathways (including vocational routes under the auspices of the National Council for Vocational Qualifications) which were specially designed for mature students in preparation for entry to (mainly) full-time undergraduate courses and came to be know under the generic term of 'access courses' (Davies and Parry 1993, Davies 1994, Parry 1996).

In the UK throughout the 1980s and into the early 1990s it could be argued therefore that the terms 'mature' or 'adult' student in effect had became a proxy for non-traditional students in higher education. By the time of the 1992 Further and Higher Education Act however, the situation had changed significantly. The number of adult learners (defined as those aged twenty-one or over on entry to higher education) comprised such a substantial proportion of the new students recruited as part of the dramatic expansion which occurred in the lead up to the Act that they were heralded in some quarters as the 'new majority'. A report in the *Times Higher Education Supplement* on the official statistics issued by the Department for Education for the year 1992 is typical of this view.

> The experience of mature students in the 1990s has changed radically from that of previous decades. It is now a misnomer to talk about 'non-traditional' students quite simply because in some universities it is the 18 to 21 year olds who are in a minority.
>
> (THES 1994)

The policy debate had also moved on, influenced by hotly contested interpretations of the concept of lifelong learning. Our starting point for the exploration of these issues lies in the dramatic changes which occurred in the shape and scale of higher education over the period in question.

The changing shape of higher education in the UK: two decades of legislative and policy overload?

Any analysis of the changing shape of higher education in the UK over the 1990s must necessarily refer to a long list of legislative changes, reports of Government commissions and a string of targeted initiatives emanating from Ministries of Education and Employment (which seemed to alter their titles on almost an annual basis), as well as the policies of the higher education funding bodies. In tracing the changes which have taken place it is difficult to distinguish between the intended outcomes of this flurry of policies directed at reform and innovation, their unintended consequences, and the impact of changes in the nature of the student body which result from broader social and economic forces.

One way or another the graphs relating to the key higher education statistics over the period are strikingly in their linearity. Overall there was a dramatic growth in terms of the total student population, which more that doubled from around 800,000 in 1980 to 1,700,000 in 1995 (QSC 1995). The 'classic' indicator of participation rates in higher education is the age participation index (API): the proportion of the relevant 'conventional' age cohort who gain entry to higher education programmes. Utilising this indicator, the API to full-time programmes across the UK as a whole tripled from 5 per cent in 1961 to around 14 per cent in 1970. It remained more or less at this level until the mid-1980s when a period of rapid and consistent growth led to a further doubling over the next decade (NCIHE 1997). The figures for Scotland, even starting from a higher base, show the same trend: from 19.3 per cent in 1986–7 to 46.7 per cent in 1996–7.

In relation to participation by women we see an even more dramatic rate of change. To take a specific benchmark, in the mid-1980s, about a century after the admission of the first women students to universities, women still accounted for less than one-fifth of all new entrants to higher education. Just a decade later however, in1997, the proportion of women students had increased to a point where they were actually in the majority in initial full-time and part-time diploma and degree programmes (Table 6.1).

Of particular interest in addressing the questions posed at the start of this chapter is the issue of the relative age balance among those entering higher education. In fact the proportion of mature entrants, in particular those over twenty-five embarking on full-time programmes, increased disproportionately when compared with younger entrants (HESA 1998).

In contrast to the situation in a number of the other country case studies in this volume, in the UK a clear distinction is made between full-time and part-time students – at both under-graduate and post-graduate levels. This distinction is applied in a very real way in terms both of the resources allocated to institutions and of the financial and other arrangements for individual students. The 'part-time' category encompasses a wide variety of different types of students, particularly when post-experience and professional development

Table 6.1 Students in further and higher education in the UK by type of course and gender (including the Open University), 1996–7

	Men (thousands)	Women (thousands)
Further education		
Full-time	414	445
Part-time	638	818
Total	1,052	1,383
Higher education (undergraduate)		
Full-time	491	528
Part-time	168	224
Total	659	752
Higher education (postgraduate)		
Full-time	75	63
Part-time	113	102
Total	188	165

Source: *Social Trends* (1999), The Stationery Office, adapted from Table 3 p. 60.

programmes are included. However, for most practical purposes, part-time students are equated with the category of adult or mature students. Including figures for the Open University, which is the largest single provider of part-time higher education opportunities, participation shows a modest, but steady increase (HESA 1998).

In total, by the mid-1990s one-third of all higher education students were studying on a part-time basis. In terms of undergraduate programmes, part-time students constituted around 16 per cent of the total. However, these figures significantly understate the situation, as they do not include a significant additional number of students, estimated at just under a million, who were enrolled in part-time adult and continuing education courses which did not lead directly to a higher education qualification (Osborne 1998).

As mentioned above, the number of institutions defined as universities also grew over this period. However, there was nothing like the institutional growth which had taken place in the 1960s (in 1960 there were only twenty-five universities). The greatly increased student numbers were therefore largely accommodated either by existing universities and other institutions of higher education or, increasingly, through taking higher education short-cycle courses in institutions not technically defined as higher education, mainly colleges of further education.

These dramatic changes were the result of a complex interplay between broad social and economic forces and policy intervention. The 1985 *Green Paper on Higher Education* was the first of many which, in a short period of time, sought to give a strong lead to the higher education system in ways which largely reflect the 'standing reform agenda' mentioned at the beginning of this chapter. Emphasis was placed on the need to demonstrate a reasonable rate of return to justify any additional investment in expansion of higher education, an argument which also applied to increasing access for under-represented groups. By the time of the 1988 Higher Education Act, while the policy rationale was still predominantly economic, arguments for expansion of the system were also supported by reference to international competitiveness and (unfavourable) comparisons with the participation rates of economic rivals.

The Act laid out plans for significant structural changes in the organisation and funding mechanisms for higher education institutions. The University Grants Committee was abolished and a new Universities Funding Council established. The polytechnics, previously linked to local ('municipal') authorities, were established as independent institutions under an equivalent national funding council, the Polytechnics and Colleges Funding Council. While the two Funding Councils were not officially defined as planning bodies for higher education, this disclaimer was, in practice, a technical nicety. These new bodies were responsible for decisions about the distribution of the overwhelming bulk of funding for teaching and research in universities and polytechnics, with the additional right to 'earmark' funds in support of particular policy initiatives; a right which, as will be shown below, they and their successor agencies used extensively.

The funding system partially fuelled expansion, while at the same time driving down the unit of resource, by allowing institutions to recruit students over and above those for which they were in receipt of 'full' funding: so-called 'marginal' students. This led some institutions, in particular some non-university institutions of higher education, into major recruitment drives both for financial reasons and also to achieve the minimal size required to obtain polytechnic and, subsequently, university status.

The pace of change continued unabated with the passing of the 1992 Further and Higher Education Act. This Act is significant for the granting by statute of degree-awarding powers to polytechnics (where most adult learners taking award-bearing courses were located) and the right of polytechnics to use the title 'university'. As a result of the legislation the number of universities and colleges with the power to award their own degrees increased to 104. (In passing it is interesting to note that existing universities could comment on proposed new names for polytechnics, which led to some lively debate in senates around the country, and opportunity for ironic comment in the pages of the Times Higher Education Supplement.) The Act also unified the two existing Funding Councils and, in an important step, set in place devolved structures with separate Councils for England, Scotland and Wales (Northern Ireland with only two universities came under the remit of the Council for England). When colleges of higher education and specialist institutions are included the total number of separately funded higher education institutions for the UK is in excess of 180.

The change in title for polytechnics can be viewed as a classic example of 'academic drift'. At the time of the OECD report of the mid-1980s, the polytechnics in the UK were held up as a model of good practice in meeting emerging needs for new forms of higher education provision (OECD 1987). The rationale underlying their establishment had focused on the need for higher education courses which contrasted with, but were intended to be complementary to, existing university provision in terms of *subject matter* (more interdisciplinary and vocationally orientated), *mode* (extensive part-time provision), *orientation* (regional and local) and *partnerships* (employers and local authorities). While not directly funded to undertake research, the primary qualifications offered by polytechnics were the same as universities (degrees, including those at honours level) and the polytechnics also offered post-graduate qualifications.

Taking 1979–80 as the base year, Watson and Taylor show how the 'traditional' universities maintained their unit of resource over the decade to 1989, while over the same period the average for the polytechnics had declined by around 25 per cent (Watson and Taylor 1998, pp. 95–6). However, resetting the baseline at the point of the abolition of the binary divide (1991–2) over the next five years the average across the system as a whole continued to decline by 25 per cent.

While these changes were being implemented in the higher education sector, from the perspective of post-compulsory education opportunities for adult learners important changes were also introduced in the *further education* sector under the 1992 legislation. A significant feature of the expansion of participation on higher education programmes already mentioned is that much of it took place on shorter cycle courses provided in this sector, mainly in the form of Diploma and Certificate qualifications.

A typology of the main forms of higher education providers in 2000 therefore includes

- 'pre-1992' universities (an increasingly differentiated group of 'old' universities)
- 'post-1992' universities (mainly the previous polytechnics)
- institutions of higher education (specialist colleges and teacher training colleges)
- the Open University
- higher education courses provided in colleges of further education.

In the UK it is thus increasingly necessary to view higher education as simply one element within the much broader environment of post-compulsory education and training.

From adult participation to lifelong learning?

In 1997 the long awaited report of the National Committee of Inquiry into Higher Education was presented to a newly elected Labour Government. Set up under the previous administration, the Committee had been charged with investigating what was widely regarded as a funding crisis in the higher education system. The Committee embarked on a wide-ranging consultation exercise and commissioned studies by experts on the implications of the dramatic expansion of the system, in particular in relation to matters of resourcing, quality and access.

The expectations of the stakeholders were high as this was the most significant review of higher education since the Robbins Committee of some thirty years earlier. (See Barnett (1999) for a comparative 'tale' of the two inquiries.) The 'Dearing' Report (after the Chair of the Committee, Sir Ron Dearing) defined the main purposes of higher education as being:

- to inspire and enable individuals to develop their capabilities to the highest potential levels throughout life so that they grow intellectually, are well equipped for work, can contribute effectively to society and achieve personal fulfillment
- to increase knowledge and understanding for their own sake and to foster their application to the benefit of the economy and society
- to serve the needs of an adaptable, sustainable, knowledge-based economy at local, regional and national levels
- to play a major role in shaping a democratic, civilised, inclusive society (NCIHE 1997, Main Report 5.11).

The issues considered by the Dearing Committee were important for the system and far reaching in their implications. When published, the recommendations received a great deal of attention and comment. The positive comments tended to emphasise the pragmatic nature of the suggestions dealing with size, resourcing and quality in higher education. The negative tended to focus on what was perceived as a lack of vision for higher education in the UK into the next century and an overly bureaucratic approach to a range of issues including proposals for the accreditation of academic staff for teaching purposes.

On matters of access and lifelong learning, however, the Dearing Report itself was very positive with a strong recommendation that resources for expansion of teaching should be concentrated in those institutions which had a track record in relation to recruiting students from under-represented sections of society. A significant emphasis was placed on areas such as continuing professional development, links with employers and flexibility in qualification structures with a view to enhancing the range of pathways by which learners might work towards higher education awards.

On the other hand, the treatment of issues relating to part-time and mixed mode study could only be described as perfunctory. The diversity lying behind the category 'part-time' was not investigated in any real depth, leading to a situation where the term became effectively synonymous with the notion of post-graduate or post-experience students. Given the significance of part-time study for lifelong learning (however defined), what could account for this relative neglect? Three hypotheses present themselves. The first is that, for all the rhetoric of lifelong learning, the equation of higher education studies with the notion of the 'classic' full-time student was still extremely influential (regardless of how far the reality may have changed).

The second relates to a confusion about categories. 'By considering all part-timers together, but omitting the Open University, a false picture was created that the majority of part time learners were engaged in postgraduate study with financial support from their employers' (McNair 1998 p. 11). As a consequence, the incentives for institutions to become more flexible remained at a rather abstract level. Third, the Report effectively ignored the very large numbers of 'lifelong learners' undertaking non-credit courses in universities.

On the key matter of resourcing, the principal recommendations of the Report sought to resolve the funding crisis by a new balance of investment between the principal stakeholders: the state, employers, and, to a major extent, students. The rationale for a greater input from students was based on projections of the average financial benefits derived by graduates over the course of their working lives. The subsequent introduction by the Government of a £1,000 fee (means tested) for undergraduate courses was widely criticised as a barrier to access. The issue became so politically charged that one of the first decisions taken by the new Scottish Parliament was to set up an Independent Committee of Inquiry on Student Finance (the 'Cubie' Committee) with a wide ranging brief (ICISF 1999).

The evidence collected by the Cubie Committee highlighted several major problem areas in relation to three issues: first, financial support while studying (the level of which had declined with the substitution of loans for grants); second, the unequal levels of support available for students in higher education and further education (even though further education attracted higher proportions of students from disadvantaged and low-income backgrounds); third, the specific financial needs of particular groups of students – single parents, mature students, the disabled and those living in rural areas. In relation to the crucial matter of fees, the Committee recommended that, that even though a minority of students were in fact liable to pay the full fee, the public perception of fees as a barrier was so strong that a different approach to sharing the costs of higher education was necessary. The report was generally well received and fuelled the debate on student support in other parts of the UK.

While higher education had formed the explicit focus of the Dearing Committee, policy formulation in the broader post-compulsory education sector – which in many respects constituted the main focus of policy attention – was the subject of two other committees. The 'Kennedy' report contained the deliberations of the committee which had been set up by the Government to study the further education sector, a sector which had been growing at an even faster pace than higher education (FEFC 1997). The

National Advisory Group on Lifelong Learning (the 'Fryer' Committee) was established in 1997 with a rolling brief to advise on strategy in relation to lifelong learning, focusing in particular on adult, non-formal and work-based learning.

In various ways, each of these reports on the post-compulsory education sector laid some claim to the territory of lifelong learning, which, as Duke comments, constituted 'the talk of the academic town in 1996, the European Year of Lifelong Learning' (Duke 1997 p. 57). The concept itself however remained both problematic and contested, reflecting similar debates to those engendered by the major international reports produced by the European Commission, UNESCO and OECD as discussed in Chapter 1 of this volume. The commonality in terminology disguised significant differences, most notably on the interrelationship between education and the economy.

Thus, the Introduction to the Green Paper on lifelong learning by the Secretary of State did indeed outline a broad educational vision:

> As well as securing our economic future, learning has a wider contribution. It helps make ours a civilised society, develops the spiritual side of our lives and promotes active citizenship. Learning enables people to play a full part in their community. It strengthens the family, the neighbourhood and consequently the nation. It helps us fulfil our potential and opens doors to a love of music, art and literature. That is why we value learning for its own sake as well as for the quality of opportunity it brings.
>
> (DfEE 1998 p. 7)

On the other hand, as the Director of the Economic and Social Research Council research programme, *The Learning Society*, points out, a closer reading contrasts this broad vision with an underlying 'determination to increase employability as *the* central policy in the development of lifelong learning' (Coffield 1999 p. 4). This view is evident when the Green Paper moves from rhetoric in favour of lifelong learning to a discussion of practical measures which, Coffield suggests, have a largely instrumental focus.

Carrots and sticks: the development of innovatory practice in relation to new groups of learners in higher education

Since the 1980s policy orientations had been operationalised through a raft of special initiatives and the unprecedented use of targeted funding (channelled to a considerable extent through the Employment, rather than the Education, Ministry) as levers to shape institutional behaviour, all accompanied by a seemingly endless array of new acronyms. This approach sought to influence the practice of higher education institutions through a complex combination of 'carrots', in the form of earmarked or targeted funding, and 'sticks', in the form of financial stringencies and increasing accountability. Much of the targeted or earmarked funding was distributed on the basis of competitive applications from institutions of higher education. While the emphases varied, in general an underlying dimension which many of them shared related to the promotion of greater 'flexibility' and 'responsiveness' on the part of higher education institutions.

The extent of this form of intervention in the year 2000 can be illustrated by the example of one single, albeit important, organisation, the Higher Education Funding Council of England (HEFCE). Under the broad heading of strategies aimed at 'widening participation', HEFCE has initiated and funded the following initiatives all of which, in one way or another, are aimed at encouraging institutions to respond to the needs of different forms of learners, including under-represented groups (in effect 'non-traditional' students) and, in different ways, employers and other corporate clients.

- premium funding whereby institutions are 'rewarded' by an additional resource allocation for recruitment of certain under-represented groups
- joint FEFC/HEFCE programme to promote collaboration between higher and further education institutions
- HEROBC (Higher Education Reach Out to Business and the Community) aimed at promoting strategic links between universities and employers
- additional student numbers, extra funding for programmes aimed at particular target groups
- special initiative funding, mainly aimed at supporting regional developments and partnerships
- widening participation co-ordination function, involving a wide range of associations and organisations with an interest in matters to do with widening access to higher education
- millennium summer schools, linking universities and schools, particularly in disadvantaged areas
- institutional strategies, requiring universities to submit to the Funding Council detailed statements on their institutional strategy in relation to widening access which are then subject to monitoring, with possible clawback of funds if specific targets are not met.

More broadly-based Government supported initiatives include: Lifelong Learning Partnerships which have an emphasis on social inclusion and regeneration involving educational institutions at the local level; the National Grid for Learning which aims to provide a focal point for learning on the Internet; the University for Industry (UFI) which has been established with the objective of stimulating the demand for lifelong learning among individuals and employers, with particular emphasis on the use of information and communications technology (Hillman 1997). By 2000 the latter had become a 'flagship' of Government policy in the area of lifelong learning although subject to continuing critical comment.

Changes are in fact evident at the institutional level compared to fifteen years ago. A review of innovative higher education practices in the UK targeted at mature and part-time students yielded many examples (Osborne 1998):

- flexible pathways leading to a variety of exit points in both undergraduate and postgraduate areas
- accreditation of prior and experienced learning (APEL) for the accreditation of either in-company training or on an individual basis for students with significant work experience
- work-based learning (WBL) programmes designed in partnership between universities and employers
- accreditation of short continuing development courses
- utilisation of individual modules from undergraduate or postgraduate courses as stand-alone short courses
- development of mixed-mode delivery combining face-to-face teaching with text-based distance learning materials, use of the Internet and other forms of computer-based materials
- structured learning contracts that include the validation and introduction to self-managed study for individuals (most frequently employees of large corporations)
- franchising of the first year of undergraduate courses to colleges of further education or offering them on an outreach basis directly from universities
- credit bearing programmes to assist transition for adult learners from adult and further education to universities
- credit bearing summer academy programmes
- non-credit bearing liberal adult education programmes targeted at specific educationally disadvantaged groupings
- programmes targeted at older citizens
- collaboration with professional bodies in the recognition of higher level vocational qualifications
- outreach non-credit bearing programmes frequently targeted at adult learners of differing educational backgrounds.

While these developments represent a real change in the nature of the higher education opportunities available, implementation is uneven across the system as a whole. The increasingly differentiated nature of higher education in the UK (in effect an ever more explicit ranking of institutions) means that universities can be found which are actively aspiring to Duke's (1992) paradigm of the 'learning university', embracing the strategies summarised above for teaching heterogeneous learners. The strategy adopted by other universities, in an increasingly hierarchical system, however, is largely to locate these types of activities and students in specialist units such as continuing education, seeking to insulate 'mainstream' departments from demands other than research and 'core' teaching.

Revisiting the concept of the 'non-traditional' student in 2000

From our attempt to investigate whether the term 'non-traditional' learner continues to have any meaning in the context of a mass system, as well as from the equity perspective of the lifelong learning agenda, it is vital to delve behind the simple participation statistics. In particular, we must look in more detail at who the students actually are, their experience of higher education, and what institutions they attend. We know that age, gender, ethnic status, social class, disability, family situation, employment, rural location are all important determining factors. Here we briefly consider five of these: adult learners, gender, ethnic group, social class and types of higher education provision.

Adult students: non-traditional no longer?

The proportion of adults may have grown over the period in question to the stage where those over twenty-one on entry constitute a statistical majority in British higher education, but of course adults are by no means a homogeneous grouping. What do we know about how the system has adapted to their differing interests and circumstances, especially in terms of the nature of the curriculum and the organisation of provision? Certainly, throughout the1980s and 1990s as we have seen, a number of developments were introduced with target sub-groupings of this clientele in mind, from the expansion of credit accumulation and transfer schemes (CATS) through to the introduction of work-based learning (WBL) programmes. However, the experience of students does not always match the intended objectives of such schemes (Haselgrove 1996). A nationally representative survey of the experiences of over 1,000 full-time and part-time students (attending 'conventional' institutions, the Open University was not included) was commissioned by the National Commission of Inquiry into Higher Education. This study concluded that

> Despite the growing numbers of mature students, higher education still appears to be catering for the traditional school leaver intake. Most mature students, and particularly those with children, did not believe that their needs, especially in relation to non-academic support, were acknowledged or met. Lone parent students were particularly dissatisfied.
>
> (Callender 1997 p. 55)

The category of lone parents is an important one in equity terms for two reasons. First, lone parents constitute a growing section of the British population because of the relatively high rates of divorce and of births to single mothers. Second, higher education can offer an important potential route out of the

Table 6.2 Participation rates in higher education in the UK by age group (%)

	UK	England	Wales	Scotland	Northern Ireland
16	0.09	0.02	0.44	0.61	0.01
17	1.34	0.29	0.39	12.23	0.25
18–20	25.14	25.12	26.94	23.82	26.65
21–24	10.69	10.65	11.94	9.38	13.47
25–29	4.14	4.12	4.72	4.07	4.19
30–39	2.99	2.98	3.38	2.94	2.81
40–49	2.01	2.00	2.24	2.00	1.79
50 and over	0.46	0.46	0.60	0.35	0.35
All ages	2.58	2.61	2.83	2.70	3.01

Source: adapted from HESA 1998a B1 p. 23.

Note: Participation rates are defined as the number of people of a particular age group who are in higher education in the year in question, divided by the population of that age group.

poverty and reliance on state benefits in which a high proportion of lone parents are trapped. The survey showed that 60 per cent of the students who were lone parents felt that institutions did not pay enough attention to the needs of mature students (compared to 10 per cent of single, childless students). Of course, this understates the situation as the respondents only included the minority of this group who had actually gained entry to higher education.

The other important feature of what has been heralded for over a decade as the 'adultification' of higher education (as discussed in Chapter 1 of this volume) is that, when measured by the most standard yardstick of the percentage of the *total* population in a given age group, the figures for adult participation do not look at all impressive. Table 6.2 clearly illustrates the 'API' for those aged thirty or over stands at less than 3 per cent. This low level points to an increasing education gap as younger members of the population have more opportunity to participate in higher education than previous generations, particularly as the figures for those over twenty-five are likely to include many graduates involved in post-graduate or continuing education programmes rather than 'second chance' learners.

Gender: lots of women, so what's the problem?

The overall figures in the move towards greater gender equality in higher education in the UK also appear impressive. In relation to undergraduate courses, to take a key example, between 1979–80 and 1996–7 enrolments by men increased by around 80 per cent while those for women increased by a dramatic 400 per cent (Social Trends 1999 p. 61). Even allowing for the relatively low base from which women started, this increase has led to a situation where at an *undergraduate* level they are now in a slight majority. But of course, as Table 6.1 has shown, this relative 'advantage' is not maintained at the post-graduate level. Just as importantly, traditional gender differences at the level of individual subject areas remain strong (QSC 1996).

An interesting group of questions arises about the extent to which, with the moves to a mass higher education system with the admission of more women students, the demonstrable economic and social advantages which in the past have been conferred by gaining a higher education are likely to continue. While it is probably too early to move towards any definitive answers, the question remains as to whether higher education is likely to demonstrate the classic situation familiar in other areas (in particular in employment) whereby the 'feminisation' of an occupation or an activity almost inevitably leads to its decline both in terms of status and economic value.

Ethnic minorities

There is considerable variation across ethnic groups as to levels of qualification in the population and rates of participation in higher education opportunities. While overall participation rates may be more or less the same as for white groups, some groups are significantly under-represented (in particular younger black men and Bangladeshi and Pakistani women) and, in common with adult and other 'new' student groups, they are more likely to be found in post-1992 universities (Madood 1993).

The national *Labour Force Survey* divides ethnic groups into four categories:

- Indian/Pakistani/Bangladeshi
- black
- white
- other groups (which includes other groups who did not state their ethnic group).

Based on these self-definitions, in 1996, 22 per cent of men from the Indian, Pakistani and Bangladeshi population had no qualifications while the comparable figures for black/white and 'other' men were around 15 per cent and 16 per cent. At the other end of the spectrum, men from Indian, Pakistani and Bangladeshi backgrounds were slightly more likely to have a degree or equivalent (18 per cent) than either black or white men (both 14 per cent). The comparable figures for women in all minority ethnic groups, particularly Indian, Pakistani and Bangladeshi, were significantly lower: one third of the latter had no formal qualifications and only 9 per cent had attained a degree or equivalent. Even allowing for the differential age profiles of the different ethnic groups and different patterns of mobility, these population figures highlight the small proportion of the total population who hold higher education qualifications. In their review of research on participation by different ethnic groups in higher education for the NCIHE, Coffield and Vignoles (1997) confirm the pattern that ethnic minority students are heavily concentrated in post-1992 universities.

Social class

Despite the enormous transformations in the higher education system between the times of the Robbins and Dearing reports, reflecting the changes in social, economic and political contexts, the social composition of participants in higher education consistently remains unrepresentative of the population at large. While variations exist depending on the indicators used to measure social class, or socio-economic status — with particular complexities for women and mature students — or the range of programmes encompassed within the definition of higher education (whether, for example, the Open University or part-time continuing education courses are included), the general patterns remain the same.

The figures in Table 6.3 speak for themselves. In 1991–2, participation rates of young students entering higher education (whether universities or other institutions) from the census categories of partly skilled or unskilled backgrounds, were only12 per cent and 6 per cent respectively. This compared with an overall participation rate of 55 per cent for those from professional backgrounds. Over the period of continuing expansion the participation rate of those from unskilled backgrounds more than doubled, but for those from professional backgrounds it had increased even faster. By 1997–8 therefore the participation rate for professional groups was in fact 66 per cent higher than for those from unskilled backgrounds, an even larger gap than in 1991–2 when the difference had been 49 per cent.

Types of institution

As this chapter has emphasised, a very important feature of the post-compulsory or tertiary sector in the UK is the extent to which much of the provision which is defined as higher education takes place in institutions which

Table 6.3 Participation rates in higher education by social class (%)

	1991–2	1992–3	1993–4	1994–5	1995–6	1996–7	1997–8
Professional	55	71	73	78	79	82	80
Intermediate	36	39	42	45	45	47	49
Skilled non-manual	22	27	29	31	31	31	32
Skilled manual	11	15	17	18	18	18	19
Partly skilled	12	14	16	17	17	17	18
Unskilled	6	9	11	11	12	13	14
All social classes	23	28	30	32	32	33	34

Source: adapted from *Social Trends* 1999 p. 61 Table 3.13.

Note: the number of home domiciled initial entrants aged under twenty-one to full-time and sandwich undergraduate courses of higher education in further education and higher education institutions expressed as a proportion of the averaged eighteen to nineteen year old population. The 1991 Census provided the population distribution by social class for all years.

are not universities, in particular, in colleges of further education. When seeking to interpret trends and compare statistics, a very important distinction must therefore be made between those figures which relate to participation in *higher education institutions* (universities and other institutions of higher education) and those which relate to participation in *higher education programmes* (which include all courses defined as higher education regardless of where they are provided).

The growth of higher education provision in the further education sector is a major trend through out the UK. The forms of such provision however vary enormously among colleges and, in particular, between the patterns which have emerged in England and Scotland (Bocock and Scott 1994, Osborne and Gallacher 1995). The main forms of provision include Higher National Certificate and Diploma courses which can also, via credit transfer arrangements, be used as an entry route to the second or third years of degree courses, and 'franchise' arrangements whereby the first or second year of a degree programme may be offered by a college in partnership with a university. These types of programme account for a good deal of the growth in higher education participation in the UK in recent years. In the case of Scotland, for example, it is estimated that some 30 per cent of all provision defined as higher education takes place in this sector (Gallacher and Thomson 1999).

In addition to the distinction between higher education courses taken in colleges of further education compared to those taken in a university or other institutions of higher education, as we have seen the most common distinction made in the literature on universities is based on the abolition of the binary divide between the pre-1992 and post-1992 universities. Here the patterns are similar to those shown in other chapters in this volume. With the exception of specialist institutions, it is in the newer universities or the colleges offering shorter cycle higher education courses that adult learners, part-time students and those from working-class backgrounds are most likely to be located.

Thus, for example, the ratio of middle-class to working-class students has been calculated by Robertson and Hillman (1997) as 75:25 at the pre-1992 universities and 68:32 at the post-1992 universities, ratios which they say have remained unchanged over many years.

Towards the future . . .

The report on England and Wales for the project *European Universities and Life-long Learning* suggests that changes in higher education which are relevant to the achievement of broadly based lifelong learning objectives have a contribution to make in one or more of the following three ways (Payne 1998):

- widening participation: involving a wider range of the population in learning

- lengthening participation: involving people in learning for a longer period of their lives
- enlarging participation: involving more people in learning.

There seems little doubt that the expansion of higher education in the UK has contributed to the latter two forms of participation. More people are involved in structured post-compulsory education over longer periods than ever before. In relation to widening participation among under-represented groups, there is also some evidence of progress. Certainly, the system is seeing more students studying in a wider variety of ways; in particular, whether by choice or by necessity, an accelerating trend towards students of all ages finding new combinations of work and study. On the other hand, as the editorial for a publication representing all of the main national networks and agencies involved in initiatives aimed at the widening of access comments,

> it is income level that remains the most prevalent and persistent indicator of participation at the end of the twentieth century. Low socioeconomic status is not only the major single remaining cause of under-representation, it also compounds disadvantage resulting from rural isolation and from age, gender, race and disability discrimination. Despite overall increases by all income groups, the participation gap between them remains stubbornly wide.
>
> (Davies *et al.* 1999 p. 2)[1]

Returning to the questions posed at the start of this chapter, there is certainly evidence of major change: more people are engaged in higher education than ever before, they are learning in a greater variety of ways with access to a wider choice of curricula and qualification routes. On the other hand we see institutional differentiation and ranking, with all the evidence pointing in the same direction: that the 'new' learners, however we define them, are largely located in institutions perceived to be at the lower end of the ranking.

It is also apparent that issues of equity and access remain as live as ever in the new mass system of higher education. Addressing these issues is crucial, not only for reasons of social justice, but also for the intellectual well-being of our universities at a time where their purposes become more and more difficult to distinguish from those of many other organisations active in the lifelong learning arena.

> The contract . . . between higher education and society offers special privileges to academics in return for a commitment to the democratic health of and progress of that society. The main contribution which universities can make to social stability is to be engaged in the life of their local communities, to research their most pressing problems and to offer constructive, if at times challenging, ways forward. *All debates*

about the future of higher education are inseparable from debates about the future of society.

(Coffield and Williamson 1997 p. 16, emphasis added)

Note

1 In 2000, the contributing networks involved with *Update on Inclusion: Widening Participation in Higher Education* included the European Access Network (EAN), Forum for the Advancement of Continuing Education (FACE), National Institute for Adult and Continuing Education (NIACE), National Open College Network (NOCN), National Task Group for Widening Participation Projects (NTG WPP), Universities Association for Continuing Education (UACE). The publication was supported by the Higher Education Funding Councils.

References

ASCETT (Advisory Scottish Council for Education and Training Targets) (1997) *Advisory Scottish Council for Education and Training Annual Report,* Glasgow: Scottish Enterprise.

Barnett, R. (1997) *Higher Education: A Critical Business,* Buckingham: Society for Research into Higher Education/Open University Press.

—— (1999) 'The coming of the global village: a tale of two inquiries', *Oxford Review of Education* vol. 25 no. 3 pp. 294–306.

Bell, R. and Tight, M. (1993) *Open Universities: A British Tradition?* Buckingham: Society for Research into Higher Education/Open University Press.

Bocock, J. and Scott, P. (1994) *Re-drawing the Boundaries: Further/Higher Education Partnerships,* Leeds: University of Leeds.

Bourgeois, E., Duke, C., Guyot, J. and Merrill, B. (1999) *The Adult University,* Buckingham: Society for Research into Higher Education/Open University Press.

Bryce, T. G. K. and Humes, W. (1999) *Scottish Education,* Edinburgh: Edinburgh University Press.

Callender, C. (1997) 'Full and part-time students in higher education: their expressions and expectations', *National Committee of Inquiry into Higher Education: Report 2,* London: The Stationery Office.

Coffield, F. (1999) 'Introduction: Lifelong Learning as a new form of social control?' in F. Coffield (ed.) *'Why's the Beer Always Stronger Up North?' Studies in Lifelong Learning in Europe,* Bristol: ESRC/Policy Press.

Coffield, F. and Vignoles, A. (1997) 'Widening participation in higher education by ethnic minorities, women and alternative students', *National Committee of Inquiry into Higher Education: Report 5,* London: The Stationery Office.

Coffield, F. and Williamson, B. (1997) 'The challenges facing higher education', in F. Coffield and B. Williamson (eds) *Repositioning Higher Education,* Buckingham, Society for Research into Higher Education/Open University Press

Davies, P. (1994) 'Fourteen years on: what do we know about access students? Some reflections on national statistical data', *Journal of Access Studies* vol. 9 no. 1.

—— (ed.) (1995) *Adults in Higher Education: International Perspectives in Access and Participation,* London: Jessica Kingsley.

Davies, P. and Parry, G. (1993) *Recognising Access: The Formation and Implementation of the National Framework for the Recognition of Access Courses,* Leicester: NIACE.

Davies, C., Taylor, R. and Woodrow, M. (1999) 'A message for the new millennium', editorial in *Update on Inclusion, Widening Participation in Higher Education* no. 2 Autumn.

DfEE (Department for Education and Employment) (1998) *The Learning Age: A Renaissance for a New Britain,* London: The Stationery Office.

Duke, C. (1992) *The Learning University: Towards a New Paradigm?* Buckingham: Society for Research into Higher Education/Open University Press.

—— (1997) 'Towards a Lifelong Learning Curriculum', in F. Coffield and B. Williamson (eds) *Repositioning Higher Education,* Buckingham: Society for Research into Higher Education/Open University Press.

FEFC (Further Education Funding Council) (1997) *Learning Works: Widening Participation in Further Education* (The 'Kennedy' report), Coventry: Further Education Funding Council.

Field, J. and Schuller, T. (1996) 'Is there less adult learning in Scotland and Northern Ireland? A quantitative analysis', *Scottish Journal of Adult and Continuing Education* vol. 2 no. 2 pp. 61–70.

Fieldhouse, R. (1996) *A History of Modern British Adult Education,* Leicester: NIACE.

Gallacher, J. and Thomson, C. (1999) 'Further education: overlapping or overstepping?' *Scottish Journal of Adult and Continuing Education* vol. 5 no. 1.

Haselgrove, S. (1996) 'What is Happening to Part-time Education?', in R. Taylor and D. Watson (eds) *Continuing Education in the Mainstream: the Funding Issues,* Leeds: UACE Occasional Paper no. 17.

—— (ed.) (1994) *The Student Experience,* Buckingham: Society for Research into Higher Education/Open University Press.

HESA (Higher Education Statistics Agency) (1998) *Higher Education Management Statistics: Sector Level 1996/97,* Cheltenham: HESA.

Hillman, J. (1997) *University for Industry: Creating a National Learning Framework,* London: IPPR.

ICISF (Independent Committee of Inquiry into Student Finance) (1999) *Student Finance: Fairness for the Future* (The 'Cubie' Report), Edinburgh: Independent Committee of Inquiry into Student Finance.

Jarvis, P. (ed.) (1992) *Perspectives on Adult Education and Training in Europe,* Leicester: NIACE.

Johnstone, D. B. (1999) 'The future of the university: reasonable predictions, hoped for reforms, or technological possibilities', in J. Brennan, J. Fedrowitz, M. Huber and T. Shah (eds) *International Perspectives on Knowledge, Participation and Governance,* Buckingham: Society for Research into Higher Education/Open University Press.

Kelly, T. (1992) *A History of Adult Education in Great Britain* (2nd edn), Liverpool: Liverpool University Press.

McNair, S. (1998) 'The invisible majority: adult learners in English higher education', unpublished paper, University of Surrey.

Madood, T. (1993) 'The numbers of ethnic minority students in British higher education: some grounds for optimism', *Oxford Review of Education* vol. 19 no. 2.

NAGCELL (National Advisory Group on Continuing Education and Lifelong Learning (1997) *Learning for the 21st Century*, London: The Stationery Office.

NCIHE (National Committee of Inquiry into Higher Education) (1997) *Higher Education in the Learning Society* (The 'Dearing' Report) London: HMSO.

OECD (1987) *Adults in Higher Education*, Paris: OECD.

—— (1999) 'Tertiary education', in *Education Policy Analysis 1999*, Paris: OECD.

Osborne, M. (1998) 'United Kingdom Report', *Thematic Network on University Continuing Education*, (THENUCE), http//www.fe.up.pt/nuce/UKIN.htmb

Osborne, M. and Gallacher, J. (1995) 'Scotland', in P. Davies (ed.) *Adults in Higher Education: International Perspectives in Access and Participation*, London: Jessica Kingsley.

Parry, G. (1995) 'England, Wales and Northern Ireland', in P. Davies (ed.) *Adults in Higher Education: International Perspectives on Access and Participation*, London: Jessica Kingsley.

—— (1996) 'Access education in England and Wales 1973–1994: from second chance to third wave', *Journal of Access Studies* vol. 11 no. 1.

Patterson, L. (1997) 'Traditions of Scottish education', in H. Holmes (ed.) *Compendium of Scottish Ethnology* vol. 11, Edinburgh: European Ethnological Research Centre.

Payne, J. (1998) 'National Report: England and Wales', SOCRATES project report, *Making it Work: European Universities and Lifelong Learning*, unpublished report, University of Leeds.

QSC (Quality Support Centre) (1995) 'Students in UK higher education', *Higher Education Digest* no. 23, London: QSC.

—— (1996) *Higher Education in the 1990s, Diversity: Too Much or Too Little*, Higher Education Digest, Milton Keynes: Open University Press.

Robertson, D. and Hillman, J. (1997) 'Widening participation in higher education for students from lower socio-economic groups and students with disabilities', *National Committee of Inquiry into Higher Education: Report 6*, London: The Stationery Office.

Schuetze, H., Paquet, P., Slowey, M., Wagner, A. (1987) *Adults in Higher Education: Policies and Practices in Great Britain and North America*, Stockholm: Almqvist and Wiksell.

Schuller, T. and Burns, A. (1999) 'Using "Social Capital" to compare performance in continuing education', in F. Coffield (ed.) *Why's the Beer Always Stronger up North? Studies in Lifelong Learning in Europe*, Bristol: ESRC/Policy Press.

Scott, P (1995) *The Meanings of Mass Higher Education*, Buckingham: Society for Research into Higher Education/Open University Press.

—— (1997) 'After Dearing', *Scottish Journal of Adult and Continuing Education* vol. 4 no. 2.

Slowey, M. (1987) 'Adult students: the new mission for higher education?' *Higher Education Quarterly* vol. 42 no. 4.

—— (1988) 'Adults in higher education: the situation in the United Kingdom', in H. G. Schuetze (ed.) *Adults in Higher Education: Policies and Practices in Great Britain and North America*, Stockholm: Almqvist and Wiksell.

—— (1996) 'Universities and lifelong learning: issues in widening access', in T. Winther-Jensen (ed.) *Challenges to European Education: Cultural Values, National Identities and Global Responsibilities*, Frankfurt am Main: Peter Lang.

Smith, A. and Webster, F. (1997) 'Conclusion: an affirming flame', in A. Smith and F. Webster (eds) *The Post-Modern University: Contested Visions of Higher Education in Society,* Buckingham: Society for Research into Higher Education/Open University Press.

Social Trends (1999) *Social Trends 29,* London: The Stationery Office.

THES (*Times Higher Education Supplement*) (1994) 'Mature approach steadily gains ground', 25 November.

Trow, M. (1989) 'The Robbins trap: British attitudes and the limits of expansion', *Higher Education Quarterly* vol. 43 no. 1.

—— (1993) 'Comparative perspectives on British and American higher education systems', in S. Rothblatt and B. Wittrock (eds) *The European and American University since 1800*, Cambridge: Cambridge University Press.

UCAS (Universities and Colleges Admissions Service) (1999) *Statistical Bulletin on Widening Participation,* Cheltenham: UCAS.

UNESCO (1972) *Learning to Be: The World of Education Today and Tomorrow* (The 'Faure' report), Paris: UNESCO

Watson, D. and Taylor, R. (1998) *Lifelong Learning and the University: a Post-Dearing Agenda,* London: Falmer Press.

Part III

North America

7   Canada

Higher education and lifelong learning in Canada: re-interpreting the notions of 'traditional' and 'non-traditional' students in the context of a 'knowledge society'

Hans G. Schuetze

Introduction: context and development

Canadian higher education has changed quite dramatically over the last four decades. Although this is most evident with respect to the growth in numbers of students, faculty and new institutions, change has also affected higher education in other, more qualitative ways.

The growth of the system

Canada has gone further than any other country except the United States in developing a mass system of higher education. In Canada 40 per cent of the population in the typical age group are enrolled in tertiary education, as compared to 35 per cent in US, 27 per cent in the UK, and 17 per cent in Germany (OECD 1998).[1] Canada spends more on public tertiary education (as a percentage both of its GDP and of total public expenditure) than any other OECD country. Between 1956 and 1968, the number of university-level institutions grew from forty to fifty-nine and now stands at almost double that number, namely seventy-five.

University enrolment expanded from approximately 90,000 full-time students in the beginning of the 1950s, to over 820,000 in the late 1990s, of whom 250,000 attended part-time. The increase in numbers was even more significant in the 195 colleges and institutes, that is the non-university institutions of advanced (post-secondary) education that had been established in the 1960s and early 1970s: by 1998 a total 490,000 students were enrolled, of whom 92,000 were attending part-time. Together the two tiers enrol now some 1.3 million students.

Correspondingly, the number of full-time university teachers increased from approximately 4,300 to 33,700 between 1956 and 1998. Together the two tiers employ over 65,000 full-time teaching staff (StatsCan 2000a).

The drivers of growth

As in the US, the change from an elite to a mass system of higher education since the Second World War is a result of three major trends. First is the adoption of egalitarian policies that aimed to increase education opportunities for returning war veterans, and later, the population at large. The aim was to make society more equitable by offering post-secondary opportunities to larger segments of the population, especially by extending access to university-level education beyond the upper middle class.

Most influential besides the principle of egalitarianism was the promise of human capital theory, according to which the expansion of education opportunities and the development of the requisite facilities were investments for enhancing both economic growth and individual levels of income from work. This economic concept, coupled with the buoyant economic climate in the 1960s and early 1970s, led to increased social demand for advanced education opportunities. This demand was further enhanced by financial assistance to less advantd students, and a major investment in publicly funded institutions of post-secondary education which greatly increased the numbers and scope of programmes offered at the post-secondary level. This expansion of programmes and curricula accommodated emerging professions such as social work, teaching, commerce and business administration, nursing and pharmacy, and met the demand for the variety of specialised skills that had become too complex to be taught at secondary level.

As in most other industrial countries, the climate of post-war optimism and economic growth came to an end in the second half of the 1970s and 1980s when economies went into recession due to the oil price shock and other factors. This also meant an end to the unprecedented growth of the education system, especially when it became clear that the massive investments in education had not resulted in the expected economic benefits, namely concomitant productivity gains, growth, and the creation of new and sustainable employment.

At present the situation is again changing significantly, even if change does not figure as prominently as in the years of massive growth. Demand for post-secondary education and training is undiminished and comes from several sources. Probably the most important is the structural change taking place in the Canadian economy. The dominance of resources-based and goods-producing sectors has given way to the production of high-value-added products and the provision of services. Consequently, the pace of change towards a more knowledge-based economy with a more highly skilled workforce has accelerated over the last ten to fifteen years. In addition to its effects on the aggregate demand for skilled workers, this change has also had consequences for individual workers, who need to expand their knowledge base and skills to adjust to new jobs and tasks.

Canadian census data provide a broad overview of these structural changes. Between 1981 and 1996 overall employment grew by roughly two and a half million jobs, while some 280,000 jobs were lost in the resource-extracting and manufacturing sectors. Thus almost all the job gains were in the services sectors. Not all of these are 'white collar' jobs requiring higher skill levels, but many do call for enhanced skills, especially in education, health, communication, and financial services.

Structural change is even more obvious from a comparison of occupational structures and levels. While management positions decreased, the demand for those with senior management functions increased. In business and finance, health, education, and the arts and culture, the share of professional positions increased disproportionately. In most cases, this upgrading of the workforce entailed an increased demand for advanced skills.

Related to these structural changes are the organisational changes taking place in many firms, which entail more job complexity, multi-tasking and multi-skilling, greater horizontal communication, and distribution of responsibility (Betcherman *et al.* 2000). For the individual worker, for work teams, or a firm's workforce as a whole, there is a need for on-going learning, both formal and informal, organised or incidental, whether on or off the job.

Another source of demand is the growing educational attainment of the Canadian population. The demand for continued learning opportunities and advanced educational credentials is steadily growing as the post-secondary education system expands and absorbs larger numbers of learners. Since to a large extent demand for, and participation rates in, further education are dependent on cultural and social upbringing and formal education, participation in post-secondary education and workplace-related training is largely dependent on prior educational attainment. Thus, the Labour Force Survey data show that 40 per cent of workers with a university degree participate in job-related education and training, as compared with 5.9 per cent of people with less than eight years of previous education.

Qualitative changes

There are a number of qualitative changes which form the context of the following discussion. The one of interest here concerns the trend towards vocationalisation and 'applied' studies as it has various consequences for institutions, faculty and students.

Although the tradition of liberal arts education is strong in Canada, there is also a clear trend towards greater vocationalism or labour market relevance in academic programmes (Fisher and Rubenson 1998). This vocationalisation of the university curriculum manifests itself in several ways, in particular through the greater emphasis on, and the growth of, so called 'applied' or 'professional' programmes.

Hand in hand with this more functional view of the teaching function of higher education goes a strong policy interest in university research that is 'applied' (as opposed to basic or 'curiosity-driven') and relevant to the needs of industry.[2] Both governments concerned with international competitiveness in a global economy and industry interested in producing and selling leading-edge products and services put strong pressures on universities and academic staff not only to produce knowledge that is economically useful, but also to assume an active role in the transfer and the commercialisation of the results of such research. More generally, this shift is due to a new neo-liberal political agenda in Canada which has opened up functions that used to be the responsibility of the public domain to the mechanisms of the market. This move towards competitiveness and the commercialisation of formerly public functions has perhaps been less drastic than in the UK, New Zealand and the US, but it is clearly manifest in Canadian universities and colleges.

Thisnda coincides with and is influenced by a concern about the size of public debt. Higher education has suffered severe budget cut-backs in public funding, forcing institutions to engage in efforts to secure additional funds from other sources. There are clear expectations on the part of federal and provincial governments that post-secondary education in the future will have to operate with reduced public resources.

While financial cuts are part of an attempt to contain the costs of the public sector overall, financial shortfalls have hit the higher education sector especially hard. Earlier expectations that enrolment levels would shrink as a result of demographic developments have not materialised; on the contrary, demand for post-secondary education, and for full time education in particular, is still growing, even if at a slower pace than in the roaring 1960s and 1970s.

In this chapter, these developments will be described and analysed with respect to three particular perspectives: first, the impact of expansion, diversification (or 'differentiation') and qualitative change on what used to be non-traditional students; second, the role of policy; and, third, the challenge of lifelong learning in a 'knowledge society' and a knowledge-based economy. Before going into these themes, it is useful in a volume on comparative perspectives, to give the reader, unfamiliar with the Canadian system, some background for a better understanding of these perspectives.

The Canadian system of higher education: an overview

Provincial and federal responsibilities

Post-secondary education is, like all education in Canada, the responsibility of the provincial governments. While the constitution is very clear about this, it does not mean that the federal government has no role at all in higher education. This federal role has developed over time and 'under conditions akin to chronic schizophrenia', caused by the attempt to 'combine constitutional propriety with political expediency' (Cameron 1997 p. 9). Thus the federal government has used a 'back-door approach' (Press and Menzies 1996) to playing a major role in higher education by adopting legislation in areas where it was constitutionally safe to do so, such as work force training, research and financial assistance to students, and through the use of federal–provincial agreements for shared-cost programmes and federal transfer payments for post-secondary education.

This covert role of the federal authorities notwithstanding, the Canadian system consists of twelve provincial and territorial quasi-systems. Although these have a few comparable structures and use much the same terminology, they have distinct rules and arrangements concerning degree-granting, access, curricula, student mobility and planning (Jones 1997), due to the distinct history and development in the various provinces.³ The resulting wide variety of institutions, structures and rules is in contrast with other federal systems such as Germany, where the federal government has a formal role in setting forth the organisational framework within which provincial systems operate, and provides nation-wide standards in such matters as structures, rules of admission, the status of the professoriate, recognition of degrees and the like, thus facilitating student and faculty mobility across the jurisdictions of the *Länder* (see Wolter in this volume).

There are nevertheless many structural similarities among the institutions of the various provinces (Skolnik 1997), including the almost uniform model of university organisation with its bi-cameral governance structure, consisting of a corporate board of governors with responsibility for administrative and financial affairs, and an academic senate with responsibility for all academic matters. Alongside such structural similarities, there is also a wide diversity of institutions in the various provinces including, besides universities and community colleges (the two dominant types), university colleges, institutes of technology, schools of craft and design, maritime institutes, open and distance colleges and universities, the *collèges d'enseignement générale et professionel* (CEGEPS) in Quebec, and aboriginal colleges (see the various provincial systems in Jones 1997).

Institutions

The two main types of post-secondary institutions are universities and community colleges. While some of the former go back to the eighteenth and nineteenth century, most of the community colleges were set up by provincial governments in the 1960s and early 1970s in response to a growing demand for non-university post-secondary education that was vocationally oriented, had close links with the community, and provided both open access and opportunities for the learning needs of various clienteles. Besides these two principal types, there is a host of other post-secondary institutions that cater to different, mostly more specialised learning needs.

Universities are institutions that award academic degrees, namely Bachelor's, Master's and doctoral degrees; some also confer diplomas and certificates which require one or two years of study in a specific field or discipline. With the exception of a few church-affiliated universities, universities are mainly publicly financed although they also have income from other sources, mainly from student fees, and from services they provide such as university-hospital-based health care and research services to industry.

Community colleges and other institutions of the same kind, such as colleges of applied arts and institutes of technology, are primarily teaching institutions which basically provide three types of programmes: technical and vocational training, general and academic education, and adult and literacy education. In addition, many colleges offer specialised post-graduate diplomas for students who already hold a first degree. The most important feature of community colleges is that they grant, in principle at least and not for all their programmes, open access. In British Columbia and Alberta, community colleges offer university transfer programmes, typically the first two years of university-level undergraduate programmes.[4] In Quebec, graduation from a two-year CEGEP programme is required for entrance to university. Colleges are much less autonomous than the universities and are seen as important labour-market instruments of government from where they receive, much like the universities, the bulk of their funding.

It is noteworthy that Canada, unlike other industrialised countries such as the US and Japan, has accommodated the growing numbers of students almost entirely through the *public* post-secondary education system. While this is still true for the university sector, which has very few non-public institutions (all with a religious affiliation), this is no longer true for the vocational and technical sector where many new private for-profit institutions have emerged over the last few years. The majority of these offers short and specialised programmes. The exact number of these institutions is difficult to ascertain but it is estimated that there are currently some 2,400, most of them small, enrolling approximately 1.2 million students. This emergence of a large private post-secondary training sector during the last decade is an indicator of both a strong market demand for vocational or job-related qualifications, and the inability of the college and institute sector to respond to the dynamics and the size of this demand.

Diversity, autonomy and co-ordination

The diversity of institutions is both an asset and a liability. While students have a wide choice of programmes, qualifications and modes of participation, student mobility between the provinces or between different institutions within the same province is a problem. This is largely due to three factors. First, there is too little standardisation which would facilitate portability of credits and credentials from one institution to another. This is due to the autonomy universities enjoy to define criteria, prerequisites for enrolment, and standards of their own for admission and credit recognition.

The second factor is that most provinces lack clearly established rules for transfer between the different parts of the post-secondary education system, a result of the largely unsystematic and uncoordinated ways the post-secondary sector was established and grew in the 1950s and 1960s. With few exceptions, provincial governments established the various categories of institutions independently from each other, with little if any regard for the linkages among them and for student mobility from one to another. Thus, in some provinces, there are two or more distinct post-secondary education sectors, governed by different legislative acts and funded according to different formulas. Co-ordination between the different institutions has been unsystematic in most provinces and in some provinces virtually non-existent (Dennison 1995, Skolnik & Jones 1993).

The third element concerns the barriers to student mobility across provincial borders. In principle, provinces are free to erect barriers against students from another province by, for instance, levying higher tuition fees from them. However, unlike in the US where most states require higher fees for out-of-state students, none of the provinces except Quebec requests differential fees from Canadian out-of-province students.

In the absence of inter-provincial agreements on credit equivalency and transfer, the Council of Ministers of Education – where all the provinces are represented, but not the federal government – agreed in 1995 to a pan-Canadian recognition of credit transfer for the first two years of undergraduate study. The Council was quick however to clarify that this would 'in no way infringe on the academic autonomy of the universities, . . . [i.e.] the right of universities to determine programme design and delivery, to determine academic prerequisites and to establish admission criteria and certification requirements of academic achievement' (CMEC 1995). The Council's reassurance to universities about their autonomy is mentioned here to demonstrate that, while the educational policy makers have seen the problem of barriers to inter-provincial student mobility, they have so far been unwilling to legislate, or regulate through other instruments such as funding, to bring universities to recognise course credit from other institutions.

Co-ordination is thus a central problem. The existence of two distinct sectors, universities and colleges, calls for some kind of articulation and efficient co-ordination between them, and in most provinces there is a clear lack of this. The need for co-ordination is particularly apparent in those provinces where community colleges have an explicit university transfer role which applies, as just mentioned, to some of the Western provinces. Here students can enrol in academic streams in the first of the first two years and then transfer to the second, or the third year in a university.

Part-time study and distance education

While most of the university level programmes, especially undergraduate programmes, are still delivered on campus to full-time ('traditional') students, many universities offer students an opportunity to study part-time through courses scheduled in the evening, on weekends, or during the summer vacations ('summer school'). This applies especially to many advanced professional programmes which accommodate the need of many of their students to combine work and study.

Colleges in particular tend to be very flexible in designing and delivering programmes that respond to the needs of their community and special groups. As part of their mandate to provide access to groups that have traditionally lacked opportunities for participating in post-secondary education, they reach out to people in remote areas and especially to the aboriginal population (the 'First Nations') who tend to live outside the urban areas. This is normally done through setting up satellite campuses in smaller villages or through on-site delivery of special programmes or courses.

There are also a number of distance education programmes that tend to cater to people whose schedules or location make it difficult to attend campus-based courses. Universities have so far not engaged in a major way in such provision, although this may soon change as interactive media, especially the Internet, provide new opportunities to reach new audiences beyond the traditional catchment areas. In Quebec, Alberta and British Columbia, special 'open universities' have been set up to serve that particular clientele, emulating the model of the British Open University (OU). Like the OU, these distance institutions cater primarily to older students, the bulk of them in the workforce, using so far mostly 'traditional' means of bridging distance such as printed materials, video and audio tapes, television and teleconferencing.

Continuing education

All universities and colleges have special continuing education units offering non-degree programmes and courses. While the majority of these were formerly financed from the regular budget, they have increasingly been made self-supporting units or 'profit centres' which need to recover costs (and sometimes overheads) from the income they generate through courses and services. This change in their financial arrangements has affected the way they operate: most courses offered now cater to professionals or corporations that can afford the fees, while classical adult education programmes are offered only to the extent that the costs are borne by government. This is particularly the case with regard to the unemployed, for whose re-training the government pays the fees.

Increasingly in universities, continuing education is provided by the mainstream departments or faculties themselves. While in some cases continuing education students are enrolled in regular programmes in order to acquire an advanced degree for career purposes, the majority participate in shorter professional programmes that either award a certificate or diploma upon completion, or that do not bear any formal credit. In particular, professional faculties such as medicine, dentistry, engineering, architecture, law, education and commerce tend to run their own continuing education programmes to serve their alumni and the professional community, not least in order to generate revenues outside the regular university budget.

Admission

To be eligible for undergraduate programmes, applicants must usually have graduated from a secondary school academic or university preparatory programme, and in Quebec they must have completed a two year CEGEP programme as already mentioned. However, since universities – and sometimes individual faculties or schools – can set their own admission standards, admission requirements are often more rigorous, depending on the particular programme or discipline and the ratio of demand to available places. Thus, some universities, faculties or programmes may require a considerably higher average grade than is required for graduation from secondary school, as well as a minimum course content. In addition, some faculties require students to have passed a standardised aptitude test, in law or in medicine for example, in order to qualify for admission.

Admission requirements for adult students, usually persons older than twenty-one years of who have been out of school for a number of years, are sometimes more flexible, depending on the particular policy of the institution to which the students apply. If applicants to graduate (i.e. master or doctorate) programmes have an undergraduate degree that is more than five years old, many universities require proof of additional qualifications or professional practice. Often, in these cases, admission is granted provisionally and students must perform to a certain standard during their first year in order to be fully admitted in the second.

Community colleges also set their own entrance requirements which tend to be somewhat lower and more flexible than those of the universities. For technical and professional diploma programmes, and for general academic and university transfer programmes, they usually require a secondary school certificate, while for programmes such as vocational, literacy and typical adult education programmes access is usually open.

Finance

Universities and colleges are, as mentioned already, supported by public funding which covers the bulk of their expenditure. Students contribute to the cost of their education by paying tuition fees which vary somewhat according to province, institution and programme of study. While professional programmes usually are more expensive (and in the case of some MBA programmes, full-cost recovery), undergraduate tuition ranges from C$1,700 annually (for domestic students) in Quebec to more than double that amount, $3,900 in Nova Scotia.[5] Except in British Columbia, where tuition fees have been frozen for the last five years except for professional programmes and international students, the level of tuition has gone up considerably over the last ten years, the result of severe cuts of funding for post-secondary education by the federal government in the early 1990s. Thus, between 1988 and 1998 tuition fees have increased by more than 100 per cent on average in Canada (CESC 1999).

As the federal and several provincial governments continue to cut back on their outlays for post-secondary education, requiring institutions to be more efficient by, among other means, finding revenues from other sources, it can be expected that this trend will continue. Correspondingly, the debt load of students has risen. Post-secondary students who had taken out student loans owed on average just over $11,000 at the time of their graduation in1995 – which was 40 per cent higher than the debt load of the class of 1990 and 60 per cent higher than that of the class of 1986 (CESC 1999).

The issue of rising student debt as a result of increases in tuition fees has become an increasingly serious concern, especially with respect to equity for persons from lower socio-economic backgrounds as well as for lifelong learners more generally. To be sure, student loan programmes are available from the federal or provincial governments, or both, and in 1997 some 380,000 students (about 30 per cent) had taken out a loan under the Canadian Student Loan Programme (CSLP). But conditions are not very attractive, especially for part-time students who have to pay interest even while still studying, so the up-take of the loan programme by these students is very low. Because the interest is quite high (at present the prime rate plus 2½ per cent), non-traditional students in general, and in particular unemployed students or would-be students from lower income strata may often be unwilling to incur sizeable debts in order to enrol in post-secondary education (Schuetze 1995). Some non-traditional groups qualify for small grants (currently at $3,000 per annum); these are disabled students, students with dependants, and female doctoral students in some selected fields where women are still under-represented.

Current participation patterns: who are the 'non-traditional' students in 2000?

The problematic notion of 'non-traditional students' has already been discussed in the introductory chapter (see Schuetze and Slowey in this volume), so suffice it here to say that in Canada too, some of the groups that were of this category in the 1970s and 1980s no longer belong to it in 2000. Women are the most obvious example. There are others however who are still under-represented in higher education, for example Canada's aboriginal population. More difficult to assess is the status of some other minorities as there are insufficient data for an analysis of the relative proportion of such students in higher education. Points in case are people with disabilities and students from a lower economic background.

The same applies to other 'visible minorities', as they are known in Canada: people of colour, mostly immigrants or their descendants. In the case of the latter it is questionable if they would really be in the 'under-represented' category as many of the more recent immigrants have, as part of the criteria by which most of them are admitted into the country, relatively high levels of educational attainment. This provides their descendants with the substantive amounts of social and cultural capital which are, as we know from many studies, a reliable predictor of participation in higher education. In this section, we shall look in some more detail into the participation of those groups of 'non-traditional' students for which we have relatively solid data: women, part-time students, adults and First Nations.

Women

Women, who were previously in the under-represented category, are now in the majority on campus both in universities and colleges. However, participation is not even. Thus, while women dominate in undergraduate studies, they are slightly fewer in graduate – especially doctoral – programmes. In terms of subjects, women are still under-represented in some of the classic male-dominated disciplines such as engineering and applied sciences, mathematics and physical sciences, but they outnumber male students in education, the arts, humanities, social studies, and, more astonishingly perhaps, in agriculture and biological studies, and in business and management studies. They also outnumber males by two to one in the health professions, not only because of their strong dominance in nursing (although this explains the breadth of the gap), but also because they now form the majority in medical studies, pharmacy and rehabilitation medicine. Only in dental studies – a very small field – are males still ahead, although the gap is closing here as well. The only field where women are significantly under-represented in universities, colleges and institutes are computer sciences and electrical and electronic technologies. However, this is not due to specific institutional barriers; on the contrary, many institutions have programmes to specifically recruit and support women in these fields.

The strong participation of women in higher education shows also at the output end. More women than men now take university degrees. While in 1972, twenty-five years ago, women gained only 38 per cent of all degrees, in 1998 58 per cent of all degrees awarded from Canadian universities were earned by women (AUCC 1999). This is explained mainly by two facts (apart from the greater participation in advanced education generally). One is that the labour market participation of women has greatly increased: whereas twenty years ago only 45 per cent of adult women (aged twenty-five to sixty-four) were in the labour force, in 1997 this percentage stood at almost double, namely 88 per cent (the rate for men stands at 91 per cent). Also, there is a significantly higher earning premium for women: female graduates earn about 50 per cent more than women without a degree (that earning differential is only 25 per cent for men).

Rather than women being under-represented, at the end of the twentieth century, it is now men who are proportionally fewer in number, and are becoming almost an endangered species in some fields of study. While this does not make them 'non-traditional', neither are women in this category any longer. It is interesting to note however that the rise of women's participation in higher education is not the effect of any particular public or institutional policy or measure aimed specifically at higher education, but stems from far-reaching societal changes, some of which were reinforced by laws, that have brought about full equality in most fields of public life. Because of their strong participation in higher education it can be expected that remaining pockets of inequality that women still face in society, for example in politics, and in the higher ranks of both the civil service and the private sector, will be eradicated as women in growing numbers embark on entrepreneurial, professional and public service careers.

Part-time students

Part-time study has been identified by many authors as being one preferred manner in which older students especially are able to combine their studies with work or other social activities (e.g. OECD 1987, Schuetze and Istance 1987, Bourgeois *et al.* 1999). The availability of programmes that could be undertaken on a part-time basis was therefore seen as an important mechanism to enhance adult participation, and some authors took the number of part-time enrolments as a proxy for the participation of adult students (Pacquet 1987). Together with the US, in the mid-1980s, Canada was in the lead at the time among industrialised countries in the level of part-time enrolment and, mainly for this reason, was regarded as particularly advanced in terms of adult participation in higher education (OECD 1987).

Until around 1992 part-time enrolment had been steadily on the rise in Canada. Over the last five years however the number of undergraduate enrolments has fallen significantly (from almost 260,000 in 1993–4 to 208,000 in 1997–8), although graduate part-time enrolment has stayed virtually the same (42,000). This pattern of diminishing part-time enrolment in undergraduate studies has not however occurred uniformly across the country. Thus in the two Western provinces, British Columbia and Alberta, part-time enrolment has continued to rise, accounting in 1998 for approximately 30 per cent of overall enrolment in degree programmes. In college programmes – both university transfer and career programmes – British Columbia has a 60 per cent majority of part-time students. How can this rather strong regional variation in the West be explained?

One explanation has to do with variations in economic cycles. For a number of structural and market reasons, the severe economic recession that hit Central and Eastern Canada in the early 1990s was felt less strongly in the East; in contrast, the slump of the Asian markets in the latter half of the 1990s had a far greater effect on Western Canada. Since part-time enrolment implies that students work to support themselves during their studies, economic cycles may explain some of the regional variations in part-time enrolment (although authors offer different interpretations of the impact of economic down-turns on part-time enrolment patterns). Another explanation which is complementary rather than alternative might lie in the fact that these two Western provinces in particular have pursued active policies to increase participation in post-secondary education, since British Columbia especially had been trailing the other provinces with respect to participation rates.

When desegregating the overall numbers with regard to age, it is important to note that the decline in part-time undergraduate enrolment was higher in the twenty-five to forty-four year old group (a loss of over 50,000 students between 1992–3 and 1998–9, which is a decline of 32 per cent or almost a third of total part-time enrolment in that age group). In comparison, the decline was only 7,000 students, or 10 per cent, in the eighteen to twenty-four year old group (StatsCan 2000b). In graduate studies however, the trend was different: the proportion of part-time enrolment of the older age groups during the 1993–4 to 1997–8 period remained stable (StatsCan 2000a).

Older students

It has been pointed out in the introductory chapter that most post-secondary students are 'adults' in the legal sense, so the term 'adult' does not make much sense if one wants to analyse the participation of older students. On the other hand, it is used in various surveys that are relevant for a discussion of enrolment patterns of older students as well as their socio-economic and demographic profile; these include the Adult Education and Training Survey in Canada (AETS) and the International Adult Literacy Survey (IALS).

Generally speaking, adult participation in organised learning activities is relatively high in Canada. According to the AETS, in 1997 some six million adults, that is 26 per cent of the population of the same age, participated in courses, seminars, workshops or other forms of structured training.[6] Of these, more than two-thirds were engaged in job-related activities and more than half (55 per cent) were employer-supported (StatsCan 2000a). Educational institutions are the most important course providers, accounting for almost 40 per cent, followed by commercial schools and employer-provided education and training, each accounting for little more than 15 per cent.

According to the IALS, which uses comparable definitions, 39 per cent of the adult population participated in educational activities in 1993 (OECD 1995, Doray and Rubenson 1997), though with important regional variations.[7] Even more prominent than in the AETS study is the proportion of activities that are pursued for job-related reasons, namely 80 per cent, again with variations in different regions and, more important, by gender; more women than men participate for other than job- or career-related reasons. With respect to providers, the IALS results are significantly different than those of the AETS, showing a polarisation between employers on the one hand, and universities and colleges on the other, with 30 per cent each (Doray and Rubenson 1997).

Regarding enrolment of older students in universities and colleges, reliable data exist only for those students enrolled in programmes leading to a degree, diploma or certificate, while data on participation in non-degree or non-credit activities is very patchy. Thus, analysing participation in credit-bearing programmes only, the widely held perception that in Canada the student body is continuously ageing is not supported by the data, or, more precisely, while the absolute number of older students (twenty-four years and older) has increased, their proportion as part of the total student population has not. To be sure, there was an increase in the 1980s and early 1990s when the proportion of undergraduate students grew from 13 to 17 per cent, yet in the late 1990s the proportion of younger students accounted for 85 per cent, and that of older students for 15 (AUCC 1999). As one might expect, this is somewhat different for graduate students. According to the 1997 survey of the graduates of the class of 1995, 35 per cent of the students graduating with a Master's degree, and 45 per cent of those graduating with a doctoral degree, were thirty-five years of age and older (StatsCan 1997).

Aboriginal students

Participation by Aboriginal people in education generally has been a problem, due to a number of factors. Major difficulties include the cultural differences that, historically, the education system was unwilling or unable to accommodate, and linguistic problems that First Nation students face. All instruction in state and, formerly, church-run schools, and almost all the educational literature and materials, are in English or French, which are not the first languages of many of the First Nation people. A third major barrier is the fact that many First Nations communities are geographically remote from the population centres where most schools and all universities and colleges are located.

For these and other reasons, school attendance and retention have been serious problems that extend into post-secondary education. According to the 1996 Census, 42 per cent of the aboriginal working age population (twenty-four to fifty-four years old) had less than a complete high school education, compared with 22 per cent of the rest of the population. Only 35 per cent of First Nation people had a post-secondary qualification, compared with 52 per cent of the rest of the population (StatsCan 1999). The percentage of the aboriginal population with a university degree, while more than doubling between 1986 and 1996, was still very low at 4 per cent (19 per cent in the rest of the population).[8] The largest increases over this ten-year period were in the rates of students who graduated from college and trade education, rising from 15 per cent to 20 per cent (CESC 1999).

In spite of recent increases in enrolment and completion rates, the overall participation rate of First Nation students is abysmally low. Thus, more than any other 'non-traditional' group, Aboriginal students are still significantly under-represented in Canadian post-secondary education.

Policy

In Canada, policies can be distinguished on three levels: federal, provincial and institutional. It has already been pointed out that the federal level has no direct responsibility for post-secondary education, but the indirect influence it exercises is considerable. The most important policy shift over the 1990s did not concern changes to any particular policy but was a general shift towards a neo-liberal agenda, the objective of which is the submission of the public functions of the state to the economic imperative of 'the market'. This move towards 'marketisation' manifested itself in several ways in higher education. Most important was the massive cut-back of federal funding for post-secondary education which went to the provinces, which meant that they had either to find extra money from their own budgets to compensate for the shortfalls of federal funding, or to cut back support to the institutions.

The net result of this policy was twofold. First, more of the financial burden was passed on to the 'consumer', namely the student, in the form of tuition fee increases. As mentioned earlier, in most provinces, student fees have more than doubled since the early 1990s (AUCC 1999). The second effect was that institutions had to do more with less. The reduction in operating budgets forced institutions to cut back on services and programmes that were seen as not cost-effective. While these cut-backs might initially have produced some efficiency or 'productivity' gains, the continuous need to produce more (visible or audible) 'bang for the (public) buck' affected the quality and the content of programmes. Thus, for example, the number of academic staff in the universities dropped by 11 per cent since 1992, in spite of increasing student enrolment. As fewer young staff are hired than before, the average age of university teachers and researchers is increasing, standing now at forty-nine years (ibid.).

As institutions in search of funding from other sources became more responsive to government and private sector demands, there has been a subtle shift to courses that were more relevant to the labour market and employment, and to applied research in fields of interest to industry. As a consequence, several observers have noted an increasing vocationalisation of the liberal arts curriculum in undergraduate studies (Fisher and Rubenson 1998) as well as a trend towards greater commercialisation of university research (Expert Panel 1999, Tudiver 1999).

For non-traditional students, the greater concern for the employment relevance of programmes might not be all that negative; in fact for students who are more practice-oriented as well as for older students with work experience, such a contextualization of knowledge might be motivating and facilitate their learning (Rubenson and Schuetze 1995). However, the cuts in staff and the focus on cost recovery and cost effectiveness of programmes and courses may work against those students who need extra help in terms of counselling or outreach activities, and who would profit from small classes or group work.

Provinces have pursued different policies with regard to non-traditional students. Thus for example, the current (conservative) government in

Ontario, the most populous and most industrialised of the provinces, pursues a neo-liberal agenda by cutting funding, promoting competition from the private sector, enhancing efficiency and productivity through the imposition of private-sector management techniques and the use of performance indicators, micro-managing planning, programming trough-targeted funding and other techniques.

In contrast, the government of British Columbia has pursued an active 'Access-for-All' policy for the last twelve years. As part of this policy, the social-democratic government has frozen tuition fees for five consecutive years in an attempt to lower the financial barriers for students and their families, and has exempted from fees some of the programmes that are mostly used by older and disadvantaged students, such as Adult Basic Education and English as a Second Language (ESL). Also, in order to increase participation by First Nation people, it has set up two institutions that are run by Aboriginal administrators and cater exclusively to First Nation students. While the Access-for All policy has yielded some impressive results with regard to some 'non-traditional' groups, the picture is not yet clear with regards to First Nation students due to problems of time lag and the lack of a reliable data base (Schuetze and Day, forthcoming).

The move towards a knowledge society and a knowledge-based economy: lifelong learning and post-secondary education

While this chapter has concentrated so far on non-traditional students and under-represented groups, as well as on the policies that are having an effect on their participation in post-secondary education, the focus of this last section is on an emerging larger picture: that of a system of lifelong learning in the context of both a knowledge society and a knowledge-based economy, as mentioned in the introductory chapter (see Schuetze and Slowey in this volume).

Canada: a polarised society

It has already been mentioned that Canada's investment in its education system is very high by international standards. As a consequence, the level of educational attainment of the Canadian population is high: in 1995, 47 per cent of the population aged twenty-five to sixty-four had completed some form of tertiary education (see Table 7.1, left-hand side), a substantially higher proportion than in any other OECD country.

If these figures are taken as a proxy for the basic cognitive capabilities prerequisite both for the knowledge-based economy and for the social skills deemed necessary for civic participation and social and economic well-being, Canada looks quite good (OECD 1997a p. 33).

The picture becomes more disturbing if, instead of educational attainment, one looks at the distribution of functional literacy as a measure of the

Table 7.1 Level of education and functional literacy in selected countries, 1995: percentage of the populations aged twenty-five to sixty-four by educational attainment and level of functional literacy (document)

	Not completed high school	High school	Non-university tertiary	University	Level 1	Level 2	Level 3	Level 4/5
Canada	25	28	30	17	19	25	32	24
United States	14	50	8	25	24	25	32	20
Germany	16	61	10	13	10	33	39	19
Sweden	25	46	14	14	7	19	40	35

Source: Rubenson and Schuetze 2000, adapted from OECD 1997a and b.

population's capability (Table 7.1, right hand side). According to the results of the International Adult Literacy Survey, a considerable proportion of Canadians are only able to do tasks that demand a low level of functional literacy.[9] Thus, on documentary literacy (success in processing everyday documents), 44 per cent of those aged between twenty-five and sixty-four scored below the level three capability deemed necessary for success in the knowledge economy. The situation for the 19 per cent that performed at the most basic level is most problematic. As Table 7.1 shows, this is not specifically a Canadian problem. However, the discrepancy between educational attainment and actual literacy distribution is particularly noticeable in North America. In fact, estimating the number of Canadian adults likely to be in need of basic education and training on the basis of actual literacy scores yields a much higher number than estimates based on educational attainment. One might think that literacy deficiencies like this would be a concern only for older adults, and it is true that the problem is most severe for those aged over fifty-five. But the troublesome fact is that 39 per cent of those between twenty-six and thirty five, 36 per cent of those between thirty-six and forty-five and 54 per cent of those aged from forty-six to fifty-five are in need of help, according to the estimates.

As it has been shown elsewhere in more detail (Rubenson and Schuetze 2000), there are a number of factors that are at the root of this polarisation of skills and knowledge in Canada. They need to be addressed by a comprehensive strategy on lifelong learning that aims at all citizens, not just those with plenty of cultural and social capital. As this chapter is concerned primarily with post-secondary education and institutional barriers that keep 'non-traditional' students from participating, we shall only discuss briefly two of them: cost and finance and the organisation of studies.

The cost of participation in post-secondary education is an important factor, especially for potential non-traditional students, when making a decision of participating in education. It has already been noted that the cost for tuition had sharply risen since the early 1990s. While several studies have found that the level of fees has no great effect on the decision to enrol, this must be questioned with respect to many of the non-traditional groups, especially older students and those from lower socio-economic backgrounds (Schuetze 1995).

Not only the cost but also the financial mechanisms supporting learning opportunities can constitute barriers. Current financial mechanisms are mostly specific to the sector, programme, or institution. For educational institutions this means that levels and modes of revenue differ depending on factors such as full-time or part-time study, field of study, or whether a student belongs to a specific group targeted for support. For the student, this fragmentation of educational finance means different rules govern eligibility, the level of support, and the terms and conditions under which grants or loans are awarded and loans paid back. Thus, the choice of whether or not to enrol and in which programme, and where and by which mode to learn, will often be determined by the availability of financial support, especially when there is no, or reduced, income from work during the period of study.

Many studies on participation in post-secondary education have found that specific institutional hurdles deter adults with work, family and social obligations from participating in formal post-secondary education. Many institutions still maintain rather rigid regimes and schedules. Universities, in particular, are traditionally organised to cater to the full-time, younger students coming directly from high school. Arrangements more suitable to adults, such as alternative access routes or admission rules, provision for distance and independent learning, the easy portability of learning credentials from one sector to another, and other flexible forms of organised learning are on the rise in Canada, and, inconvenient scheduling or the lack of appropriate courses is now rarely seen as a hindrance to engaging in post-secondary education. However, flexible schedules and relevant programmes for working students are not yet the norm throughout all institutions, nor in all fields of study. They are still the exception in university level programmes that require the use of laboratories and other specialised equipment or settings, such as medicine or engineering.

Beyond the individual and structural barriers already discussed, institutional barriers affect accessibility and mobility across different types of learning opportunities. As mentioned already, the lack of portability of credits across institutional and provincial boundaries severely limits learners' choices and mobility. This is not only an obstacle to the mobility of professionals and people with vocational certificates. It also affects students who have not yet completed their studies and want to continue in another institution or province.

Policies for lifelong learning

A major challenge in setting up a system of lifelong learning is extending organised learning opportunities to the least qualified. With literacy skills becoming increasingly important in the workplace, low-skill adults, young as well as old, are at risk of being excluded from the labour market. The large number of adults with low literacy levels (IALS levels 1 and 2) is thus a major problem. Many studies reveal that the people most in need of expanding their skill levels in fact seldom participate in organised education and training. They also tend to live and work in contexts, at or outside work, that do not stimulate a readiness to learn (Rubenson and Schuetze 1995).

Financial support is crucial for any viable policy. A vital issue, therefore, is how existing funding regimes affect the recruitment of those who traditionally do not participate. In a market-driven system, it is obvious that advantaged groups will strongly influence patterns of provision. However, even organisations with pronounced ambitions to reach disadvantaged groups actually provide services that correspond best to the demands of the advantaged, mainly because existing funding regimes do not compensate for the increased costs involved in recruiting, and working intensively with, those who are not used to learning (Nordhaug 1991). When government policies seek to increase efficiency through the adoption of more market-oriented approaches and outcomes-based funding, the likelihood is that organisations will cater to those students most easy to recruit and likely to succeed.

Since few employers take an active role in providing opportunities for workers with limited literacy skills to learn or actively use such skills, it is left to the public sector to provide the foundation for lifelong learning to a large segment of the adult population. The cost scenarios for undertaking this provision are staggering (OECD 1999). The discrepancy between available public funds, present funding regimes and the extent of the task is a major barrier for 'lifelong learning for all'.

If the state is to provide its citizens with equal learning opportunities, it is not sufficient to leave the task to institutions of post-secondary education. Rather, the task calls for co-operative efforts with and among several other policy sectors such as welfare, employment, and cultural affairs, sectors that often work in isolation from each other. It is easier to call for such co-operation than to actually accomplish it, especially when such co-operation, in order to be efficient, must extend to the private and the voluntary sectors as well. To be realistic, one must note that past experience in Canada of co-operation between different policy sectors, and especially between the various levels of government, has not been very positive. That does not mean it cannot be improved if the task at hand is seen as a policy priority.

Conclusions

The analysis of some of the issues of lifelong learning in Canada shows that the general enthusiasm and uncritical hype about the necessity and inevitability of the advent of the 'learning society' must be challenged as must the neo-classical credo that reliance on market mechanisms will achieve what the welfare state has failed to achieve.

The difficulties of designing an equitable and efficient strategy for a learning society – characterised not only by access to learning opportunities throughout life but also by the enhanced capacity of all members of that society to take advantage of them – are apparent. Canada would need to make an effort – co-ordinated not only among the federal and various provincial governments but also among different policy sectors and between the public and the private domain – to turn investment in public education and private sector training into effective learning opportunities for the entire population, not just its upper half. The role of post-secondary education in such a transformation towards a system of lifelong learning is important, but it is only one part of the system and must therefore be prevented from trying to exercise more and continued control over access, standards, and the proper definition of legitimate knowledge.

Notes

1 The 'typical' age group in Canada, the US, Mexico and the United Kingdom is eighteen to twenty-one; in Germany where high school lasts a year longer and where males must serve a year in the compulsory military (or, alternatively, civic) service, the typical age group is twenty-one to twenty-five.

2 This more utilitarian view of the university's research and teaching functions has its tradition in the US where 'land grant' colleges and universities had been set up in the middle of the nineteenth century with the explicit mandate to benefit agriculture, the rural regions and farmers and, especially in the Western provinces, this model was later emulated in Canada. The policy emphasis today on applied and industry-relevant research and a technology transfer function finds its conceptual base in various economic theories, e.g. the 'new growth' theory, the concept of the emerging 'knowledge-based economy' (Rubenson and Schuetze 2000), and the theory of 'innovation systems', all of which consider knowledge to be the pivotal factor of innovation, competitiveness and growth in the 'new economy'.

3 There are ten provinces in Canada and two (and, as of 1999, three) territories. The latter are in the North of the country where the climate is severe. They are therefore very sparsely populated and have no universities.

4 Besides these transfer programmes, some colleges ('University Colleges') in Alberta and British Columbia also offer, as of the mid-1990's, full four-year bachelor programmes making them hybrid or comprehensive institutions, since they still retain their non-academic programmes.

5 Quebec universities charge higher fees for out-of-province students which are comparable to those required in the other provinces. Average fees for all students, both in and out of province, are $2,300.

6 The AETS defined 'adults' as persons aged seventeen and over, not attending an institutional institution on a full-time basis, or full time students who are twenty and over and attending elementary or secondary education, or who are twenty-five and over and attend post-secondary education.

7 In British Columbia, participation was at 48 per cent, and 45 per cent participated in the other three Western provinces, compared to 31 per cent in Quebec and 31 per cent in Atlantic Canada.

8 While there has clearly been real improvement over the ten- year period, caution is advised in taking this increase at face value as some of it may be due to incomplete reporting and to 'ethnic mobility' as the number who reported that they belonged to one of the First Nations in 1996 was higher than in 1986 (CESC 1999).

9 The International Adult Literacy Survey (IALS) is a collaborative effort by twelve countries with the support of the OECD, UNESCO and the European Union. The IALS data set consists of a large sample of adults (ranging from 1,500 to 8,000 per country) in Belgium, Canada, Germany, Ireland, the Netherlands, New Zealand, Poland, Sweden, Switzerland, the UK and the US. The persons involved in the study were given the same wide-ranging test of their literacy skills, and a questionnaire collecting information about family background and literacy practices in the home, work situation, leisure activities and involvement in everyday learning activities as well as organised forms of adult education and training. Using multivariate analysis (logistic regression) these data have been used to critically examine who is involved in different forms of lifelong learning, the barriers to lifelong learning, and the structural inequality in learning opportunities.

References

AUCC (Association of Universities and Colleges of Canada) (1999) *Trends*, Ottawa: AUCC.

Betcherman, G., Leckie, N. and McMullen, K. (2000) 'Learning in the workplace: training patterns and training activities', in K. Rubenson and H. G. Schuetze (eds) *Transition to the Knowledge Society: Policies and Strategies for Individual Participation and Learning,* Vancouver: UBC Press (Institute for European Studies).

Bourgeois, E., Duke, C., Guyot, J. L. and Merrill, B. (1999) *The Adult University,* Buckingham: SRHE/Open University Press.

Cameron, D. (1997). 'The federal perspective', in G. Jones (ed.) *Higher Education in Canada: Different Systems, Different Perspectives,* New York and London: Garland.

CESC (Canadian Education Statistics Council) (1999) *Education Indicators in Canada,* Council of Ministers of Education, Canada.

CMEC (Council of Ministers of Education, Canada) (1995) *Pan-Canadian Protocol on the Transferability of University Credits,* http://www.cmec.ca/postsec/ transferability.stm.

Dennison, J. D. (1995) 'Organization and function in higher education', in J. D. Dennison (ed.) *Challenge and Opportunity: Canada's Community Colleges at the Crossroads,* Vancouver: University of British Columbia Press.

Doray, P. and Rubenson, K. (1997) 'Canada: the growing economic imperative', in P. Belanger and S. Valdivielso (eds) *The Emergence of Learning Societies: Who Participates in Adult Learning?* Oxford: Pergamon and UNESCO Institute of Education.

Expert Panel on the Commercialisation of University Research (1999) *Public Investment in University Research: Reaping the Benefits.* Report to the Prime Minister's Advisory Council on Science and Technology, Ottawa: Government of Canada.

Fisher, D. and Rubenson, K. (1998) 'The changing political economy: the private and public lives of Canadian universities', in J. Currie and J. Newson (eds) *Universities and Globalization: Critical Perspectives,* Thousand Oaks: SAGE.

Jones, G. (ed.) (1997) *Higher Education in Canada: Different Systems, Different Perspectives,* New York and London: Garland.

Nordhaug, D. (1991) *The Shadow Education System: Adult Resource Development,* Oslo: Oslo University Press.

OECD (1987) *Adults in Higher Education,* Paris: OECD.

—— (1995) *Literacy, Economy and Society: Results from the First International Adult Literacy Survey*, Paris: OECD.

—— (1996) *Lifelong Learning for All*, Paris: OECD.

—— (1997a) *Literacy Skills for the Knowledge Society*, Paris: OECD.

—— (1997b) *Education at a Glance: 1997*, Paris: OECD.

—— (1998) *Education at a Glance: OECD Indicators*, Paris: OECD.

—— (1999) 'Resources for lifelong learning: what might be needed and how might it be found?' in *Education Policy Analysis*, Paris: OECD.

Pacquet, P. (1987) 'Adults in higher education: the situation in Canada', in H. G. Schuetze (ed.) *Adults in Higher Education: Policies and Practice in Great Britain and North America*, Stockholm: Almqvist and Wiksell.

Press, H. and Menzies, T. (1996) 'The federal role and post-secondary education', in S. B. Lawton (ed.) *Financing Canadian education*, Toronto: Canadian Education Association.

Rubenson, K. and Schuetze, H. G. (1995) 'Learning at and through the workplace: a review of participation and adult learning theory', in D. Hirsch and D. Wagner (eds) *What Makes Workers Learn? The Role of Incentives in Workplace Education and Training*, Cresskill, N.J.: Hampton Press.

—— (2000) 'Lifelong learning for the knowledge society: demand, supply, and policy dilemmas', in K. Rubenson and H. G. Schuetze (eds) *Transition to the Knowledge Society: Policies and Strategies for Individual Participation and Learning*, Vancouver: UBC Press (Institute for European Studies).

Schuetze, H. G. (1995). 'Funding, access and teaching: the Canadian experience of a mass system of higher education', in T. Schuller (ed.) *The Changing University?*, Buckingham, UK: SRHE and Open University Press.

Schuetze, H. G. and Day, W. L. (forthcoming) *Access for All: Policies and Funding Mechanisms in British Columbia 1988–1998*, Vancouver: UBC (Centre for Policy Studies in Higher Education and Training).

Schuetze, H. G., and Istance, D. (1987). *Recurrent Education Revisited: Modes of Participation and Financing*, Stockholm: Almqvist and Wiksell.

Skolnik, M. (1997) 'Putting it all together: viewing Canadian higher education from a collection of jurisdiction-based perspectives', in G. Jones (ed.) *Higher Education in Canada: Different Systems, Different Perspectives*, New York and London: Garland.

Skolnik, M. and Jones, G. (1993). 'Arrangements for co-ordination between university and college sectors in Canadian provinces', *Canadian Journal of Higher Education* vol. 23 no. 1.

Slaughter, S., and Leslie, L. L. (1997) *Academic Capitalism: Politics, Policies and the Entrepreneurial University*, Baltimore: Johns Hopkins University Press.

StatsCan (Statistics Canada) (1997) *National Graduate Survey 1997*, Ottawa: StatsCan.

—— (1999) 'Education achievements of young aboriginal adults', *Canadian Social Trends*, Spring, Ottawa: StatsCan.

—— (2000a) *Education in Canada 1999*, Ottawa: StatsCan.

—— (2000b) *Education Quarterly Review* vol. 6 no. 3.

Tudiver, N. (1999). *Universities for Sale: Resisting Corporate Control over Canadian Higher Education*, Toronto: James Lorimer.

8 The United States
Heterogeneity of the student body and the meaning of "non-traditional" in US higher education

Seth Agbo

Introduction

Since the 1980s, thinking about higher education policy and practice in the United States has been heavily influenced, if not dominated, by ideas about the ability of higher education to continue to meet the changing and the developing needs of the nation effectively. The passing of the industrial age and advent of the information era have created new forms and modes of knowledge and information production, presentation, and distribution that directly affect our traditional system of higher education. The passage of the GI Bill or the Servicemen's Readjustment Act in 1944 was a major political shift providing a massive influx of veterans into higher education (Millard 1991). Adult students have not only continued to flow into post-secondary institutions but their numbers have increased significantly. Quinnan (1997) contends that within a period of twenty years, from 1971 to 1991, the enrolment of students aged twenty-five or older increased by 171 percent. Within the same period, the enrolment of students aged twenty-five to twenty-nine increased by 99 percent, of those thirty to thirty-four by 201 percent and of those above thirty-five years by 48 percent.

Issues shaping current policy agendas in higher education today concern lifelong learning, the current role of education in workforce development, better job opportunities, the education–labor-market mismatch, the competitive global economy and equality of educational access. Although these issues make varied assumptions about a new clientele in higher education, non-traditional age and non-traditional route students, this new clientele remains hidden in the background of the education debate. This chapter looks more closely at the current status of non-traditional age and non-traditional route students in the United States.

Structural characteristics and organization of higher education in the United States

The face of higher education: composition of student body

At the dawn of the twentieth century, higher education enrolment was less than a quarter of a million students. Enrolment rose to more than 2.5 million in 1950 and by the fall of 1965 there were about 6 million students in institutions of higher education. This enrolment represented about 50 percent of the relevant age cohort in higher education. Enrolment of traditional students in the eighteen to twenty-four age cohort peaked in 1981 and then began to experience a downward trend that continued into the 1990s.

The distribution of total enrolment in public and private institutions changed little between 1972 and 1995, with public institutions enrolling nearly 80 percent of the total student population. By the end of the 1970s and the early 1980s non-traditional students, particularly older women and part-time students, began to participate in higher and further education, and this is reflected in the greater share of enrolments in two-year institutions. As a result of this new clientele of non-traditional students, enrolment reached a high of 12.5 million in 1983 and 14.5 million in 1992 (National Center of Education Statistics (NCES 1998a)). Although enrolment decreased to 14.3 million in 1996, it is expected to rise to 16.1 million by 2008 (NCES 1998b). As is indicated in Table 8.1, the increase in minority students was primarily due to an expansion in the enrolment of Hispanic and Asian/Pacific-Islander students, whose enrolment as a percentage of all post-secondary students increased about 4 percent between 1976 and 1995.

Structure

Higher education in the United States is an array of independent private and state institutions. There are institutions of all conceivable kinds, with

Table 8.1 Percentage distribution of total enrolment in higher education institutions, by race/ethnicity and type of institution, 1970–95

Fall year All institutions	US residents[1]						Non-resident alien
	White (resident)	Minority					
		Total minority (resident)	Black	Hispanic	Asian/ Pacific Islander	American Indian/ Alaskan Native	
1976	82.2	15.4	9.4	3.5	1.8	0.7	2.0
1980	81.4	16.1	9.2	3.9	2.4	0.7	2.5
1990	77.6	19.6	9.0	5.7	4.1	0.7	2.8
1995	72.3	24.5	10.3	7.7	5.6	0.9	3.2
By control and type of institution: 1995							
Public	71.6	25.7	10.5	8.4	5.8	1.0	2.7
Private	74.6	20.4	9.9	4.9	5.0	0.6	5.0

Source: NCES 1998a p. 150.

Note: includes US citizens and resident aliens. Details may not add up due to rounding.

striking differences in total enrolment, functions and quality. To cater for the 15.4 million students attending higher education institutions there are 3,842 institutions offering post-secondary education and training (Chronicle of Higher Education 1999). About 8.9 million are full-time students while 3.5 million are studying part-time. Of more than 3 million graduate students, about 1.3 million are full-time and 1.7 million are part-time.

The structural pattern of higher education in the United States suggests that the major types of post-secondary education can be classified by the duration of courses and the type of degree. Two-year community colleges enroll more than one-quarter of all higher education students and provide relatively short course programs in institutions that are usually not research oriented. Four-year institutions enrolling about 54 percent of all higher education students offer relatively long course programs that emphasize breadth of education and some low-level specialized professional degrees. There are striking differences as regards control, funding, staffing, enrolment, the range and types of degrees granted, and in the quality of students and teachers. However, accreditation boards ensure a certain number of common elements in the seemingly diverse trends as well as minimum quality standards. This type of standardization that is common with many program areas ensures the integration of the system to the extent that students can transfer from one institution to another or from one level to another. The various entrance requirements, the kinds of services offered, the cost of attendance, and the availability of student financial aid affect student choices and selection of institutions.

Access

Partly because of technological changes at the workplace and growing educational requirements for all types of occupations, post-secondary education has become a route to social and economic success. As the proportion by which the earnings of post-secondary graduates exceed those of their high school counterparts has been going up since the 1980s, there has been a tremendous increase in demand for higher education in the 1980s and the 1990s. Although the population of twenty to twenty-four year olds has been decreasing for the past decade, the number of enrolments has been increasing, driven by female enrolment and participation rates of non-traditional students.

The proportion of high school graduates who enrolled in post-secondary institutions increased from 49 percent in 1972 to 62 percent in 1995 (Cuccaro-Alamin 1997), and to 65 percent in 1996 (NCES 1998a). The proportion of high school graduates aged sixteen to twenty-four enrolled in higher education between 1972 and 1995 increased for whites, blacks, and Hispanics, and across the income spectrum. However, high school graduates from low- and middle-income families were less likely to proceed on directly to post-secondary education than those from high-income families. Part of the explanation may lie in the fact that high school graduates may work and save money for post-secondary education and thus delay their immediate enrolment.

Costs

The NCES report (1998a) indicates that between 1985 and 1995 tuition and fees in public institutions per full-time-equivalent (FTE) student increased from $3,121 to $4,426 in constant dollars and from 18 to 24 percent as a share of all revenue, while in private universities average tuition and fee revenue per FTE increased from $12,023 to $16,344 per year (all figures in 1997 constant dollars) (NCES 1998a).

The average total annual cost (including living expenses as well as tuition and fees) for all students was $12,600. For students who attended public four-year institutions, the total cost amounted to $10,800, while the total cost for attending a private four-year not-for-profit institution was about double the price for a public institution ($20,000). The total price for a two-year public institution was $6,800 (NCES 1998a). The rise in average prices for undergraduate higher education was mainly due to rises in the costs of tuition, room, and board. Between 1986–7 and 1996–7, the average post-secondary costs of tuition, room and board increased by 31 percent at private institutions and 20 percent at public institutions.

The increase in tuition fees has been due to a number of reasons: most significantly, as will be discussed in more detail later in this chapter, there has been a decrease in public levels of support for post-secondary education. Access depends on low tuition charges in public institutions, and also on the availability of scholarships and grants to dependent undergraduates from low-income families. Growth in competition among higher education institutions to enroll more students may become a significant factor for institutions to increase access through their own financial aid and scholarship programs.

The focus of the remainder of this chapter will be on the profile of non-traditional age and non-traditional route students in higher education. The first part begins with a brief look at the characteristics of non-traditional students and trends in their enrolment in higher education, while the second part explores the nature of courses and programs needed by non-traditional students and the reasons for their participation in higher education.

Non-traditional age and non-traditional route students in higher education

Profile of non-traditional students in higher education

Universities and colleges in the United States have traditionally focused almost exclusively on the education of the young and academically qualified

(Millard 1991, Fisher 1992, Quinnan 1997). However, in the last two decades, non-traditional age and non-traditional route students have become an important group in higher education institutions. Previously, even in the few institutions having a tradition of academic provision for adult students, the participation of adults was always marginal and limited to non-degree studies through short courses administered by extra-mural or external departments designated as continuing education (Millard 1991). Now, however, adult participation has transgressed the boundaries of extra-mural studies and is moving to the center of the mission of the university or college (Parnell 1990, Merriam and Caffarella 1991, Quinnan 1997).

The concept of the non-traditional student

There is ongoing controversy among scholars and practitioners over the definition of the non-traditional student. A cursory examination of the student body in the United States reveals a large proportion of students that does not fit the definition of the traditional student. In accordance with the definition adopted for this book, "non-traditional" students include part-time, as well as students from under-represented groups. Horn and Carroll (1996) identify at least three broad characteristics that elicit differences of perception between traditional and non-traditional students:

- *Financial and family status*   The utilization of financial and family status to define non-traditional students assumes that such students are financially independent from parents, that they have family responsibilities and financial constraints such as dependents beyond their spouses, that they may be single parents, or that they may be working full-time while enrolled. The Department of Education considers all students of twenty-four years or older to be independent students (Horn and Carroll 1996). Students who work thirty-five or more hours per week are considered non-traditional. Furthermore, students who declare financial dependents such as children, elderly parents, siblings or other family beyond their spouses are also specified as non-traditional.
- *Enrolment patterns*   The use of enrolment patterns assumes that traditional students enroll immediately after secondary school and attend full-time. Therefore, students who delay enrolling in higher education by a year or more after high school and students who attend part-time do not fit into the traditional student category and are termed non-traditional.
- *High school graduation status*   Finally, students who do not earn a regular high school diploma but who receive certification such as General Education Development (GED) or a high school certificate of completion are also considered to be non-traditional students.

As many of the attributes used to distinguish non-traditional undergraduates are interdependent, students may have one or several of the characteristics of a non-traditional student. For example, a delayed entry student may also attend part-time, be a single parent, be independent and responsible for dependents, and so on. Consequently, it is likely that a student with any non-traditional characteristic usually has more than one such characteristic. A scale used by Horn and Carroll (1996) measures the number of non-traditional characteristics, from zero to seven, with zero indicative of the traditional student. They consider students with only one characteristic, such as "older than typical" or "attend part-time" to be *minimally non-traditional*; students with two or three non-traditional characteristics are deemed as *moderately non-traditional,* and *highly non-traditional* students have four or more non-traditional characteristics.

Trends in non-traditional student enrolment

Horn and Carroll (1996) report that a clear majority of 1992 undergraduates (about 70 percent) were at least minimally non-traditional, and about 50 percent were either in the moderately or highly non-traditional categories. Between 54 and 59 percent of all undergraduates were older than traditional students. About 40 percent were enrolled part-time while between one-quarter and one-third worked full-time. About 48 percent declared they were financially independent of their parents. 20 percent had dependents, and about 7 percent were single parents. Between 4 and 7 percent were students without a high school diploma, gaining admission to post-secondary institutions with the General Education Development (GED) exam.

Almost half of the minimally non-traditional students were older than typical, and about a third were enrolled as part-time students. While only about 12 percent of these students worked full-time in 1986 and 1992, the proportion of those who worked full-time rose to about 30 percent in 1989. In the three survey years, about 11 percent of the minimally non-traditional students indicated that they were financially independent of their parents. The proportion of the minimally non-traditional students enrolled through non-traditional routes was below the average for all undergraduates.

Students with two or three non-traditional characteristics classified as "moderately non-traditional" accounted for about 25 to 30 percent of undergraduates in 1986, 1989 and 1992. About 90 percent of the moderately non-traditional students were older than typical. About 73 to 75 percent of those students were independent, and between 45 and 56 percent were enrolled as part-time students. Between 25 and 30 percent worked full-time. Over 70 percent were financially independent of parents, and about 12 percent had dependents.

Students with four or more characteristics identified as "highly non-traditional" accounted for almost the same proportion as the moderately non-traditional students. Almost all the students identified as highly non-traditional were older than typical and were financially independent. Two-thirds had dependents and about one-quarter were single parents. In 1986, about one-fifth of the students were enrolled in non-traditional routes, with the proportion declining to about 12 percent in 1992.

Generally, non-traditional students are likely to be women, to belong to a racial/ethnic minority group, and to have less well-educated parents than traditional students (Table 8.2).

Trends for individual non-traditional characteristics

In order to determine the pattern of change in the enrolment of non-traditional students between 1986 and 1992, and also to look at the enrolment pattern of students in 1997, it is useful to examine each non-traditional characteristic separately.

Enrolment trends of older than typical age students

Although much of the discussion on non-traditional students has focussed on "adult students" it might be useful to concentrate instead on students that are older than typical college age, since the "definition of 'adult' students is somewhat arbitrary and varies both within and across national systems of higher education" (Richardson and King 1998 p. 65). NCES classifies all students of seventeen years of age and older as "adults." While this is correct from a legal perspective, it blurs the line between traditional and non-traditional students with regard to age. Therefore, the "older than typical" criterion appears more meaningful than "adult student." Horn and Carroll (1996) define older than typical students as those undergraduates who are twenty years and older in their first year, twenty-one or older in their second year, twenty-two or older in their third year, or any student who is twenty-three years or older.

The percentage of undergraduate students enrolled in higher education who were older than typical increased by 10 percent within six years, from 54 percent in 1986 to 60 in 1992 (Horn and Carroll 1996). The bulk of these older students were enrolled in non-degree programs: in two-year and shorter programs, and in private for-profit institutions. Substantial increases of older than typical students occurred in private, not-for-profit,

Table 8.2 Composition of 1992 undergraduates according to gender, race/ethnicity, and parent education levels for traditional and non-traditional students

	Traditional students	Non-traditional students
Percent female	53	56
Percent racial-ethnic minority	18	23
Percent with a parent who graduated from college	51	37

Source: Adapted from Horn and Carroll 1996 Figure 2, p. 11.

four-year institutions where their proportion rose from over one-third (38 percent) to almost one-half (47 percent) between 1986 and 1992. But even in the public four-year institutions the numbers have increased and in 1992 stood at 44 percent (Horn and Carroll 1996).

Financially independent students

Between 1986 and 1992, there was no substantial increase in the overall percentage of students identified as financially independent of their parents, although one might have expected that expansion in the older than typical age group would also mean an increase of financially independent students. This is not the case, and suggests that the increase in older than typical students may be occurring under the age of twenty-four, the criterion for financial independence.

Part-time enrolments

Part-time enrolment is an option for older or returning students, especially those students twenty-five years or older, who are more likely than younger ones to have family responsibilities, full-time jobs, or other time or financial constraints. However, there may also be others enrolling part-time for undefined reasons (NCES 1998a).

In 1997, from a total of 15.4 million students enrolled in post-secondary institutions in the United States, about 7 million or 45 percent were enrolled on part-time bases (Chronicle of Higher Education 1999). Where part-time study has remained around 30 percent over the last twenty years, indicators demonstrate that the part-time mode of study is more prevalent among graduate students. Data on undergraduate students (Table 8.3) show, not unexpectedly, that older students are much more likely to attend part-time than younger ones. Female students are more likely to enroll part-time than their male counterparts, which can probably be explained by the need to combine parenthood and other family obligations with the pursuit of academic studies. Also, some part-time students are more likely to enroll in two-year than in four-year institutions.

Table 8.3 Percentage of undergraduate students enrolled in college part-time by age, sex, and type of institution, 1976–95

		Age			Sex		Type of institution	
	Total	*18–24*	*25–34*	*35 or older*	*Male*	*Female*	*2-year*	*4-year*
1976	27.9	14.6	61.7	80.2	26.8	29.0	48.2	17.6
1980	30.9	15.8	68.7	82.3	25.7	35.5	50.4	18.9
1990	31.9	15.8	60.1	74.9	28.1	35.0	51.1	21.3
1995	30.6	16.7	53.3	67.7	28.1	32.5	48.2	22.1

Source: Adapted from NCES 1998a p. 164.

Full-time employment

In the United States, combining work and study has become common practice. Faced with higher tuition costs at post-secondary institutions, many undergraduates, particularly financially independent ones, rely heavily on work to defray their education expenses. The past three decades have been characterized by increasing employment among post-secondary students. Before turning to employed non-traditional students, it is illuminating to look at the percentage of full-time post-secondary students aged between sixteen and twenty-four who were in gainful employment full-time. The US Department of Education, NCES (1998a) data show that the proportion of post-secondary students between the ages of sixteen and twenty-four who were employed full-time for twenty hours or more increased from about 34 percent (14 percent of whom worked for twenty hours or more and around 4 percent for thirty-five or more hours) in 1970 to about 47 percent (27 percent for twenty or more and 7 percent for thirty-five or more hours) in 1995. This shows that substantially more students are in gainful employment, working increasing amounts of hours.

Effects of work on post-secondary education

The effects of such a combination on the student's ability to study successfully are not quite clear, but the generally accepted view appears to be that their success is by no means guaranteed. Working during the school year may leave such students less time to concentrate on academic work, and participation in extracurricular activities combined with long working hours may even lengthen the time it takes them to complete their degrees. However, working can be advantageous in that students may gain experiences that prepare them for the workplace and increase their prospects for future employment alternatives (NCES 1998a).

Not surprisingly, the NCES survey shows that the more students work the more likely they are to report that their job requirements limit their class schedule, reduce their course choices, limit the number of classes they could take, and negatively affect their academic performance (see Table 8.4).

Non-traditional route enrolment

The lack of a high school diploma does not preclude students from post-secondary study. Many adults without such a diploma take the General Education Development (GED) exam to enter a community or four-year university. GED exams serve a diverse group of adults who seek a second opportunity to acquire a high school diploma and be recognized by employers and higher learning institutions throughout North America. While in 1986–7 percent of all undergraduates had no high school diploma but had acquired a GED or a high school certificate of completion, this number dropped to 4 percent by 1992.

Table 8.4 Percentage of undergraduates who worked to pay school expenses who reported various effects of work on their studies, by average hours worked while enrolled, academic year 1995–6

Average hours worked while enrolled	Course-taking effects			Effect on grades*		
	Limited class schedule	Reduced class choices	Limited number of classes	Positive effect	No effect	Negative effect
Total	39.5	36.1	30.4	14.8	48.4	36.8
1–15	21.7	16.3	15.0	22.3	60.7	17.1
16–20	31.4	27.8	23.5	13.8	51.8	34.3
21–34	41.9	38.4	31.9	11.5	42.6	46.0
35 or more	61.1	59.8	50.6	9.7	35.0	55.4

Source: NCES 1998a, p. 152.

* Only dependent students (67 percent of students who worked to pay school expenses) were asked this question.

The extent and nature of demand for higher education and training from non-traditional students

This section explores how developments in the labor market affect demands for particular skills and competencies, and how the economy influences the choices of fields of study. A second, yet equally important, question relates to the nature of courses and programs required by non-traditional students, and their reasons for participating in higher education.

Higher education and the labor market

Higher education is greatly valued in the United States, mainly because it yields both individual and public returns. As society becomes more technologically advanced, the skills and knowledge required to be successful in the workplace are changing constantly. Many view higher education as a panacea for economic success. There is growing recognition that education and training are inextricably linked to employment opportunities and economic wellbeing (NCES 1998a). Post-secondary graduates with a Bachelor's degree generally earn more than their counterparts who hold only a high school diploma (NCES 1999). Put simply, for the purposes of obtaining and keeping a job, postsecondary education makes a significant difference.

Wages and salaries by educational attainment

Since 1970, there has been a widening gap between the median annual earnings of workers aged from twenty-five to thirty-four who had no high school diploma and those who had graduated from high school. In 1996, for example, annual earnings of workers who had not completed high school were 31 percent lower for males and 36 percent lower for females than for their counterparts who had completed high school. Holders of Bachelor's degrees earned substantially more than those with either high school diplomas or certificates of completion (54 percent more for males and 84 percent more for females). Female young adults who obtained a Bachelor's or higher degree have, since 1970, had a very high earnings advantage rising from 52 percent in 1980 to 200 percent in 1992 (Horn and Carroll 1996).

Similarly, in documenting the mean annual earnings for workers aged eighteen and over by level of education in 1992, Rodriguez and Ruppert (1996) determined that salaries for those without high school diplomas and those with professional degrees ranged from \$12,809 to \$74,560 respectively. In 1992, associate's degree holders earned nearly twice as much as did individuals without high school diplomas, while high school graduates earned 57 percent of the salaries of Bachelor's degree recipients. Doctorate degree recipients earned nearly twice as much as did Bachelor's degree recipients, and more than three times the salaries of high school graduates. Professional degree holders earned four times the salaries of high school graduates while Bachelor's degree recipients earned far less than half the income of those holding professional degrees. The conclusion based on this evidence is that post-secondary education is linked closely to higher salaries. There is no doubt that there will therefore be continuing demand for higher education.

Earnings by field of study

Although students may consider other non-pecuniary benefits in their choice of fields of study, one cannot underestimate the effects of anticipated starting salaries in determining students' choices. There is therefore a high premium placed on the value of the skills students acquire from post-secondary education and the supply and demand of post-secondary graduates in particular fields. A study conducted by NCES (1997) on median staring salaries for post-secondary graduates indicates that, between the late 1970s and early 1990s, starting salaries for students who specialized in Computer Science, Engineering, Business, and Management were much higher than graduates from any other fields of study. In 1980, for example, Computer Science and Engineering graduates' starting salaries were 61 percent above the median for graduates in all fields; and Business and Management salaries were 13 percent above all fields, while Education graduates' salaries were 19 percent below the median for all graduates. Starting salaries for graduates majoring in Humanities or Education have fluctuated over the years, but were generally notably lower than the starting salaries of all graduates.

Employment opportunities

Like higher earnings, employment opportunities are closely associated with educational attainment. Between the early 1970s and late 1990s, the employment rate of young adults was generally higher among those individuals who had attained a higher level of education (NCES 1999). In 1971, the employment rate of males was higher for holders of a high school diploma than for holders of a Bachelor's degree. In the 1980s and 1990s, 94 percent of males and 84 percent of females who had a Bachelor's degree were more likely to find employment (in 1998) as compared to 87 percent of males and 70 percent of females who had a high school diploma or GED.

The labor market and lifelong learning

As an increasingly knowledge-based and science-dependent business and service economy replaces the industrial economy, it is increasingly recognized that the traditional concept of one-time front-end education no longer provides an adequate foundation for a lifetime of work (Rubenson and Schuetze 2000, Millard 1991, Parnell 1990, Merriam and Caffarella 1991). Consequently, traditional systems of education must make efforts to respond adequately to the demands for widespread accessibility to appropriate and timely information and knowledge required by a rapidly changing economy, the post-industrial workplace, and the seemingly insatiable demand for higher education.

Adult education in the United States

The Economic Opportunity Act of 1964 established the adult basic education (ABE) program, and led Congress to pass the Adult Education Act in 1966. Inherent in the initial Adult Education Act is the need to educate financially constrained, unskilled adults through a system of local adult education service providers. These providers include school districts, community colleges, and other public and private agencies using state funds and federal government formulae. The provision of adult education falls into three main categories. The first is adult basic education (ABE) that is equivalent to grades 1 through 8. The second is adult secondary education (ASE) that is equivalent to grades 9 through 12; and the third category is English as a second language (ESL), provided to those whose first language is not English. The transformation of the concept of adult education is highlighted by new interpretations of adult learning that reflect concepts far beyond those of simple basic education to include the modalities of the labor market.

Participation in adult education

According to NCES (1998a), in 1995 some 76 million adults, constituting 40 percent of the adult population, participated in adult education activities. These activities included short-term training, seminars, workshops, and specific coursework in educational institutions or at the workplace on part-time bases (see Table 8.5).

In both 1991 and 1995, working adults were more than twice as likely to participate in adult education as those without employment (41 percent in 1991 and 51 percent in 1995). Adults with some college or higher levels of education were more likely to participate in adult education activities compared with their counterparts who completed only high school. In 1995, 58 percent of participants in adult education activities had Bachelor's degrees as compared with about 31 percent who had high school diplomas or General Education Development (GED) certificates.

Apart from the increase in expectations expressed in such common goals as the eradication of illiteracy or universalization of higher education in the United States, the labor market plays a crucial role in its impact on higher education.

Providers of adult education

Adult education is provided by elementary and secondary schools, post-secondary institutions, trade organizations, business organizations, and others. According to NCES (1998a), about 60 percent of adults took courses provided

Table 8.5 Adult education participation rates in the past twelve months, by type of adult education activity, educational attainment, and labor force status, 1991 and 1995

	1991 total	1995 total	Type of adult education activity			
			Basic skills	Creden- tial	Work- related	Personal develop- ment
Total	31.6	40.2	1.2	6.1	20.9	19.9
Educational attainment						
Grades 9–12	14.3	22.9	5.6	1.6	6.9	10.4
High school diploma or GED	22.5	30.9	0.8	3.5	14.2	17.7
Vocational/technical school	31.7	41.9	0.6	5.4	21.9	21.1
Some college	39.4	49.3	0.5	12.1	22.3	25.3
Associate degree	49.1	56.1	0.4	10.9	32.1	27.4
Bachelor's degree or higher	52.2	58.2	–	7.7	37.9	27.9
Labor status						
Employed	40.8	50.7	1.1	8.2	31.1	22.0
Unemployed	27.5	36.6	5.0	5.5	11.1	17.4
Not in labor force	14.5	21.3	0.9	2.2	3.4	16.2

Source: Adapted from NCES 1998a p. 58.

Note: The participation rate of adults age seventeen or older was determined by their involvement in one or more of six types of adult education activities in the twelve months prior to the collection of data; therefore, percentages may not add to totals because people participated in more than one type of activity (9 percent in 1995).

by business, industry, or professional associations in 1995. During the same period, the proportion of adults who took work-related courses in post-secondary and government organizations was more than five times that enrolled in work-related courses in elementary/secondary institutions.

Participation rates in work-related courses varied according to educational attainment. It is worth noting that as trade organizations provide apprenticeship programs that offer formal and on-the-job training at the workplace, individuals with low or middle-level educational qualifications were more likely to take courses with trade organizations than were those with Bachelor's or higher degrees.

In 1995, unemployed adults were more likely to take courses in post-secondary institutions than their counterparts who were employed (NCES 1998a). White adults were found to be more likely to take work-related courses within business organizations (61 percent) than either Blacks (48 percent) or Hispanics (57 percent). Both Blacks and Hispanics were more likely to take work-related courses in post-secondary institutions. Blacks, however, were more likely to enroll in work-related courses in government and trade organizations than whites or Hispanics.

Main reasons for participating in adult education

Kopka and Peng (1993) contend that reasons for adult participation depend highly on the participants' age, gender, racial and ethnic categorization, and educational attainment. Among the reasons for participation cited by the majority of adults were skills advancement, job advancement, personal enrichment, new job training, and the attainment of credentials.

Adults aged twenty-five years or older were likely to participate in adult education to improve and advance themselves at the workplace. Like the overall participation rate, the rate for job improvement peaked during the mid-career points of individuals (Kopka and Peng 1993). Individuals who were more likely to participate in adult education to enhance their career opportunities were between the ages of thirty-five and thirty-nine (27 percent), forty and forty-four (32 percent) and forty-five and forty-nine (28 percent). On the other hand, young adults aged seventeen to twenty-four were more likely to participate for reasons of obtaining credentials such as diplomas or degrees, to train for new jobs, or to improve basic skills. Senior citizens of sixty-five and older enrolled in adult education classes mainly to enhance their personal, family, or social lives (Kopka and Peng 1993).

Today there is a trend towards a wider concept of adult education and away from the narrow confines of conventional basic literacy and math skills. This new concept of lifelong learning is now complemented by the expressed need for contemporary forms of literacy, with an emphasis on developing individuals' capacities and opportunities for continuous learning. Thus, adult education now equates more closely with traditional concepts of education.

Public policy and higher education responses to learning needs of non-traditional students

The final section of this paper provides an overview of public policy and its embodiment in the provision of access to higher education in the United States. As the various states are ultimately responsible for establishing policy and overseeing the structure and functions of post-secondary and public education, this last section examines federal and state policies that enhance or impinge upon access to higher education.

Educational finance

Financing is a major interplay between public policy and higher education at all levels of government in the United States. While governments may occasionally impose organizational or structural changes, most changes in public policy concern the levels and modalities of funding (Wagner 1987). The efficacy with which federal and state governments encourage participation in higher education lies in the extent to which they support programs that make post-secondary education accessible. Federal, state, and local governments currently undertake a range of schemes to encourage participation in higher education.

Throughout the whole development of higher education in the US, many of the policy initiatives in higher education reforms emphasize equal educational opportunity for anyone willing to undertake post-secondary education. This notion of educational equality grew with the development of a system of tax-supported public schooling, leading to the establishment of state colleges and universities and to an increase in the provisions of community colleges (Farrel 1992). As it became increasingly evident in the past several decades that large numbers of students were unable to take advantage of educational opportunities because of their social origin, there have been large increases in scholarships and fellowships for non-traditional students.

To support programs that encourage participation in higher education, national and state governments have particularly endeavored to reduce the costs of study through subsidies to public institutions (NCES 1998a). The rationale behind state subsidies is to enable public institutions to charge tuition fees that are significantly below the actual cost of education. There are also federal and state grants, loans, and work-study programs that provide financial aid to students demonstrating need (NCES 1998a).

Federal policy on higher education

The Higher Education Act (HEA) of 1965 has directed the expansion of higher education systems in the United States. This is the federal law that provides for student aid and other federal programs for higher education. Periodic amendments to the Act relate to the way the federal government can use federal student aid in making post-secondary education more affordable and accessible (AGB 1997).

The cost of attending higher education provided the focus for the Congress-appointed National Commission on the Cost of Higher Education. The Commission's final report, *Straight Talk About College Costs and Prices* (January 1998), reshaped perceptions of the cost of higher education by establishing evidence that the cost of higher education had risen by 400 percent since 1976 (cited by McKeown-Moak 1999). This has led to recognition that there is a need for government intervention to create equitable access to higher education. Meanwhile, new federal income tax credits, new federal income tax incentives for post-secondary savings, and new federal income tax provisions regarding student loans have now become part of the package to make higher education accessible.

Federal income tax credits

Given the growing disparities between post-secondary tuition and other fees on one hand and the rate of inflation and family income on the other over the past two decades, President Clinton made tuition tax credits a platform for his 1996 re-election campaign. The 105th Congress subsequently enacted several tuition tax provisions in the Taxpayer Relief Act of 1997 (Conklin 1998), providing a new mechanism to increase access to higher education and training. Given that most student aid programs provide for loans, grants, scholarships, and work-study programs to assist students and their families to pay for post-secondary education, the Taxpayer Relief Act makes higher education more accessible by providing tax credits, incentives for savings for post-secondary education, and a deduction of interest on student loans (Conklin 1998).

Hope scholarship tax credit

The Hope scholarship tax credit is intended for upper income earners and is available to independent students or to families who pay tuition and other fees for their children. Students must be enrolled at least half-time in their first two years of post-secondary education to be eligible for a refundable tax credit of up to 100 percent federal income credit on the first $1,000 of their required fees. They would also be eligible for up to 50percent credit on the second $1,000 (Conklin 1998).

The Hope scholarship and tuition deduction proposals could cost the federal government over $33 billion within the next six years. While the higher education community generally compliments the Hope scholarship policy, critics have raised a number of concerns. The most serious of these is that the concentration of the economic advantage of the scholarship falls into the hands of the better-off, and not into those of disadvantaged students. Furthermore, there are far-sighted predictions that tax credits and deductions could offset established modes of student aid, and that it would be of greater benefit to fund higher education through student aid and the expenditure side of the budget rather than through tax holidays. There is also a provision that students eligible for benefits under the Hope scholarship should prove they earned a B average (AGB 1997). This could cause concerns with post-secondary faculty and administrators about the paper work involved, and could also involve the Internal Revenue Service (IRS) in regulating grading practices and academic standards (AGB 1997).

Federal income tax provisions regarding student loans

Whereas the federal government funds other post-secondary education pro-grams through the annual budget process, student loans fall under the cate-gory of federal entitlement programs and thus are not subject to annual appropriations (AGB 1997). There are two categories of student loan that must be paid back by the student after graduation: subsidized and unsubsi-dized loans. Subsidized loans are awarded on students' ability to pay, and the government pays the interest on subsidized loans as long as the student bor-rower is attending an educational institution. Unsubsidized loans are also available regardless of need, and are offered to students at lower interest rates than most loans available privately.

Pell grants and supplemental educational opportunity grants

Pell grants are awarded to economically disadvantaged students to provide access to post-secondary education. Pell grants represent the largest federal student-aid program, currently providing $7 billion in awards to 5 million students (AGB 1997). They are awarded to disadvantaged students to better their chances of gaining access to higher education. In 1997, Congress raised the Pell grant award from $2,700 to $3,000, and increased the program by $400 million to increase the number of eligible low income and non-traditional students (Conklin 1998).

State policy on higher education

A major part of policy relating to access to higher education stems from state policies on post-secondary education. The fiscal year 1999 saw the largest total of state appropriations ever made to higher education. The appropria-tions amounted to $52.8 billion representing an increase of $3.2 billion or 6.5 percent over the 1998 fiscal year, and a $6.2 billion or 13.3 percent increase over the 1997 fiscal year. Legislatures in states such as Colorado, Indiana, Maine, New Jersey, Virginia and Washington reviewed methods to increase appropriations to offset tuition freezes or to reduce the rates of increase (McKeown-Moak 1999). Although reductions or freezes in tuition fee increases in higher education have somehow become dependent on increased state appropriations, there are signs of declining levels of confidence in the ability of appropriations to reduce or freeze tuition and fees.

New York State funding programs

There is a great deal of variety in funding schemes across the fifty states, so an example from New York State may suffice to illustrate state-level involvement in student finance.

The Tuition Assistance Program (TAP) is one of the main student-aid programs in New York State. The TAP is the dominant template of State student aid in New York, providing about 86 percent of student-aid programs (New York State Department of Education 1998). The TAP is awarded to low-income undergraduate students. The New York State Department of Education (1998) reported that the State provided about $619.8 million in the Tuition Assistance Program in the 1996–7 academic year to 236,609 dependent undergraduate students. The State government has now reduced the TAP for "proprietary non-degree dependents from $1,000 to $800 or 90 percent of tuition, and for independent students from $800 to $640 or 90 percent of tuition" (New York Department of Education 1998 p. 3).

Besides the Tuition Assistance Program, the state created a new program in 1997, *Scholarships for Academic Excellence,* which grants 2,000 scholarships of $1,000 each, and up to 3,000 additional scholarships of $500, to be granted to top graduating students of each high school in New York State. The 1998–9 Executive Budget recommended extending the scholarship "program to make 2,000 of New York's 'top scholars' eligible for annual $1,500 awards, and 6,000 'academically distinguished' students eligible for annual $500 awards" (New York State Department of Education 1998 p. 3).

Conclusions

In the United States, non-traditional students, particularly adults, have become an important group in universities and colleges. The image of a college or university student as a twenty year old full-time resident studying for a professional career has become an anachronism. Non-traditional students have clearly become a new majority that constitutes a new subculture in higher education.

As the imperatives of the knowledge-based and global economy have emphasized the needs of adults to meet changing workplace demands, long established patterns of educational preparation and transition to work are being questioned. Access to post-secondary education has been expanded for adults and hitherto non-traditional students, by expanding the number and types of programs and post-secondary education institutions. Other factors have increased in importance as compared to ten years ago. The more widespread access to information and telecommunication media in the 1990s has had a positive impact on adult participation in post-secondary education programs. New priorities are being designed to reflect and shape current state policy agendas regarding the role of higher education in workforce development (see Rodriguez and Ruppert 1996). The thrust of such changes has been to make access to education and training programs more readily available to the general population. Recent policy reports indicate a renewed interest in lifelong learning, in the aging of today's workforce, and in ways in which to provide workforce preparation services to older adults.

Particular features and mandates of the university/college have changed from generation to generation (Perkin 1984, Altbach 1992). However, the uniqueness of the university/college lies in its polymorphous capacity to change its form and purpose to suit its ephemeral and sociopolitical environment while preserving its culture. Like all human institutions, the university maintains a tenacious endurance over time with a stubborn resistance to change in spite of external pressures and internal transformations (Perkin 1984). Nevertheless, the university, traditionally an elite institution, has provided social mobility to previously disenfranchised groups (Altbach 1992), even if it continues to maintain some internal social differentiation whereby some members are more highly valued or rewarded than others. The degree of such differentiation and its significance for the way individuals live their lives varies dramatically across institutions. Moreover, there are many different bases or criteria for such differentiation. Among the most common are age, race, ethnicity, regional origin, sex, and income (Quinnan 1997). Both across and within institutions of higher education, there is considerable variation in which one of these, or which set of them, is most powerful as a determinant of how students live their lives. Set against this backdrop of academic culture, it is clear that non-traditional students are still assigned a marginal status.

This is somehow expressed by the view that the best way to provide educational opportunity to non-traditional students, particularly adults, is in the form of adult or continuing education. This means that the education of adults should be separated from the mainstream, with organizational structures resembling auxiliary enterprises and not integral parts of the mission of higher education (Millard 1991). Quinnan describes adults as an "at-risk" group on our campuses: a group of significant "Others" who dwell in educational "borderlands." He observes that "the disadvantaged status put upon adult learners by universities designed to serve a younger population is somewhat mitigated by the adults' intense inner drive to prevail" (Quinnan 1997 p. 31).

Practicing college and university educators have long been aware that how much and how well people learn, how much they change and grow, is highly dependent on the context and the possibilities for application of new skills and knowledge. There lies at this juncture a whole field of critical research and experimentation in what we might term the "edifice of lifelong learning." What are the implications of the edifice of lifelong learning for the way in which non-traditional and traditional students learn and grow and the way in which universities and colleges function to meet their combined needs? The question, therefore, is how to adapt higher education missions, objectives, and structures most effectively to provide equal educational opportunities for non-traditional as well as the traditional students.

References

Altbach, P. G. (1992) 'Patterns in higher education development: toward year 2000', in R. F. Arnove, P. G. Altbach and G. P. Kelly (eds) *Emergent Issues in Education: Comparative Perspectives*, Albany: State University of New York Press.

AGB (Association of Governing Boards of Universities and Colleges) (1997) *Ten Public Policy Issues for Higher Education in 1997 and 1998* (AGB Public Policy Series No. 97–1), Washington D.C.: Author (ERIC Document Reproduction Service No. ED 412 830).

Boyer, E. L. (1987) *College: The Undergraduate Experience in America*, New York: Harper and Row.

Chronicle of Higher Education (1999) *1999–2000 Almanac Issue* vol. 46 no. 1 (August 27).

Conklin, K. D. (1998) *Federal Tax Tuition Credits and State Higher Education Policy: A Guide for Policy Makers*, Washington, D.C.: National Center for Public Policy and Higher Education.

Cuccaro-Alamin, S. (1997) *Findings from the Conditions of Education: Postsecondary Persistence and Attainment* (Report no. 13, NCES 97–984), Washington D.C.: US Government Printing Office.

Farrel, J. P. (1992) 'Conceptualizing the role of education and the drive for social equality', in R. F. Arnove, P. G. Altbach and G. P. Kelly (eds) *Emergent Issues in Education: Comparative Perspectives*, Albany: State University of New York Press.

Fischer, R. B. (1992) 'Post-retirement learning', in R. B. Fischer, M. L. Blazey and H. T. Lipman (eds) *Students of the Third Age: University/College Programs for Retired Adults*, New York: Macmillan.

Horn, L. J. and Carroll, C. D. (1996) *Non-traditional Undergraduates: Trends in enrollment from 1986 to 1992 and Persistence and Attainment Among 1989–90 Beginning Postsecondary Students* (Report No. NCES 97–578), Washington, D.C.: NCES.

Kopka, T. L. C. and Peng, S. S. (1993) *Adult Education: Main Reasons for Participating* (NCES 93–451), Washington, D.C.: US Department of Education.

McKeown-Moak, M. P. (1999) *Financing Higher Education: An Annual Report from the States, 1999*, (Report No. HE 031 972), Denver, Col.: State Higher Education Executive Officers. (ERIC Document Reproduction Service No. ED 428 638).

Merriam, S. B. and Caffarella, R. S. (1991) *Learning in Adulthood,* San Francisco: Jossey-Bass.

Millard, R. M. (1991) *Today's Myths and Tomorrow's Realities: Overcoming Obstacles to Academic Leadership in the 21st century*, San Francisco: Jossey-Bass.

NCES (US Department of Education) (1997) *Starting Salaries of College Graduates*, Washington, D.C.: US Government Printing Office.

—— (1998a) *The Condition of Education* (NCES 98–013), Washington, D.C.: US Government Printing Office.

—— (1998b) *Projections of Education Statistics to 2008*, Washington, D.C.: US Government Printing Office.

—— (1999) *Annual Earnings of Young Adults, by Educational Attainment* (Indicator of the Month, June, NCES 1999–009), Washington, D.C.: US Government Printing Office.

New York State Department of Education (1998) Report by the Board of Regents to the Governor and Legislature on State student financial aid programs, Albany: State University of New York.

Parnell, D. (1990) *Dateline 2000: The New Higher Education Agenda*, Washington, D.C.: Community College Press.

Perkin, H. (1984) 'The historical perspective', in B. Clark (ed.) *Perspectives on Higher Education: Eight Disciplinary and Comparative Views*, Berkeley: University of California Press.

Quinnan, T. W. (1997) *Adult Students 'At Risk': Culture Bias in Higher Education*, Westport, Conn.: Greenwood.

Richardson, J. T. E. and King, E. (1998) 'Adult students in higher education: burden or boon?' *Journal of Higher Education* vol. 69 no. 1.

Rodriguez, E. M. and Ruppert, S. S. (1996) *Postsecondary Education and the New Workforce* (SHEEO Publication No. PLLI 96–8005), Washington, D.C.: US Department of Education.

Wagner, A. P. (1987) 'Adults in higher education: the situation in the United States', in H. G. Schuetze (ed.) *Adults in Higher Education: Policies and Practice in Great Britain and North America*, Stockholm: Almqvist and Wiksell.

Part IV

Australia, Japan and New Zealand

9 Australia

Higher education and lifelong learning: an Australian perspective

Richard James and David Beckett

A nation in transition

Australia is a vast island continent, sparsely populated with 19 million people. Until the 1960s and 1970s the cornerstones of national economic prosperity were primary industries – pastoral, agricultural and mining – which capitalised on Australia's abundant natural resources and advantages. However, the economy underwent substantial structural change in the latter part of the twentieth century. The catchcry of the 1990s was for the 'lucky' country to become the 'clever' country.

Successive governments had begun to see Australia as economically vulnerable in global terms. The clever-country transition was to be achieved through a deregulated economy exposed to worldwide competition, the consolidation of robust secondary manufacturing industries, and growth in the areas of tourism and other service sectors. In addition, federal government policy in a range of portfolios was underpinned by the belief that the nation's wealth would be dependent on the production of 'knowledge' goods by a sophisticated tertiary workforce.

Along with these macroeconomic changes, the technological transformation of work and the rapid growth of knowledge in many fields contributed to the requirement for a more highly educated nation. Demand for all forms of education increased, especially post-secondary education. In universities, enrolments in postgraduate education climbed steeply: tight labour markets and more sophisticated workplaces initiated the re-entry to formal education of people in early or mid-career seeking retraining or to gain career advantage.

During the 1990s the Australian geopolitical environment became less Anglo/Eurocentric. The cultural and economic future of Australia was now depicted in the context of South-East Asia. Australian higher education became a prominent industry in the region, with most universities benefiting from the revenue provided by fee-paying international students. By 1998 there were 68,000 international students enrolled in Australian universities – in the main part citizens of neighbouring Asian countries – making up 9.6 per cent of the total student population (DETYA 1999a). The majority of international students reside in Australia during their studies, although technological delivery and collaborative arrangements with Asian universities rose in the late 1990s and 'off-shore' campuses were established in Asian cities.

Which Australians traditionally have been less likely to participate in higher education? There is an egalitarian spirit among Australians and they do not like to admit to the existence of class divides, yet socio-economic differences in the Australian population, which possibly broadened in the 1990s, are closely associated with persistent patterns of educational advantage and disadvantage. People of lower socio-economic backgrounds are significantly under-represented in universities and there are marked variations in higher education participation between metropolitan regions.

Similar imbalances are found in the educational participation of urban and rural people. Though Australia is a vast continent it is highly urbanised, and most Australians are city-dwellers concentrated along the south-eastern seaboard. Around 30 per cent of Australians, however, are classified as living in rural or isolated areas. Large distances from major cities, dispersed populations, and depressed rural micro-economies create difficulties in the provision of education and health services. School retention rates are lower in rural areas and fewer rural and remote dwellers on a per capita basis attend university.

Ethnicity also shapes a definition of the non-traditional student. Australia is a polyethnic nation. Its indigenous people are the descendants of people who lived on the continent for 40,000 years prior to European settlement in 1788. Indigenous people live in both urban and rural Australia, many in remote areas. The conditions for many indigenous communities, especially in the distant outback, are far from acceptable. They have poor access to amenities and infrastructure, and educational participation is low. Health problems are acute and life expectancies are appallingly short. The policies of successive Australian governments have failed to make major inroads into these problems.

The nation's polyethnicity is also the outcome of various waves of immigration in the post Second World War period. Immigrant recruitment on labour market and humanitarian grounds brought people from Europe and more recently from Asia, Central America, and Africa, producing a cosmopolitan society. About 20 per cent of Australians have a first language other than English; about 40 per cent of Australians have at least one non-English-speaking parent. It is quite common for schools in the metropolitan areas of the major cities to have astonishingly diverse populations, with perhaps several dozen immigrant languages represented in a school population of a few hundred (Beckett 1997).

This brief description of the social, cultural and economic context of Australia flags some of the major influences on higher education as the nation enters the twenty-first century. The concept of a non-traditional learner invites a number of interpretations in Australia. It is not circumscribed solely by age, since factors such as socio-economic background, ethnicity, and geographical location historically have been potent factors in the likelihood of tertiary educational participation. With the expansion of the higher education system, much headway has been made in removing barriers and improving the perceived relevance, attainability and outcomes of university study for non-traditional students. However, persistent patterns of educational disadvantage remain. As we argue in this chapter, the Australian higher education system has reached a critical cusp.

The Australian higher education system

Australia is a federation of six states. These have responsibility for schooling, which is free in public sector schools, while the federal government substantially funds and has responsibility for higher education. In addition, the federal government plays a policy coordinating role with the states in the provision of vocational education and training. In contrast to the United Kingdom and the United States, there is no involvement of local government in educational provision.

Australia's early nationhood was a cultural transplant of the British Isles and many aspects of Australian life were modelled on English examples, including the first universities and the early 'grammar schools'. The first 'sandstone' universities were established in Sydney and Melbourne in the 1850s, as were some small technical schools – for mining, domestic arts and industrial technology. The university system expanded massively following the Second World War, and a further large expansion took place in the 1960s. In 1964, the Martin Report was the basis of federal legislation that consolidated a divide between liberal and vocational curricula, the establishment of the so-called 'binary' system of vocationally-oriented Colleges of Advanced Education and Institutes of Technology alongside the traditional academically oriented universities.

More sweeping changes were ahead. In 1987, the federal government dissolved – through a series of mergers and amalgamations – the binary system of nineteen universities and sixty-nine Colleges of Advanced Education, creating a Unified National System (UNS) comprised of thirty-six universities. In 1999, universities numbered forty. Four of these are small, specialist institutions. In addition there are two private universities. All universities are teaching and research institutions, though they are highly differentiated.

The massive upheaval involved in the formation of the Unified National System was justified on both social justice and human capital grounds. The architect, the Hon. John Dawkins, then federal minister for higher education, sought to remove endemic participation imbalances while at the same time significantly expanding the nation's knowledge and skill base (Dawkins 1988). The Dawkins reforms ambitiously attempted to build a higher education system with a capacity to provide education and training commensurate with a new economic environment. The alignment of higher education with national economic objectives heralded a new era of vocationalism in universities.

The expansion from an elite towards a mass system ushered in dramatic changes in funding arrangements. Fees had been abolished in 1974 but this constrained the revenue available to fund expansion. In response, the government crafted the Higher Education Contribution Scheme (HECS), a unique income-contingent loan scheme. With the exception of postgraduates, who in the main part pay fees, and a small proportion of fee-paying domestic undergraduates, Australian students make either an up-front or a deferred payment under the HECS scheme. Deferred payments are repaid through the taxation system once income has reached a threshold level. HECS charges have increased since their introduction ,and by the late 1990s were estimated to constitute 37 per cent of the actual cost of provision. Annual HECS charges ranged between AU$3,409 and $5,682 in 1999, differential charges applying across fields of study according to the relative cost of provision.

Although the total operating grants to universities increased over the period following the creation of the Unified National System, a steadily shrinking proportion of Gross Domestic Product was allocated to higher education. In 1989, 77.1 per cent of university revenue came from government; by 1999 the proportion had fallen to 53.8 per cent. Universities were encouraged to generate alternative revenue from overseas students, fee-paying postgraduates, and, more recently, a capped proportion of fee-paying undergraduates in designated fields.

In the face of declining public revenue, the modern Australian university has become adaptive and entrepreneurial in order to diversify its revenue base. New technological opportunities have hastened the imperative for internationalisation, with on-line global provision by overseas consortia being viewed as a threat to lucrative markets in the Asian region. Domestically, universities compete vigorously for students and course marketing is extensive. At the same time, paradoxically, collaborative and cooperative arrangements between universities and other educational and commercial organisations have grown. Universities have a new interest in vocational programmes, alliances with industry and workplace-based training. Increasingly, universities conceptualise the student as client and are reaching out to non-traditional markets and non-traditional students.

These trends, in particular the new vocationalism and enhanced industry linkages, bring universities into close alignment with the major public provider of vocational education and training, the Technical and Further Education sector (TAFE). TAFE is not part of the Unified National System, but both systems fall under the responsibilities of the federal Department of Education, Training and Youth Affairs. A number of tertiary institutions are dual sector, offering both higher education courses (crudely, for the award of degrees) and TAFE courses (for the award of diplomas as well as non-award programmes).

TAFE was born in 1974. Commonwealth legislation that year established state-specific systems of technical and further education, provided in close connection with industry and intending to service apprenticeship and other training programmes, as well as broader social justice, access and bridging courses. Despite a history of flexibility and responsiveness to student and industry needs, TAFE has had a perennial image problem. Sandwiched between the top end of liberal studies secondary schools preparing students for academic and professional futures, and the tertiary destinations which would fulfil those futures, mainstream TAFE courses have always led to less high-status outcomes, despite these outcomes having traditionally underpinned earning a living. In diverse ways, TAFE meets the needs of school-leavers and of adults seeking to upgrade their employability. This is achieved through courses in pre-employment skills, such as in literacy and numeracy, and in employment skills in para-professional work and apprenticed trades. In addition, TAFE provides recreation and personal fulfillment courses, not directly vocationally-oriented. Until quite recently, modest fees, or none at all, were charged.

Since the early 1990s a national 'training reform agenda' has required TAFE to integrate into national vocational education and training policies, primarily through the exposition and development of competency-based curricula and assessment. Legislation in 1992 established a new authority to administer the total Australian governmental provision of vocational education and training, both nationally and in each state: the Australian National Training Authority (ANTA) shapes and funds, in partnership with each state, the field of vocational education and training (including TAFE and adult and community education),

Like the Dawkins reforms in higher education, the training reform agenda is also intended to galvanise new global market initiatives through a more sophisticated labour force characterised by new skills and competence. The convergence of common imperatives in both higher education and vocational education and training – and the establishment of unified national approaches in both areas – has raised new questions about the relative roles, responsibilities and status of the two sectors.

In all, a complex picture of post-secondary education and training in Australia in the 1990s emerges. At the beginning of the decade, Marginson produced a thumbnail sketch of national educational participation that is still relevant:

> Of every hundred Australians in 1991, approximately eighteen were enrolled in schools, three in higher education, six in mainstream TAFE programmes and three more in the recreation and leisure programmes also offered by TAFE. Note that all school students and 61 per cent of higher education students were enrolled on a full-time basis, but only 10 per cent of TAFE students are full-time.

There is another large group – estimated at 2,000,000 Australians, or fifteen in every hundred people – involved in private training. Most of this private training does not lead to formal qualifications, and is not publicly regulated. There are no accurate data on this group.

(Marginson 1993 p. 4)

Equity of access, meaningful participation, and finally, successful outcomes for traditional and new claimants upon university studies are all policy areas that confront the new political imperatives. It is increasingly apparent that globalisable enterprises require the widest possible pool of talent from which to shape the new 'knowledge-based' markets – and universities are caught up in this in two ways. First, they are themselves players in such globalised markets, since academia is itself a knowledge-based industry. Second, their students-as-graduates are increasingly expected to demonstrate their acquisition of self-directed or lifelong learning capacity.

The concept of lifelong learning in Australia

Lifelong learning has become an umbrella term in Australia. On the one hand, it is used to signify intellectual autonomy and non-reliance on formal educational participation. On the other hand, it evokes a diametrically opposite concept, that of repeated engagement with education and training programmes, whether in educational organisations or in the workplace. This leads to a frequent contradiction in the portrayal of the lifelong learner. He or she is someone whose learning is independent of educational organisations. Equally, he or she is also someone who is motivated and able to engage in formal learning throughout his or her lifespan. The breadth of the concept has made it a convenient rhetorical slogan and its over-use has threatened to undermine its significance and impact.

The report *Developing Lifelong Learners through Undergraduate Education* (Candy *et al.* 1994), prepared for the National Board of Employment, Education and Training, was a landmark in the discussion of lifelong learning in Australian higher education. The authors responded to a brief to identify and describe the characteristics of undergraduate education which enable and encourage graduates to participate in formal and informal learning throughout their lives (Crean 1994). The report adopted a curriculum focus, being concerned in the main with the teaching and learning conditions that create the skills, dispositions and capacities for learning after graduation, yet the 'profile' they outlined (see Figure 9.1) has interest and significance well beyond university experiences.

These proposed attributes of the lifelong learner suggest that learning across the lifespan intimately relates the processes and the products of learning. Traditionally, universities have not paid much explicit attention to the processes of learning, but have insisted on the integrity and standing of the product. Yet learners of any age, and with almost any sort of involvement with the labour market, bring to their daily activities a rich array of

An inquiring mind

- a love of learning; a sense of curiosity and question asking
- a critical spirit; comprehension monitoring and self-evaluation.

Helicopter vision

- a sense of the interconnectedness of fields
- an awareness of how knowledge is created in at least one field of study, and an understanding of the methodological and substantive limitations of that field
- breadth of vision.

Information literacy

- knowledge of major current sources available in at least one field of study
- ability to frame researchable questions in at least one field of study
- ability to locate, evaluate, manage, and use information in a range of contexts
- ability to retrieve information using a variety of media
- ability to decode information in a variety of forms: written, statistical, graphs, charts, diagrams and tables
- critical evaluation of information.

A sense of personal agency

- a positive concept of oneself as capable and autonomous
- self-organisation skills (time management, goal-setting, etc.).

A repertoire of learning skills

- a knowledge of one's own strengths, weaknesses and preferred learning style
- a range of strategies for learning in whatever context one finds oneself
- an understanding of the differences between surface and deep level learning.

Figure 9.1 A profile of the lifelong learner

Source: Candy *et al.* 1994 pp. 43–4.

attributes, not many of which have been highly regarded by universities. Many of these attributes are the kind of thing that can be learnt (or at least strengthened by learning, especially by formal learning through sustained, systematic encouragement). Equally, they in turn enrich learning processes, whether formal, non-formal or informal. In other words, these attributes make learning processes more likely to be educational. So process and content interact dialectically, and do so right across the human age span.

Following the Candy propositions, the Karpin Report (1995) also influenced thinking in higher education. As did Candy, but from a different perspective, Karpin advocated a holistic managerial model of workplace learning, especially in the overt support given to the 'higher order social and cognitive competencies', which Karpin calls 'soft skills'. These are the interpersonal and communicative capabilities of strategic thinking, vision, flexibility and adaptability, self-management, team membership, problem-solving, decision-making and risk-taking. Of course these capabilities – or attributes – are not adequately characterisable as merely cognitive in a narrow sense, since they involve the social and affective. Indeed the tag 'soft skills' is a pejorative misnomer. It is quite difficult to educate for these capabilities, and even more so to have them count in corporate structures for productivity and promotion outcomes, yet lifelong learning at its broadest is about acquiring these capabilities and exercising them in a sophisticated fashion.

So, in both the education and the corporate world in Australia in the early to mid-1990s, there was an emergence of interest in more sophisticated and more holistic adult learning capabilities and strategies. In the years following the Candy and Karpin reports the concept of lifelong learning centred less on curriculum and more on structural issues. Attention shifted — arguably narrowed – to the institutional arrangements that encourage and allow entry and re-entry to formal learning at various stages in life and career.

The report of the 1998 Review of Higher Education Policy, *Learning for life* (West 1998), colloquially the 'West Review', again endorsed the role of higher education in developing a learning society, declaring in its first recommendation the need for 'a commitment to establishment of a learning society in which all Australians, of whatever social, cultural and economic background, have access to a post-compulsory education of excellent value'. The review proposed key changes as cornerstones of this goal, including achieving universal completion of secondary education, improving 'first time access' to post-secondary education, and new student-centred funding arrangements: a voucher-like lifelong learning entitlement. Contentiously, the Review argued that a student-centred funding model would achieve two complementary outcomes: the incentive to encourage students to choose their studies carefully, and, equally, encouragement for providers to compete vigorously in terms of the nature, price and quality of their offerings. Subsequently, leaked government planning documents alluding to the prospect of deregulated university fees and the potentially rising cost of a university degree to the individual drew widespread student protest and public concern.

For nearly a decade, then, lifelong learning has been the principal focus of national educational objectives and has stimulated reconsideration of the appropriateness of policies and processes across all education sectors. While the federal government is yet to adopt the recommendations of the West

Review in full, the review provides perhaps the clearest picture to date of some of the deep structural changes that might be necessary in Australian educational systems to convert the learning society objective into reality.

Numbers

This seems an appropriate point at which to assess the progress that has been made in higher education towards the lifelong learning objective. Here the proof of the pudding lies in the eating, since the sector's performance can be readily examined through access and participation trends following the creation of the Unified National System. Four broad observations can be made about these data. First, while participation rates increased considerable during the late 1980s and early 1990s, expansion stalled in the late 1990s. Second, the relative participation rates of certain population subgroups have been remarkably stable despite dramatically improved access (DETYA 1999a). Third, though there have been major gains in access for identified equity target groups, some groups remain seriously under-represented in participation share (DETYA 1999b). Finally, substantial differences are apparent in the social and demographic composition of the student populations across fields of study and across institutions (James *et al.* 1999).

The higher education student population rose dramatically in Australia during the last twenty years of the century, most steeply in the late 1980s soon after the Dawkins reforms. In the 1960s, 10 per cent of each age cohort could be expected to participate in higher education at some stage during their lifetime, compared with the present estimate of around 45 per cent for today's teenagers. Three-quarters of these higher education participants enter directly from secondary school. In addition, about 45 per cent will enter vocational education and training at some stage, bringing the proportion of young people who are expected to undertake tertiary education to 90 per cent.

Universities have coped with a massive expansion in student numbers. In 1987 there were 394,000 university students; by 1997 this had climbed to 659,000 (all data from DETYA 1998 unless indicated otherwise). The number of undergraduate students grew by 58 per cent, from 330,500 to 521,500. The strongest growth, however, was in postgraduate education. The number of coursework students more than doubled, rising from 49,000 to 102,500 during this period. The number of postgraduate research students grew even faster, climbing by a staggering 145 per cent – from 14,500 in 1987 to 35,000 in 1997. The growth in student numbers has been accompanied by significant shifts in the popularity of various disciplines. The field of education had the largest decline in share of enrolments: from 21 per cent in 1983 to 11 per cent in 1997. The largest growth in enrolments was in health (boosted by the transfer of nurse education from hospitals to universities) and the broad business and economics field. Approaching one-quarter of higher education students now study in business and economics related courses; in 1998, these courses commanded 41 per cent of the nation's enrolments in higher degrees by coursework (DETYA 1999a).

In addition to the growth in the number of domestic students, more overseas students came to Australia to study, a result of extensive marketing and rising disposable incomes in South East Asian countries. The international enrolment share rose from 4.3 per cent in 1985 to 9.6 per cent in 1997. Demand for Australian higher education withstood the Asian economic crisis of the late 1990s and the number of commencing overseas students leapt from 37,292 in 1998 to 45,000 in 1999 (DETYA 1999a).

Throughout the 1990s there was considerable stability in the distribution of student ages. Since the expansion of the higher education system following the Second World War, Australia has had a tradition of adult participation in higher education. The share of students aged thirty years or more hovered between 26 and 28 per cent between 1987 and 1997, defying the common belief in the predominance of school-leaver entry. Enrolment type has also been relatively stable. In 1997, 59 per cent of students were enrolled full-time, 27 per cent part-time, and 13 per cent were external students. Two-thirds of part-time students were twenty-five years or more. The creation of Open Learning Australia, a consortium of six universities, expanded external study options but has not markedly affected the proportion of students choosing this study mode. Open Learning Australia had 6,600 students studying off-campus units in 1998, the equivalent of 1,800 full-time students.

Despite growth in the system, there has been mixed success with regard to non-traditional students. Since the late 1980s federal policy has identified equity target groups (Table 9.1), including women, particularly in non-traditional areas. With the expansion of access to higher education of the past decade, the higher education participation rates of all groups has improved, but the relative participation share of some has altered little.

Overall, the rising participation of women in undergraduate education is a success story. By 1997, women occupied 55 per cent of all higher education places, slightly above their population share of 52 per cent. Women are over-represented in education and health but remain under-represented in engineering. They also remain under-represented in some postgraduate areas.

Higher education has also been successful in attracting people from non-English-speaking backgrounds (though equally this could be seen as a great success by some ethnic communities and families in achieving their aspiration to gain 'first generation' higher education entry for their children). Overall, students from non-English-speaking backgrounds are presently slightly over-represented on population share, but there are marked differences between ethnic groups that may require closer monitoring.

There has been less success with other subgroups. Indigenous people are seriously under-represented. The participation share of indigenous Australians increased slightly during the 1990s to 1.2 per cent of non-overseas students in 1997, but indigenous Australians were 1.7 per cent of the

Table 9.1 Higher education participation by equity groups in Australia: percentage of enrolled non-overseas students

Equity group	1991	1992	1993	1994	1995	1996	1997	Reference values
People with a disability	na	na	na	na	na	1.0	1.3	4.0
Indigenous students	1.0	1.0	1.0	1.2	1.2	1.2	1.2	1.4/1.7
People of non-English speaking background	4.3	4.7	5.0	5.2	5.5	5.4	5.1	4.9/4.8
People from rural backgrounds[1]	18.5	18.7	18.5	18.0	17.7	17.7	17.4	24.3
People from isolated backgrounds (est.)[2]	1.9	2.0	1.9	2.0	2.0	1.8	1.8	4.5
People from lower SES backgrounds[3]	15.0	15.0	14.8	14.8	14.9	14.4	14.5	25.0

Source: adapted from Andrews *et al.* (1998).

Notes:
1 Reference value based on data obtained from the 1991 Census.
2 Reference value is based on data from the 1991 Census.
3 Reference value is set at 25 per cent of the population.

national population on the basis of the 1996 census. Retention and success rates for indigenous Australians are below average.

Disturbingly, two large population subgroups are markedly under-represented. People from lower socio-economic backgrounds are defined as 25 per cent of the national population, yet occupy only 14.5 per cent of university places. Correspondingly, people of medium and higher socio-economic backgrounds are over-represented, considerably so in the case of the latter group. Roughly speaking, per capita estimates suggest that people from lower socio-economic backgrounds are only half as likely to attend university as those of medium or higher socio-economic backgrounds.

The situation for people from rural and isolated areas is only slightly better; people living in rural or isolated Australia make up 29.8 per cent of the nation's population, yet their participation share in universities is only 19.2 per cent. Roughly speaking, urban people are almost twice as likely to attend university as rural/isolated Australians. The isolated group is one of the most under-represented groups in Australian higher education. A pattern of higher tertiary participation for people living in metropolitan areas is evident for both university and TAFE courses, though there are larger variations in the university participation (Stevenson *et al.* 1999). Regional TAFE participation does not offset lower university rates, despite speculation that there might be some substitution in rural areas. Variations in university participation between regions in metropolitan areas, according to socio-economic profile, are as substantial as the variations between rural and metropolitan regions.

These imbalances show that, despite expansion and progress towards equity goals, there remains a significant social stratification in higher education participation. Indeed, aggregate figures mask important variations in the patterns of the participation of non-traditional students by institution and by field of study. Overall, non-traditional students, as we have broadly defined them, are more likely to apply to and gain access to the newer, lower status universities, and are significantly under-represented in the more prestigious professional fields (Postle *et al.* 1995). People of lower socio-economic background range in population share from 5 to 45 per cent across universities, with a share of below 10 per cent in six of the eight older, 'sandstone' institutions

One of the significant developments in the context of patterns of lifelong learning in Australia is emerging evidence of extensive student movement not only from TAFE to higher education but also from higher education to TAFE. Of course TAFE-to-university movement is expected, for it conforms with commonplace assumptions about a hierarchical relationship between the sectors and the notion of upward educational 'progression'. Yet the work of Golding (1995) reveals a largely unforeseen pattern of student movement in the reverse direction, university-to-TAFE. This development in itself is evidence of the blurring boundaries and the reduction in 'barriers', real or imagined, to participation.

Progress towards the learning society

The broad participation figures indicate that Australian universities achieved major improvements in post-secondary educational participation throughout the 1990s. More Australians than ever before are likely to engage in tertiary education at some stage during their lives. When higher education and vocational education participation rates are added together, Australia is not far short of universal tertiary participation. While the demographic distribution of students on-campus does not yet mirror the national population, the overall number of non-traditional students has expanded considerably during the past decade. In all, these are significant achievements during a period of steady decline in per capita public funding.

Progress towards the goal of lifelong learning is evident in measures other than aggregate participation figures. The higher education sector has also become more responsive to the needs of non-traditional students. Four trends are worth noting. First, a decade of emphasis on quality assurance has brought a new client-focus to universities and enhanced efforts to monitor student feedback and to adapt programmes to student needs and expectations. Second, contemporary Australian universities are aware of and sensitive to cultural diversity in its many manifestations. The recognition of student diversity is evident in the extensive access and support programmes offered by all institutions. Third, the concept of flexible delivery is a defining feature of curriculum planning in many institutions, with the objective of providing learning in a manner, time and place that suits the individual learner. The communication capacity of new technologies has provided much of the impetus for this trend.

Fourth, universities have taken steps to improve articulation – especially between higher education and TAFE – and to encourage and recognise two-way student movement. These developments include the introduction of collaborative higher education and TAFE courses. In recognition of the non-linear educational mosaics of many people, the objectives of these initiatives are the dissolution of hierarchical barriers and the creation of seamless pathways and transitions.

These trends mark the ascendancy of student-centred thinking in higher education. The university is increasingly the catalyst for self-guided learning and academics are conceptualising their roles as supporters and mentors in addition to their subject expertise. Curriculum emphases forego ever-expanding content in favour of transferable investigative skills and information acquisition and analysis skills. In some cases, students have been handed the opportunity to shape their own programmes. By and large the philosophy underpinning these trends is congruent with the Candy model for the preparation of autonomous learners with the capacity to pursue learning outside the guidance (and constraints) of formal educational programmes.

In acknowledging these developments, we do not wish to overstate the extent or rate of change. The trends outlined are not universal. Not all Australian universities have reshaped their cultures and pedagogical practices, nor would all academics see themselves as guides and critical friends. Many admission procedures, teaching practices and assessment methods would be instantly recognisable to students of the 1960s and doubtless earlier. Flexibility and responsiveness to student needs and expectations are not yet core academic values, though progress in this direction could be said to be promising.

Arguably, the major pedagogical challenge that still confronts the Australian academic community is understanding and responding to student diversity. An implicit assumption of the elite era was that university teachers taught cohorts with roughly comparable levels of preparedness and 'ability'. Greatly expanded access has diversified the lecture room in tangible ways. Not only is this diversity apparent in gender, age and ethnicity, but also in values and objectives. Many non-traditional students are unfamiliar with the culture of universities and may be less deferential to it. Correspondingly, the complexity of academic teaching has risen and a broader set of educative understandings and skills is needed. This creates stresses and strains at the daily academic–student interface. The non-traditional student may be most strongly identified with these tensions and may continue to bear the label of the 'weaker' student.

Gaps and constraints

No account of gaps in, and constraints upon, participation in university studies would get very far without interrogating the categories of 'traditional' and 'non-traditional' students.

If traditionally students have moved straight from schooling to tertiary studies, changing labour market conditions, both for adolescents and for young graduates (those who emerge from the seamless school–tertiary pathway), increasingly confront the assumption that the full-time study mode is the norm. In Australia, federal government policy in the vocational education and training sector is designed to filter down to senior secondary school, in that adolescents are encouraged to blend part-time studies with part-time work and part-time training – all alongside each other in the typical week! Coupled with this is additional encouragement to undertake subjects with count for 'dual recognition'. This means that English, for example, perhaps re-badged as Communication, is available both for tertiary entry calibration, and simultaneously as a subject on the first rung of a vocational credential pathway, leading towards a certificate, then a diploma and so on, with employability as the target.

The net effect of these two initiatives at the top end of secondary school is to relax the exclusively academic tertiary focus – which generates the traditional full-time school leaver entry route to universities – in favour of a looser set of non-traditional arrangements. Given that the full-time adolescent labour market has completely collapsed in Australia, and the personal costs of university studies (even including, more recently, vocational education in colleges) continue to rise, part-time enrolments predictably will increase. As Marginson observes:

> Full-time jobs for young people aged fifteen to sixteen years have practically disappeared. . . . The proportion of teenagers with part-time jobs has risen significantly, from 4 percent in 1966 to 23 percent in 1992. . . . These trends are independent of economic recessions. . . . For teenagers, participation in education has become a substitute for work as well as a preparation for it.
>
> (Marginson 1993 pp. 11–12)

Many of those with part-time jobs are also full-time students, whether in TAFE or tertiary courses. Those young people with incomplete secondary schooling, no further (or continuing) studies in train, and no niche in the workforce have no future in the labour market, although they may hold casual short-term jobs.

Curiously, there are no reliable national figures on the various admixtures of part-time work, part-time studies, and full-time versions of these, nor of involvement in the hybrid of training as a variable. Similarly, there are no hard data as yet on the patterns of part-time employment of notionally full-time students, though anecdotal evidence from the academic community strongly suggests that study is less central to the lives of many undergraduate students and that the demands of balancing education, work and other commitments are increasingly a source of pressure for many students. Student involvement and engagement with the university experience does appear to be changing.

There are also no reliable figures on the mature-age version of the various admixtures. That is to say, when non-school leavers enrol for tertiary studies (both in universities and vocational colleges), it is not possible reliably to measure the extent to which these mature-age people, who are typically part-timers, are *entering*, as opposed to *re-entering*, the sector.

These gaps in the data are central to any discussion of extent of participation in university studies by reference to lifelong learning ideals. On the Candy definition of lifelong learning, which centres upon the self-direction of generic learning capabilities, what else these students (both the school-leaver and the mature-age part-timers) are doing can be factors in the likelihood of their success once they engage in tertiary studies. But a narrow definition of lifelong learning – more institutional, less experiential – assumes that 'lifelong' learning refers to the propensity of certain groups to dip in and out of formal studies. This latter definition runs the risk of remaining self-serving: to those students who have much, more will be given. Participation debates then are reducible to data on outcomes. What is overlooked, because the policy definition is narrow to start with, is how experiences of life and work mediate access in the first place (at whatever age the access is sought), and any second and subsequent points of access. A wider definition of lifelong learning such as Candy's acknowledges this depth and breadth of experience, and the enrolment trends towards part-time studies right from school leaving onwards signal that gaps and constraints in participation may start with the very conceptualisation of the issue – and may indicate why good data is hard to find on new 'non-traditional' participation patterns. Hence our earlier claim that the Australian higher education system has reached 'a critical cusp'.

In making this methodological and definitional point, we want to underpin its significance by drawing out some socio-cultural considerations. Lifelong learning in its narrower definition becomes a code, or a *telos*, for those with the employment status and access to funds to re-engage in formal training at various career points. Yet as we have signalled, the more fundamental question is: if lifelong learning in the broader sense is a 'Good Thing', under what conditions do people choose to participate in its tertiary provision?

In answering this question, certain evidence does identify gaps and constraints, clustering around an increasingly educationally bifurcated society.

Class and rurality: the persistent imbalances

Class and geographical location continue to shape the conditions for participation in lifelong learning. Australia still has a higher education system significantly stratified by social class. Students from lower socio-economic backgrounds are significantly less likely to believe that a university course will improve their chances of getting a job or offer them the chances of an interesting and rewarding career (James *et al.* 1999). Similarly, rural students (and especially those from lower socio-economic backgrounds) are on average significantly less likely than urban students to believe that a university course would offer them the chance of a career they would wish to follow, or that their parents want them to do a university course. In addition, rural students are significantly more likely than urban students to believe that their families cannot afford the costs of supporting them at university, and the cost of university fees may stop them attending.

Overall, the educational disadvantage of these non-traditional student groups has two main causes: they are more likely to perceive 'discouraging' inhibitors and barriers, such as the cost of higher education, while at the same time they are likely to experience lower levels of 'stimulating' factors, such as parental encouragement or the belief that a university course will offer them an interesting and rewarding career.

Despite the explicit barrier or disincentive created by the growing cost of attending university, expense is not the only or major influence on student attitudes. James *et al.* (1999 p. xvi) make this point:

The present imbalances in higher education participation in Australia also reflect differences in family and community attitudes towards the relevance of education. The effects of these powerful social influences are apparent well before the final years of senior schooling or eligibility for university entry; as school completion rates are lower in rural areas, many rural students do not reach the point at which it is meaningful to speak of potential barriers to higher education. For rural students in families and communities where higher education is seen as less relevant to life and employment, completing school and going on to university is not yet the norm.

School retention and transition: cultural considerations

We know across the Western world that incomplete schooling forecloses the chance of early entry to higher education. There are particular problems in school retention in rural and remote areas of Australia, because so much else is expected of the younger generation in the local achievement and sustenance of livelihood. Policies and programmes that address the problem of educational disadvantage in terms of expanding choices at the transition point to tertiary studies will not, therefore, be successful. Serious efforts to equalise participation cannot be delayed until that point of transition. Improving higher education participation is not merely a matter of removing or reducing inhibiting effects, but also involves raising perceptions of the relevance and benefits of higher education, and building incentives and encouragement in communities and families, especially in non-metropolitan areas of Australia. Boosting the 'encouraging' factors is critical in achieving long-term gains. This involves universities focusing more energy on reaching back into the early stages of the creation of educational ambition.

New and original equity initiatives are required during the junior and middle secondary years to encourage students not to foreclose their options

(Wyn and Lamb 1996, Dwyer 1997). These need to address raising student, parent and community awareness of the value of completing school, the material attainability of higher education and other post-secondary education and training in regional Australia, and in changing the culture of some universities.

The rhetoric of choice: 'option-driven' hypocrisy

The new rhetoric in Australia of expanding student choices is based on political confidence in the capacity of the market to exert pressures on universities that will ultimately improve quality and efficiency. Yet market forces are unlikely to bring in those disadvantaged in the two main ways outlined in the preceding two points. The West Review's strong advocacy of the adoption of student-centred funding arrangements is a sign of the pervasiveness of the new 'student choices' policy paradigm. On a broader definition of lifelong learning, the formation of the ability to choose is itself a factor in participation in tertiary studies.

'Too many medicos': expectations of work and the labour market

During the 1980s and well into the 1990s, inflated expectations held by parents and their children centred on professional careers such as medicine, law, commerce and the like. However, Australia did not then, and does not now, require larger numbers of such tertiary graduates. Instead, vocational education and training – a component of the 'Cinderella' sector, adult education – was recognised in government policy as the idea whose time had come (see Senate Select Committee on Employment, Education and Training 1991). Yet for many families, the elite professions – and the dedication of additional years of full-time studies for school leavers – remain the sole focus of tertiary studies.

All this persists, when, as we have noted, boundaries between study and training and work are blurring, and the shape of a new professional formation is emerging (Hager and Beckett 1998). More attention to actual labour-market learning capabilities (Beckett 1999), rather than formal credentialled achievements, is increasingly apparent (Boud and Garrick 1999, Garrick 1998).

The retrieval of the vocational education and training sector, which includes TAFE, from its lowly status, on the margin of policy initiatives in education with little realistic funding, thus began with a recognition of the ways adults were learning *for* work, *in* work, and *from* work, and how important this would be for Australia's participation in revitalised international markets (NBEET 1990a, 1990b, 1991, 1992, National Training Board 1990, 1991). And the universities have 'vocationalised' themselves with the same motive.

The labour market has evolved quite dramatically in the 1990s in

Australia. In common with other Western nations, substantial downsizing and middle-level job losses have been accompanied by increasing employment in part-time, often low-skilled, areas, particularly in human services such as the financial and hospitality industries. 'Winners' here are women, who have found the part-time hours and generic skill requirements congruent with family responsibilities, and early school leavers sought after for 'McJobs' in the fast-food industry. Other winners are in the high-technology and value-added private enterprise areas, where Reich's (1993) 'symbolic analysts' have cornered the new knowledge-based work. There is, in short, a polarisation of the labour market, with implications for access to tertiary studies.

This is in dramatic contrast to the post-war period, when the most desirable immigrants were deemed to be European adults of employable age. The employment available to these new arrivals in the early days was mainly in unskilled rural development (irrigation and other infrastructural schemes) and inner-urban manufacturing. Australians' reliance on a huge pool of immigrant labour, replenished and adapted to stable labour market conditions, came to be seen as inefficient and socially undesirable. Their version of lifelong learning, which was profound, consisted in the accumulation of experience from a multiplicity of jobs, and the achievement of affluence which a sustained income could provide. Yet the expectation which these post-War settlers had of their children – that professional formation via tertiary studies was the key to security – is no longer feasible, given labour market changes. Only some professionals can confidently call themselves 'secure', and there are many newer ways to find that labour market niche.

Realising the learning society

A commitment to lifelong learning and the creation of a knowledge society remains a cornerstone of federal education policy. In 1999, the federal Minister for Higher Education the Hon. David Kemp reiterated the pattern of policy thinking of the entire decade (Kemp 1999):

> There is little doubt that the nations which will succeed in the 21st Century will be 'knowledge societies' – societies rich in human capital, effective in their capacity to utilise and deploy their human resources productively and successful in the creation and commercialisation of new knowledge. In such a world there will need to be greater opportunities than ever before for lifelong learning – for preparation not just for the first job but for succeeding jobs.
>
> (Kemp 1999)

If the argument is accepted that the nation's wealth and prosperity is increasingly bound up in knowledge – rather than capital – as the principal factor of production, and that it is the 'knowledge workers' who will be empowered to control their own and their communities' destinies, then there is a compelling social obligation and imperative to ensure that all Australians have an opportunity to participate in the 'knowledge society'.

In this chapter we have raised an important issue: the way that the very notion of lifelong learning is framed will determine perceptions of participation. Our discussion of gaps and constraints on participation, given a broad, self-directive definition of lifelong learning, leaves much for universities and other providers of post-secondary education to be concerned about.

The present social imbalances in school completion rates and higher education participation have far-reaching consequences for the nation as a whole, and especially for the development of rural Australia. The lower participation rates of rural and isolated people and of people from lower socio-economic backgrounds are an integral component in a cycle of disadvantage. Outdated expectations of university studies, a new emphasis on various admixtures of part-time studies and work, on entry and re-entry to formal learning, and on learning in informal and semi-structured ways at work itself, are all important in locating participation debates more broadly in labour market changes. Disadvantage is at the heart of the emergence of new class divisions and tensions in Australia, seeming to revolve around individuals' ability to enter and re-enter the 'New World of Work'. This affects school-leavers, but also early school-leavers, and mature entrants and re-entrants to tertiary studies. Lifelong learning is then perhaps definable in non-traditional ways.

What universities, in particular, can do is address anew this shift in their student populations, taking a broad and generic view of what these experientially-enriched adults bring to their studies, and discarding any narrow perceptions of lifelong learning which assume it is what students dip in and out of, each time they formally enrol. A knowledge-based economy can ill-afford such a lucky-dip model of participation in higher education.

The policy implication of a reliance on a lucky-dip model is obvious. Australian governments in the 1990s have demonstrated a growing faith in the efficacy of the market and its capacity to expand the range of options open to prospective university students. Since the reforms of the late 1980s the emphases of federal higher education policy have changed considerably, from a model largely based on political theory, in which the objective was maximising participation, to an economic-rationalist model concerned with outcomes, and, by the late 1990s, to a student-choice, quasi-market approach that has its genesis in public choice theory and faith in market mechanisms. With these changes and the increasing de-regulation of the system, the notion of student choice is gradually supplementing or replacing the tradition of equity. But choice-driven change, if uninformed and capricious, is fickle. Market forces alone generate a lucky-dip provision, on both the supply side and the demand side.

Whether educationally disadvantaged Australians will participate in a student-choice market in higher education is uncertain. In Australia, there is a manifest gap between the 'intelligent country' rhetoric and the capacity of educational systems to realise it and involve all Australians in it. An ideology of student choice ignores the formation of that capacity to choose, and is perhaps the uncomfortable strategy of a government which, despite an espoused commitment to the 'knowledge society', is unable to find a way to fund a truly mass higher education system, with broadly-based lifelong learning principles at its heart.

Acknowledgements

We wish to thank Dr Carole Hooper for preparing an overview of recent participation trends. We are also very grateful to Dr Geoff Caldwell (Australian National University) for granting access to preliminary research he had undertaken for this chapter. Any errors are ours alone.

References

Andrews, L., Aungles, P., Baker, S. and Sarris, A. (1998) *The Characteristics and Performance of Higher Education Institutions*, Canberra: Australian Government Publishing Service.

Beckett, D. (1997) '"*Case study: Australia*", Project: vocational education and training in foreign countries', in U. Lauterbach, W. Huck and W. Mitter (eds) *Internationales Handbuch der Berufsbildung* [International Handbook of Vocational Education], German Institute for International Educational Research, Carl Duisberg Gesellschaft, and Bundesminister für Bildung und Wissenschaft, Frankfurt.

—— (1999) 'Past the guru and up the garden path: the new organic management learning', in D. Boud and J. Garrick (eds) *Understanding Learning At Work*, London: Routledge.

Boud, D. and Garrick, J. (eds) (1999) *Understanding Learning At Work*, London: Routledge.

Candy, P., Crebert, G. and O'Leary, J. (1994) *Developing Lifelong Learners through Undergraduate Education*, Commissioned Report no. 28, National Board of Employment, Education and Training, Canberra: Australian Government Publishing Service.

Crean, Hon. S. (Minister for Employment, Education and Training) (1994) *The Enabling Characteristics of Undergraduate Education: Advice of the National Board of Employment, Education and Training and its Higher Education Council*, Canberra: Australian Government Publishing Service.

Dawkins, Hon. J. S. (1988) *Higher Education: A Policy Statement (The White Paper)*, Canberra: Australian Government Publishing Service.

DETYA (1998) *The Characteristics and Performance of Higher Education Institutions*, Occasional Paper Series, Higher Education Division, Canberra: Australian Government Publishing Service. http://www.detya.gov.au/highered/otherpub/characteristics.pdf

—— (1999a) *Students (Preliminary) 1999: Selected Higher Education Statistics*, Canberra: Australian Government Publishing Service.

—— (1999b) *Equity in Higher Education*, Occasional Paper Series, Higher Education

Division, Canberra: Australian Government Publishing Service. http://www.detya.-gov.au/highered/occpaper/99A/equityhe_all.pdf

Dwyer, P. (1997) 'Outside the educational mainstream: foreclosed options in youth policy', *Discourse* vol. 18 no. 1.

Garrick, J. (1998) *Informal Learning in the Workplace: Unmasking Human Resource Development*, London: Routledge.

Golding, B. (1995) *Tertiary Transfer: The Unacknowledged Pathway between University and TAFE*, TAFE Pathways Issues paper 2, Melbourne: Office of Training and Further Education.

Hager, P. and Beckett, D. (1998) 'What would lifelong education look like in a workplace setting?' in J. Holford, P. Jarvis, and C. Griffin (eds) *International Perspectives on Lifelong Learning*, London: Kogan Page.

James, R., Wyn, J., Baldwin, G., Hepworth, G., McInnis, C. and Stephanou, A. (1999) *Rural and Isolated Students and their Higher Education Choices: A Re-examination of Student Location, Socioeconomic Background, and Educational Advantage and Disadvantage*, Canberra: Australian Government Publishing Service. http://www.-detya.gov.au/ nbeet/publications/hec/studentchoices.pdf

Karpin Report (1995) *Enterprising Nation: Report of the Industry Task Force on Leadership and Management Skills* (D. Karpin, Chair), Canberra: Australian Government Publishing Service.

Kemp, Hon. D. (1999) *Preparing Youth for the 21st Century: The Policy Lessons from the Past Two Decades*, Paper presented in Washington D.C., 23–4 February 1999.

Marginson, S. (1993) *Education and Public Policy in Australia*, Cambridge, UK: Cambridge University Press.

National Training Board (1990) *Setting National Skill Standards*, Canberra: National Training Board Ltd.

—— (1991) *National Competency Standards: Policy and Guidelines*, Canberra: National Training Board Ltd.

NBEET (National Board of Employment, Education and Training) (1990a) *The Recognition of Vocational Training and Learning* (Commissioned Report no. 1), Canberra: Australian Government Publishing Service.

—— (1990b) *A Clever Country? Australian Education and Training in Perspective*, (Conference Proceedings 1–3 November, Coffs Harbour), Canberra: National Board of Employment, Education and Training

—— (1991) *Progress and Prospects in Improved Skills Recognition* (Commissioned Report no. 10), Canberra: Australian Government Publishing Service.

—— (1992) *Education, Training and Employment Programs, Australia, 1970-2001: Funding and Participation* (Commissioned Report no. 11), Canberra: Australian Government Publishing Service.

Postle, G. D., Clarke., J. R., Skuja, E., Bull, D. D., Batorowicz, K. and McCann, H. A. (eds) (1995) *Towards Excellence in Diversity: Educational Equity in the Australian Higher Education Sector in 1995: Status, Trends and Future Directions*, Toowoomba: USQ.

Reich, R. (1993) *The Work of Nations: A Blueprint for the Future*, London: Simon and Schuster.

Senate Select Committee on Employment, Education and Training (1991) *Come In Cinderella: The Emergence of Adult and Community Education*, Canberra: Parliament of the Commonwealth of Australia.

Stevenson, S., Maclachlan, M. and Karmel, T. (1999) *Regional Participation in Higher Education*, Occasional Paper Series, Canberra: Australian Government Publishing Service. http://www.detya.gov.au/highered/occpaper/99B/1.htm#/ 5regionalparticipation

West, R. (1998) *Learning for Life: Review of Higher Education Financing and Policy* (The West Review), Canberra: Australian Government Publishing Service.

Wyn, J. and Lamb, S. (1996) 'Early school leaving in Australia: issues for education and training policy', *Journal of Education Policy* vol. 11 no. 2.

10 Japan

From traditional higher education to lifelong learning: changes in higher education in Japan

Shinichi Yamamoto, Tomokazu Fujitsuka and Yuki Honda-Okitsu

Introduction

Since the early 1980s, various social and economic changes have prompted the promotion of the education of non-traditional students in universities and other institutions of Japanese higher education. The greatest attention has been paid to those who, having left the school system, have had some work experience and then return to higher education. Numerous political measures aiming at aiding this type of non-traditional student have been implemented to increase their numbers rapidly. Changes and developments, however, have barely begun and there are many problems to be tackled.

This chapter attempts to describe the changing situation of non-traditional students, especially non-traditional students in Japanese higher education, in order to forecast the direction in which Japanese society is moving.

The higher education system in Japan

Structure of the higher education system

The first modern university established in Japan was the University of Tokyo in 1877, which was reorganized as the Imperial University in 1886. The missions of the Imperial University were to train the future "elite" and to introduce or interpret Western science into Japanese society, both of which were necessary for the modernization of Japan. Soon, people had realized that the practical value of university education would guarantee them good jobs and prestigious social status. This belief was prevalent around the 1900s in the mid-Meiji era when the present Japan established its hierarchical higher education system, from the private schools to imperial universities. Within this system, even students born into poor families could move up to a higher social status.

The education system featured a so-called European-style "double-track" secondary education system, in which a narrow university-track was separated from other pathways to the labor market. Tuition for university was expensive at that time, and people's aspirations of access to higher education were not easily realized. The trigger for the rapid increase in higher education enrolment occurred after the Second World War with the introduction of an American style "single-track" secondary education system. This was followed by the enormous growth of the Japanese economy in the 1960s and 1970s.

Since the inception of an American-style education system, six years of primary education, three years of lower secondary education and three years of upper secondary education are required before admission to higher education. Higher education is divided into short-term (two years) and long-term (four years) courses, the latter being pursued at universities. After the completion of undergraduate education at a university, individuals can proceed to postgraduate education at the Master's or Doctoral level.

Among two-year junior colleges, colleges of technology, and special training colleges, colleges of technology are peculiar in that they give five years of specialized technical and engineering education to graduates of junior high schools. The number of new entrants to colleges of technology is about 10,000 every year, which is relatively insignificant when compared to the enrolment of other institutions. Junior colleges, with predominantly female students (more than 90 percent), have shifted their educational emphasis from humanities and home economics to professional and business education. Special training colleges, legislated for in 1976, provide practical vocational training such as engineering, information processing, accounting, nursing, and hairdressing.

Today, about 90 percent of an age cohort completes upper secondary education in Japan. The proportion of those entering employment directly upon completion of high school declined from about 60 percent in the 1960s to 23 percent in 1997. Of all high school graduates in 1997, 27 percent entered universities, 13 percent entered junior colleges, and 17 percent entered special training colleges. The remaining 20 percent entered miscellaneous schools or were unemployed. About 9 percent of undergraduates proceeded to postgraduate education.

Specific features of the higher education system

In 1998, 74 percent of the 604 universities, 86 percent of the 588 junior colleges and 90 percent of the 3,573 special training colleges were private institutions. The rapid increase in enrolment in universities and junior colleges in the 1960s and 1970s was made possible by the growth of the private sector. Unlike national and public universities, which have laid stress on engineering education and the training of teachers, private universities have expanded into the fields of social science and the humanities. Special training colleges are more successfully run by flexible private bodies than public ones because they provide practical and professional training in close conformity with the skill needs of the labor market. These private institutions vary in their prestige, history, student numbers, and the quality of education and training.

A second important feature of higher education in Japan is the diversity of private universities. This is closely related to the hierarchical structure among universities. This hierarchy is based not only on the history and the prestige of each university, but also on the selectivity of admission. In Japan, each university conducts its own admissions procedure. Applicants for national universities must undergo a common examination prepared by the University Entrance Examination Centre prior to undertaking the university-specific examinations. Entrance into a university itself is not as difficult for an applicant as it used to be because of the decrease in the youth population. Further, admissions bodies increasingly consider recommendations from high school principals. In order to enter a prestigious university, however, excellence in academic achievement is still required. On the other hand, many special training colleges do not impose any selection criteria for admission. Once a student is admitted to a higher education institution, it is usually not very difficult to graduate. Most institutions do not require high standards of educational achievement for completion.

A third significant feature of the Japanese higher education system is that companies that employ new university graduates do not typically expect them to have acquired specialized vocational skills. The particular characteristics of Japanese work patterns include lifelong employment and on-the-job training of employees. Companies do not expect their new employees to have specific skills, but they do expect them to be trainable. In the case of those who complete undergraduate or graduate courses in engineering and technology, however, employers hold relatively high expectations of the skills and aptitudes that they will acquire through their post-graduate experience. Further, graduates of junior colleges or special training colleges are usually expected to have acquired practical vocational skills.

A fourth important feature of the higher education system in Japan is the geographical gap in educational opportunities. About 60 percent of enrolment in all types of institutions is concentrated in the metropolitan areas of Tokyo, Osaka and Nagoya. This geographical concentration is especially intense in the case of private institutions.

Finally, a fifth feature of significance within Japan's system of higher education is that enrolment in graduate schools is very small, and varies widely across the fields of study. The number of graduate students per thousand people is only 1.31, far less than the US (7.74), England (5.24), and France (3.54). In addition, more than 40 percent of Master's students in Japan major in engineering. Although most of those who have completed Master's courses in engineering secure jobs, about 30 percent of Master's students in the humanities, social sciences, or physical sciences go on to doctoral programs to become university professors. Graduate schools in Japan, except for

Master's programs in engineering, specialize in the training of scholars, the future university faculty.

Although the preceding five features of the higher education system in Japan have been criticized for a long time, it was not until the mid-1980s that substantial reforms were initiated. The efforts to increase the number of non-traditional students in the higher education system constitute an important part of these reforms.

Relation between the social functions of universities and types of student

The functions assigned to the higher education system largely determine the type of student found in higher education in Japan today. Japanese higher education, especially in the universities, follows the modern university model of production (research), knowledge transmission (teaching), and knowledge transfer, not only for industry but also for the public (Yamamoto 1998). Further, the Japanese university system has been an effective means of identifying young people who have the potential to play important roles in Japanese society. Universities select students through a difficult examination process, and these students are valued for passing the admission procedures rather than for the specializations they acquire in their studies.

Traditionally, the identification of students with potential tended to be effective only for young students who advanced to universities following graduation from high school. For non-traditional students over thirty years old, graduation from a prestigious university does not necessarily guarantee better careers. Japanese industry, which offers the largest number of job opportunities to university graduates, prefers young students who show potential to adults who already have knowledge and skills that industry requires. The system of employment at leading Japanese companies has had a strong influence on people's attitudes toward university education.

This principle of "the younger, the better" has deeply affected the higher education system in several ways. First, the enrolment of non-traditional students, though growing, is smaller than in other major developed countries. This may be attributable to the fact that Japanese educational statistics do not refer to the number of students classified by age cohort. Instead, there are detailed statistical figures classified by school grade, and by numbers of freshmen, sophomores, juniors, and seniors. Second, the graduate school system is very small compared with its huge undergraduate counterpart. Most students get jobs immediately after finishing undergraduate programs. The only exception is engineering, where graduate education in a Master's degree program has become widespread.

Non-traditional students have not been in the mainstream of the higher education system, and the universities have been educational institutions for the young. Every element of the university system, teaching, student services, and so on, has been so focused on young people that Japan now needs to reorganize its system for ever-increasing numbers of non-traditional students.

Concepts and measures for non-traditional students

Various measures aimed at the development of higher education for non-traditional students have been implemented in Japan since the end of the 1980s. Most of these measures are to relax restrictions on the provision of higher education to make it more compatible with the conditions specific to adults: for example, living conditions, abilities and interests. Although these measures have had some effect on promoting non-traditional higher education, the presence of new types of students in higher education is still the exception (Okitsu 1996).

"Refresh Education"

The concept of "Refresh Education" is defined as "the education given at higher education institutions in order that adults with work experience acquire new knowledge and skills or refresh outdated knowledge and skills." This concept appeared for the first time in a report produced by a committee in the Ministry of Education, Science, Sports and Culture (Monbusho) in 1996.

Refresh Education can be seen as a sub-concept of the well-known notion of "recurrent education," which refers to further periods of formal learning after having left the school system. Refresh Education is a specific type of recurrent education in which the target of education is adults with work experience who pursue vocational training at higher education institutions. This concept was devised because of the perceived ambiguity of concepts such as recurrent education and lifelong learning. Typically, they are perceived as including cultural activities, sports, recreation, outdoor activities, hobbies, volunteer activities, and so on (Okamoto 1994). Since the mid-1980s, educational policy makers in Japan have been emphasizing the vocational flavor of lifelong or recurrent education, thus necessitating a new catch phrase to express a specifically vocational reference.

Special admission for adults

Non-traditional student applicants would be at a disadvantage if they were required to tackle the traditional entrance examinations, as they have been out of the school system for extended periods of time and are typically too busy to prepare themselves adequately. To lessen this disadvantage, a Special Entrance Examination for Adults evaluates occupational skills acquired through work experience. Further, interviews and essays replace much of the usual academic examination process. In 1998, 616 university departments and 536 postgraduate courses provided this type of examination.

Evening courses and day-and-evening courses

Evening courses provide opportunities for adults with jobs who would otherwise have difficulty in attending courses during the day. Legislation for such programs was passed for Master's courses in 1989 and for Doctorate courses in 1997 through revision of the Chartering Standard. The number of postgraduate evening courses increased from five in 1989 to twenty-five in 1998.

In undergraduate programs at universities and junior colleges evening courses have a much longer tradition. In contrast to postgraduate evening courses, however, the numbers of courses and students are decreasing.

With the rapid increase of these provisions, mainly in postgraduate education, the number of graduate students participating in these types of courses is 1,694 (as of 1998), an increase of seventeen times across the previous eleven years. However, the share of these students among all graduate students was only 0.9 percent.

The University of the Air and correspondence courses

The University of the Air has provided education through radio and television since 1985. It has its own broadcasting station to transmit lectures eighteen hours per day. The cost of each course is 9,000 yen ($90 US), and each is worth two credits. A Bachelor of Arts degree requires the completion of 124 credits. The on-air courses are supplemented by printed materials, instruction by correspondence, and face-to-face instruction. The University of the Air does not impose any admissions selection criteria on applicants. In order to meet the diversified needs of the general public, the University provides programs in a Faculty of Liberal Arts only. This faculty is divided into three areas of study: "Science in Everyday Life," "Industrial and Social Studies," and "Humanities and Natural Sciences." The majority of participants are classified as regular students; other types of students include one-year or one-semester (six month) non-degree students. In 1998, 26,892 regular students and 41,098 students of other categories were enrolled in University of the Air programs, the former twice and the latter five times more than compared to ten years ago.

Long before the establishment of the University of the Air, universities and junior colleges were already providing correspondence courses. In 1998, 142,000 students were enrolled in correspondence courses at universities, and 34,000 students were enrolled in similar programs at junior colleges. Although correspondence doctoral studies have not yet been approved, the University Council approved distance Master's courses in December 1997.

Non-degree students, contracted researchers, joint researchers

Non-degree students may study particular subjects without necessarily wishing to graduate from a specific institution. Credits earned by non-degree students are recognized as equivalent to those earned by regular students and can be counted toward degrees.

The posts of contracted and joint researchers result from cooperation schemes between institutions of higher education and industry. Firms often send employees to universities or other institutions on a short-term basis to participate in research projects as contracted or joint researchers. In 1997, 817 contracted researchers and 2,394 joint researchers operated within national universities. The increase in such posts is more remarkable for joint researchers than for contracted researchers; however, the amount of contracted research and the value of grants for it from corporate interests is rapidly increasing.

Non-credit extension courses at universities

The goal of these courses is to make intellectual resources at universities available to local communities. In 1996, 525 universities provided 9,299 courses, and about 650,000 people participated, a number that had tripled in ten years. The increase is more remarkable for private and public universities than for national universities.

Most public and some private universities have newly established lifelong learning research centers on campus. They are mandated to pursue academic research into lifelong learning, to developing curricular plans for lifelong learning initiatives, and to provide information service and advertisement of their programs.

According to one survey, by providing extension courses most universities aim to provide a social service, improve the public image of the university, and improve its research activities of the university; this implies that these kinds of courses are rarely profitable for universities (Yamada 1993).

Finally, there is one other kind of institution that provides options very similar to extension courses. This category encompasses public service institutions such as Citizen's Public Halls, Youth Education Centers, and Public Corporations on the one hand, and private institutions organized by various bodies such as the so-called "Culture Schools" on the other. The non-credit extension courses of universities are in competition with these institutions.

Various measures aimed at increasing the acceptance of non-traditional students in higher education have been implemented in Japan since the end of the 1980s. Many quantitative indicators point to the fact that the measures taken have had a fairly large effect in promoting non-traditional higher education. The presence of non-traditional students in higher education, however, is still very insignificant. Furthermore, as a result of emphasis being placed on the postgraduate level, the promotion of non-traditional education in other institutions, especially short-term higher education, is relatively slow. However, the growing number of non-credit students and extension courses is making the boundary between higher education and other sources of lifelong education more vague.

Actual circumstances of non-traditional students: an empirical perspective

This section examines the conditions of non-traditional students, focusing on access, motivation, needs, learning conditions, consequences of learning, and obstacles in the development of education for non-traditional students. There is a considerable amount of data about students studying in Master's program, a level of higher education that is expected to fill a very important role in terms of refresh education and non-traditional study. It was for this reason that the Japan Institute of Labor undertook a nation-wide survey of non-traditional Master's level students.

Access to educational opportunities

The National Institute of Educational Research (Kokuritsu Kyoiku Kenkyusho 1993) conducted a survey of lifelong learning activities among 2,042 employees in 1991. The results indicate that only 4 percent of the sample were sent by their employers to institutions of higher education. The use of higher education is very limited when compared to training courses provided by the human resource departments of companies (82 percent of employees) or seminars and courses provided by private training agencies (61 percent of employees). A survey conducted by the Ministry of Labor in 1996 indicated that of 6,792 employees, 54 percent experienced some learning activities during the previous year compared to only 1 percent who had studied at an institution of higher education (Ministry of Labor 1997a).

According to a Japan Institute of Labor (Japan Institute of Labor (JIL) 1997) survey of 1,618 individuals involved in Master's courses, two-thirds of non-traditional students on Master's courses are male and one-third are female. The proportion of women is larger among non-traditional students than it is among traditional young students on Master's courses. Unlike male non-traditional students who are concentrated in the early thirties age bracket, female non-traditional students are scattered evenly over all age groups.

About one-third of non-traditional students are full-time workers. Those sent on Master's courses by their employers on full or partial leave of absence tend to be male. Among female students, the proportion of those working part-time and those who left previous employers in order to be full-time students, is higher than for male students. The jobs in which non-traditional students are typically engaged are teachers (37 percent), business workers (22 percent), and technological workers (18 percent).

Non-traditional students

Although at the undergraduate level non-traditional students tend to learn with the consent of their employers, at the graduate level those students who leave their employers in order to learn and those students who are sent by their employers are more frequent (Nikkei Research 1995).

Among students of the University of the Air in 1996, 45 percent were male and 55 percent female. One of the reasons for this difference is that the University of the Air has a Faculty of Liberal Arts only. Although the proportion of students in their twenties (29 percent) and thirties (23 percent) is as high as that of non-traditional students on university Master's courses, the proportion of older students is higher in the University of the Air. In university correspondence courses, 23 percent of students are aged between eighteen and twenty-two, whereas students over the age of thirty account for 43 percent of enrolments. Twenty percent of male students and 11 percent of female students already have Bachelor's degrees. Among participants in university non-credit extension courses, female student make up almost 70 percent, suggesting that these courses are functionally equivalent to public and private "Culture Schools."

Motivation of learners and social needs

It is also revealing to look at the motivating factors behind non-traditional students' educational experiences. To the question of motivational factors, the most frequent response is that the students are seeking to acquire a broader perspective of things. The next most common goals are to obtain a degree, and to acquire knowledge and skills useful in enhancing job performance. Promotions and pay increases are rarely cited as motivational factors. Individuals who are sent by employers on full or partial leave of absence are more frequently motivated by the desire for knowledge and skills directly related to their jobs. Of those who had left their employers, 40 percent intended to become scholars.

The motivations of non-traditional students in university undergraduate courses are as follows: to acquire a broader culture (44 percent), to learn a specific discipline systematically (43 percent), to heighten general ability (40 percent), to obtain a degree (39 percent), to obtain a skill qualification (22 percent), and to acquire practical knowledge and skills (21 percent). Non-traditional students in undergraduate programs seem still to have less practical goals than those on Master's courses.

Non-traditional students

According to the afore-mentioned survey by the National Institute of Educational Research (Kokuritsu Kyoiku Kenkyusho 1993), more than 60 percent of the respondents had been directed by their employers to join university seminars or special training colleges. Those who wished to be regular or non-degree students, however, accounted for only 31 percent. While 84 percent expressed a desire to join private training agency seminars and 78 percent hoped to visit and inspect factories and offices of more influential firms, the surveyed employees' indicated need for higher education was not very strong. However, if one takes into consideration the fact that the actual rate of people experiencing higher education as continued training is quite small, the percentage of those who wish to do so is quite high. In general, however, employed people prefer to attend concentrated courses.

The same survey asked employees to state freely what they would wish to learn if they were to study voluntarily at higher education institutions. The responses were of three types: cultural studies, studies leading to some form of certification, and practical vocational studies. Cultural studies also included learning related indirectly to careers, such as foreign languages, economics and business management, law, and pedagogy. The respondents perceived practical vocational studies as including advanced technologies, computer skills, and management skills.

Conditions of non-traditional study

In considering the learning lives of non-traditional students, attention must be given to their economic circumstances. According to the JIL (1997) data about students in Master's courses, more than 80 percent of non-traditional students pay all their school expenses themselves. Approximately 15 percent are paid in full by their employers. Ironically, the income of those paid by their employers is typically higher than that of those paying for themselves. This seems to indicate a double financial pressure for the latter group. In addition, although about half of the traditional young students obtained scholarships, only 15 percent of non-traditional students received such monetary aid.

It is difficult for non-traditional students to find housing or childcare service on campuses, even of public universities, services that are now commonplace at European and North American universities. Furthermore, graduate studies are very expensive. The fees graduate students have to pay during their first year total 750,000–1,000,000 yen ($10,000 US).

In regard to time, non-traditional students attend campus an average of 3.3 days per week; this is about one day less than younger students. Non-traditional students working full-time go to campus 2.4 days per week. When asked about attendance, 78 percent of non-traditional students report that they are rarely absent from classes. Adults also spend an average of sixteen hours per week studying off-campus, over an hour more than younger students. Working adults manage their time in various ways: 52 percent spend less time associating with colleagues and friends; 27 percent study secretly during business hours; and 24 percent occasionally leave work earlier than usual. Fifty-six percent of non-traditional students' superiors and 48 percent of their colleagues are supportive of their studies; 34 percent of their superiors and 42 percent of their colleagues do not pay any attention to their circumstances. Though 64 percent of their families actively support their lives as non-traditional students, another 16 percent of families respond negatively to the decrease of family time and 12 percent dislike the added financial burden.

Consequences of learning

With all the extra pressures that non-traditional student learners face in Japan, one would assume that the burden is somehow reflected by certain rewards. The survey of adults who are enrolled or have finished learning at eight graduate schools compares the students' expectations and the actual results of learning experienced by graduates. Surprisingly, and contrary to what one might expect, employers in Japan hardly recognize the results of non-traditional student learning, particularly when employees study on their own initiative.

Response of higher education institutions

Structure of educational opportunities

According to the JIL (1997) survey, among 778 courses with some non-traditional student participation, 73 percent are traditional day courses and 24 percent are day-and-evening courses. In contrast, evening courses account for only 2 percent. As seen above, provisions aimed at adjusting the time schedule of education to the living conditions of adults are still quite limited.

In terms of locality, 78 percent of the institutions offering Master's courses to non-traditional students are located in three metropolitan areas. In these areas, the proportion of private institutions is quite large. In contrast, national institutions provide the most opportunities for non-traditional student education in Master's courses in local areas. Geographical discrepancy in opportunity is not peculiar to non-traditional student education, but rather a reflection of the unequal distribution of higher education opportunity in general. Although opportunities abound in metropolitan areas, there is also intense competition for admission in these areas, suggesting that the educational demand exceeds the supply. Among non-traditional students, the social sciences are the most popular courses, unlike the rest of the students, many of whom are studying engineering at Master's level.

Organizations for managing the education of non-traditional students

As with information about non-traditional students in general, reliable data are rather limited. According to a survey conducted by the National Institute of Educational Research in 1991 (responses were given by 558 universities and 469 junior colleges), the methods of organization for the management of extension courses can be classified into five types (Yamada 1993):

- Whole Institution, managed by a specialized body in addition to decision-making by the representatives of all departments or courses of the whole institution.
- Practical Management, managed through the decision-making process of the whole institution without a specialized body.
- Specialized Management, managed by a specialized body separate from the decision-making of the whole institution.
- Decentralized Management, managed by each department or course without the involvement of the whole institution.
- No Extension Courses.

About a half of all national universities and junior colleges belong to the Decentralized Management category. Among private institutions, the share of No Extension Courses and Practical Management type management are relatively large.

Decentralized Management is not active in the operation of extension courses, suggesting that management by each department or course is not effective. But even if institutions have a specialized body for management, such as those in the Whole Institution and Specialized Management categories, they rarely have facilities for the exclusive use of extension courses (Yamada 1993).

Problems in higher education institutions

Many surveys indicate that the main obstacles to adult participation in higher education are the time schedule it entails and procedures for admission. Because most adults have jobs and do not wish to resign their current posts in order to learn at higher education institutions, they cannot attend classes in the daytime as full-time students. The provision of education after five o'clock or at weekends, however, has recently started in a small number of institutions. Moreover, many adults have had no experience of academic study for a long time and are unlikely to pass the ordinary entrance examinations. In order to enlarge higher education opportunities for adults, it is crucial to take steps to address these issues.

Adults already learning at some higher education institutions also face problems. The biggest of these is the content of education. According to the JIL (1997) survey, 44 percent of non-traditional students enrolled in Master's courses wish institutions to "provide a greater variety of practical subjects," 41 percent want "a greater variety of advanced subjects," and 36 percent wish for "a greater variety of optional subjects." However, a comparison between non-traditional students and staff as to what they think important about Master's courses reveals that non-traditional students attach more importance to the academic or cultural contents of education and less to practical or vocational education than the staff. Although the results of the survey about problems and demands in the content of non-traditional student education are complicated and sometimes inconsistent, it is clear that non-traditional students are not satisfied with the course content offered in higher education institutions.

On the other hand, institutions of higher education also suffer from problems with the education of non-traditional students. For example, the biggest problem for universities and junior colleges that provide extension courses is "the shortage of material, manpower and financial resources for education." This problem may exert a negative influence on the usual operation of institutions beyond the sphere of extension courses through, for example, the deterioration of teaching conditions within faculties. The second biggest problem is "how to plan course programs." For institutions, it is always a perplexing task to differentiate themselves from other institutions both inside and outside higher education, and to arrange programs that are both advanced and attractive to a variety of people at the same time.

Background of policy measures for education of non-traditional students

Rationale for the promotion of lifelong learning

So far, we have described and analyzed the current trends and conditions of non-traditional students in relation to higher education. The Monbusho has acknowledged three key reasons why non-traditional or lifelong learning is needed. Although they are officially spoken about with regard to special consideration for administrative purposes (thus necessitating a deeper analysis as will be discussed later in this paper), they offer rich implications for the role of higher education in Japan.

The first reason that the Monbusho gives is the need to respond to a changing social and economic situation. People need to acquire new knowledge and technology continuously if they are to keep pace with social and economic changes, including the advance of science and technology, the shift to an information-oriented society, internationalization, and changes in the industrial structure. Higher education is expected to provide adults with new and advanced knowledge and skills.

The second concern is the "maturation" of Japanese society. This comprises a combination of such phenomena as rising income levels, expanding leisure time, the growth of the aged population, and other factors. This maturation is reflected in an increasing demand for learning as a means of achieving richness of spirit and a sense of purpose in life. In this sense, unlike the European context, learning for pleasure is one of the rationales for lifelong learning in

Japan. There are many places, run by both public and private organizations, for the learning of non-vocational subjects such as reading classical Japanese literature, flower arrangement, dancing, painting and so on.

The third point is the "academic credential issue" in Japan: people tend to evaluate others by their academic backgrounds acquired when they were still young. Many Japanese believe this is the most serious of the various educational problems. To remedy the harmful effects of society's present pre-occupation with academic credentials, the Monbusho says that it is necessary to build a society in which there is proper evaluation of learning achievements throughout an individual's life by the encouragement of lifelong learning. In this sense, increasing enrolment of non-traditional students at higher education institutions may be a sign that the situation is improving.

The Japanese university system faces new hardship

The promotion of lifelong learning is intended to relax the rigid age system of higher education as well as to solve the credential problem. Since the Recommendation of the National Council on Educational Reform in 1987, the relation of higher education with the lifelong learning system has become closer, and the Monbusho has implemented numerous policy measures, as discussed in the first section of this chapter. In addition to these, we must look at another circumstance that forces universities to accept non-traditional students.

Japan experienced rapid growth in higher education twice after the Second World War. The first surge came in the 1960s to early 1970s. The participation ratio of the eighteen year old population in higher education grew rapidly to 39 percent in 1976, from only 10 percent in 1960 (Monbusho 1997). This growth was triggered by various factors, and the result was the 'massification' of higher education. Massification means not only the growth of higher education in population, but also a radical change in character of the system. Higher education is no longer for the "elite" but for the mass that needs higher education. Demands for education have diversified from academic to applied.

The second stage of massification started at the beginning of the 1990s. The participation rate of the eighteen year old population in higher education grew from 36 percent in 1990 to 47 percent in 1997. This rapid increase was triggered by the growth of the eighteen year old population in the late 1980s. This second stage of massification, however, is and will be followed by a difficult situation: the steady decline of the eighteen year old population, which is expected to fall to two-thirds of today's population within twenty years (from 2.05 million in 1992 to 1.20 in 2009). Except for a few prestigious universities, most institutions of higher learning must confront the problem of how to deal with the future shortage of applicants and also how to attract students.

Along with the massification of higher education, a growing number of people have complained about the content of education. Faculties tend to teach too much academic subject matter while many students prefer to take practical courses that they think useful for their future jobs outside academia. Another difficulty is the students' declining incentive to learn. As many students, who might not have enrolled in higher education two decades ago, are not accustomed to learning abstract subjects or dealing with academic language, universities must respond by improving teaching methods and the structure of their curricula. So-called "faculty development" (FD) has become a fashionable phrase in Japan when we talk about improvement of teaching. Together with FD, universities will be forced to reform by the fear that they could lose their attraction unless they adequately respond to new situations.

Introducing a policy for increasing the ratio of non-traditional students will affect the university system on two dimensions. First, non-traditional students may help universities to cope with the shortage of young students. So far, the enrolment of non-traditional students in both undergraduate and graduate programs is not large enough to supplement the decreasing number of traditional ones. However, recent trends show that the enrolment of non-traditional students will steadily increase.

Second, non-traditional students will stimulate the efforts of universities to improve teaching and, to some extent, research activities. In the lifelong learning system, people have strong expectations of the quality of teaching because non-traditional students have strong incentives to learn. What they need is not an empty diploma, but practical benefits from learning.

Toward a new concept in non-traditional student learning

The higher education system is expected to be a key vehicle for promoting the lifelong learning system. The great advantage of higher education compared to other educational sectors is that it has numerous resources, including staff and facilities. The Monbusho is implementing a number of policy measures at the higher education level to provide diverse learning opportunities, including the expansion of access to higher education for non-traditional students and the establishment of new types of institutions and facilities to the public.

However, it is still new for the Japanese to think of lifelong learning or non-traditional student learning in combination with the higher education system. In Japan, there is a long tradition of non-formal education which was called "popular education" or "social education," and which was regarded as nearly equal to lifelong education or lifelong learning until the mid-1970s. The introduction of the OECD's discussion on recurrent education sounded very new to the Japanese because it was strongly oriented towards vocational education, and also combined vocational training and formal education aimed at creating job opportunities for those who were returning to the educational sector.

The traditional Japanese meaning of lifelong learning thus has several specific features. The first is that it focuses on educational activities in non-school education sectors. The second is that its main concern is non-vocational learning perceived as being primarily for the enrichment of people through learning. The third is that it mainly emphasizes the "input" of the learning opportunity but is less concerned with the "output" of the learning (i.e. its practical use).

Through its inclusion in higher education, the concept of lifelong learning or non-traditional student learning has broadened its scope to include not only non-vocational, non-formal, and input-centered learning, but also vocational, formal and output-concerned learning. In this sense, the Monbusho's aim to reduce the negative effects of the preoccupation with academic credentials calls for a subtle discussion. If we try to increase the usefulness of university learning for non-traditional students, the academic credentials they gain should be more applicable to their future careers. And this is precisely what the Monbusho intends to achieve by the promotion of non-traditional student learning. The solution will be not to limit the effectiveness of the academic diploma for the young, but to have it act as an extension to non-traditional students. However, this means that Japan must change the employment and vocational training systems within the major companies that have predominated in Japanese society and education.

It may be quite incidental, but the decline of the eighteen year old population can only reduce the traditional functions of the university (i.e. the selection of the students). Instead of selecting applicants through the admissions process, universities will have to offer attractive programs for both young and non-traditional students, and provide assurances that the diploma will be useful to both groups.

The impact of technological and labor market changes on lifelong learning

The impact of industrial changes on non-traditional students in the 1990s can be divided into two parts: technological change, and change in the labor market. Technological change requiring higher technology may motivate the retraining of workers. The labor market may change in the direction of greater flexibility due to shorter-term contracts and more performance-based salaries. An increase in labor market flexibility may in turn motivate workers to undertake retraining upon leaving their jobs.

Educational experience of workers in the information industry

In recent years, employment in tertiary industry has grown to more than 60 percent of the national total. The growth of service industry employment has been rapid. In contrast, the share of primary industry employment has been decreasing. For example, between 1985 and 1995, the employment of information engineers increased 81.2 percent overall (Ministry of Labour 1997b), and was particularly rapid in the real estate, service, electricity, gas, heat supply, and water industries.

In the ten-year period between 1985 and 1995, the proportion of information engineers who were programmers or computer operators with junior college degrees increased, but the proportion with university degrees decreased significantly. In contrast, the proportion of information engineers who are system engineers with junior college or university degrees has increased because of the requirements of higher technology (Japan Institute of Labor 1997b).

The labor market under a post-Bubble crisis

From the late 1980s to the early 1990s, the Japanese economy experienced unprecedented prosperity, which brought about an economic condition dubbed the Bubble Economy. Shortly thereafter it fell into a serious recession, causing the burst of the Bubble. In terms of its scale and duration, this recession has had a graver effect on the Japanese economy than did the Oil Crisis of the 1970s. However, as a decrease in the annual GDP growth rate was experienced in all Western countries in the 1990s, Japan's post-Bubble depression was not unique. In contrast, the East Asian economy experienced remarkable growth in the early 1990s.

For a very long time, Japan's employment system was said to have the unique features of "lifelong employment" and a "seniority system." Within the corporate giants, the internal labor markets are clearly defined. Japanese enterprise has no choice but to amend its employment system as it has experienced both a serious shortage and surplus in its work force during the last decade. In the mid-1990s, most articles concerning the Japanese economy included the words "Collapse of the Japanese Management System." To what extent, then, has the Japanese Management System in fact collapsed?

From 1991, the labor market took a turn toward a surplus in the work force and a rising unemployment rate. In particular, unemployment increased among young workers (under the age of thirty-five) and older workers (over the age of fifty-five). This meant that the main strategy for employment control of Japanese companies was the promotion of early requirement and restriction on the hiring of new graduates. Furthermore, in the period of higher unemployment in the 1990s, the rate at which people left their jobs and sought employment in other companies decreased while the rate at which people were changing their positions within the same industry was increasing (Ministry of Labor 1997b). Since most wages have traditionally been based on length of service, wage differentials between Japanese workers have been small. Equality and seniority are the main characteristics of the Japanese wage system. We did not see any change in Japan's wage differentials during this decade (OECD 1996).

Employer and employee attitudes toward education affected by industrial changes

Under such industrial changes, the attitudes of employers have begun to change. According to a survey of 313 companies, the types of training they are willing to contract out to higher education institutions in the future are: highest level technologies (62 percent), upper level technologies (55 percent), basic technologies (52 percent), internationalization (49 percent), system-engineering (45 percent), and upper-level management (42 percent). In the case of large companies with more than 5,000 employees, 76 percent wish to contract education and training at the highest level of new technology out to higher education institutions. On the other hand, medium-sized and small companies with less than 1,000 employees wish to commission not only education and training of technology, but also the training of newly hired employees. There is strong demand from employers, particularly large companies, for training at higher education institutions and in high-level technologies.

The starting salaries of graduates with Master's degrees correspond exactly with the salary of graduates who have already worked for two years. This is because Japanese companies usually apply the same salary system to both categories of workers, at least at the beginning of their career. Choosing to matriculate into a graduate school and paying costly tuition does not give one any advantage when receiving a starting salary, at least not in one's initial career.

The majority of non-traditional student learners pay for their own tuition and do not receive any scholarships. Students are demanding a more supportive system, but such a system may be inadequate. Opportunities to raise money for tuition, through savings for example, are extremely limited. This becomes an enormous obstacle for those going back to graduate school. In fact, the standard income of non-traditional student learners is quite high before returning to school.

Certainly, many Japanese companies continue seriously to review and restructure their employment system. Macro-economic data, however, do not show that the Japanese labor market is becoming explicitly more flexible. One of the main reasons is that the long recession has affected it too much. A decrease in labor mobility, a constant wage differential (in contrast with most Western countries where the wage gap is becoming greater), and an increase in the unemployment rate among young workers about to seek their first employment in the internal labor market are some of the factors which indicate that the Japanese employment system, and its basic treatment of workers, remains largely unchanged.

For non-traditional students in Japan, flexibility in the labor market is important and provides great motivation to learn. Some individual firms also pursue new ways of employment, for instance earlier retirement, short-term contracts, or short-term evaluation of a worker's abilities. After all, the pace at which labor market flexibility progresses depends on business, and workers are less willing to run a risk or to invest in themselves for future opportunities during a recession. In other words, non-traditional learners become more conservative about giving up a job in order to study during a recession. Economic factors influence adults' consciousness and behavior in regard to education.

Governmental promotion of human resource development and science technology

The government has positively promoted development of technology and human resources in preparation for a knowledge-based society in the near future. Under its policies and plans, the number of adults studying in higher education on their own incentive is steadily increasing.

On the basis of the Sixth Basic Plan for Development of Occupational Abilities, the Ministry of Labor promotes the development of workers' abilities by providing subsidies and administering various training institutions. Considering spontaneous education that acknowledges personal and technical development in line with industrial change as one of its central issues, the Sixth Basic Plan for Development of Occupational Abilities expresses the governmental policy for education and training from 1996 to 2000.

The main grants offered by this government initiative are:

- the Subsidy for Labor Mobility Skills Development which aims at developing labor mobility and at avoiding a rise in the unemployment rate
- the Grant for Lifetime Development of Vocational Abilities which aims at promoting a development of worker's abilities
- the Subsidy for Highly Developed Skills which is paid to employers who provide training for development of high value-added products or new markets
- the Subsidy for Self-education which is paid to employees who provide an extended paid recess for the education and training out of the company, or they share the tuition costs.

Koyo Sokushin Jigyodan, a governmental organization dedicated to promoting employment, has established public training institutes in local areas. Most effective among its programs are the short-term special training programs of the Human Resources Development Center and the Polytechnic College that, within six months, provide training in high technology and specialist knowledge for workers. In 1996, nearly 20,000 workers took the program. Recent changes in labor force composition have also seen white-collar workers in urgent need of retraining.

In spite of the decrease in labor mobility, the total number of adults in higher education is increasing on account of the political endeavor of all government bodies. Correspondingly, many workers have been demanding opportunities to study and develop their abilities on their own in order to adjust and keep pace with job restructuring in their companies.

Recent reviews of Japanese management systems

From numerous studies, we know that the Japanese employment system has performed well in training laborers in applied skills and knowledge. While the internal labor market developed by the Japanese employment system has usually been regarded as an obstacle to non-traditional student education, we can also see good performance in in-house training supported by this system. Therefore, as have educational institutions, Japanese companies have trained their workers both formally and informally.

Increasing the number of non-traditional students in higher education will still depend on businesses in the future. Many companies are no longer willing to train their workers. Moreover, they have begun to be more interested in employing well-trained workers under shorter contracts and higher salaries. The expansion of non-traditional student education includes moving some educational activities from within companies to the educational institutions. Universities are urged to improve their teaching skills and to accept more non-traditional students. However, they may be among the most difficult institutions to change in Japan. If universities are successful in responding to social demands more quickly, they will be ideal institutions for non-traditional students because of their human resources and facilities.

From the perspective of technological and labor market change, the next issue for discussion must be what kind of education it is appropriate for the higher education institutions to offer, and what kind of education should they take charge of for the more efficient sharing of non-traditional student education and training.

Conclusion: from traditional mode to lifelong learning mode; why and how the higher education system should be changed

The 1990s witnessed a decade of University Reform, initiated by the recommendations of the University Council (an advisory committee to the Minister of the Monbusho). The most important task for university reform is to make universities more accountable to students, customers, and the general public, a task which has sometimes run counter to the traditional notions of university and faculty autonomy. People have realized, in view of the massification of higher education and the progress in scientific research, that the university system in Japan no longer fits the new requirements of the people.

As for teaching, students prefer more practical courses to academic-oriented ones, and they require the curriculum to be more systematically organized. When considering research, people feel that the outcomes should be more applicable to society's needs. The government also considers that basic research at academic institutions is essential for the maintenance and improvement of the national economy and international competitiveness.

In the twenty-first century, knowledge has become a more crucial factor for individual life as well as for national prosperity. Indeed, knowledge is the engine for a prosperous future. Just as other countries regard the promotion of science and technology as important for economic competitiveness and national security, more people have come to regard having knowledge or learning new skills as necessary for the betterment of their lives and for job security. Preparing for a lifelong learning society has become one of the top priorities for educational policy in Japan.

Universities, the center of the higher education system, have traditionally been places for the young in Japan, and curricula and systems of study have been tailored for them rather than anyone else. This traditional mode of higher education has been closely connected to the Japanese lifelong employment system, under which finding a better job is believed to be much more difficult for non-traditional students than the young. The problem of academic credentialism also played an important part.

These conditions, however, are now rapidly changing. The demand for lifelong learning is increasing. Therefore, Japanese higher education is expected to transform itself into a new lifelong learning mode not only as soon as possible, but also as much as possible.

References

Japan Institute of Labor (JIL) (1997) *Daigakuin Shushi Katei ni okeru Shakaijin Kyoiku* (Non-Traditional Student Education in Master's Courses), Report no. 91, Tokyo: Japan Institute of Labor.

Kokuritsu Kyoiku Kenkyusho (The National Institute of Educational Research) (1993) *Shogai Gakushu no Kenkyu* (A Study of Lifelong Learning), Tokyo: Emuti Shuppan.

Ministry of Labor (1997a) *Minkan Kyoiku Kunren Jittai Chosa* (Survey on Training in Industry), Tokyo: Ministry of Labor.

—— (1997b) *White Paper on Labor*, Tokyo: Japan Institute of Labor.

Monbusho (1997) *Japanese Government Policies in Education, Science, Sports and Culture, 1996*, Tokyo: Government Printing Bureau.

Nikkei Research (1995) *Daigaku Kaikaku no Kongo no Kadai ni tsuiteno Chosa Kenkyu Hokokusho* (A survey of the Future Problems of University Reform), Tokyo: Japan Institute of Labor.

OECD (1996). *Employment Outlook*, Paris: OECD.

—— (1997) *Thematic Review of the First Years of Tertiary Education: Comparative Report*, Paris: OECD.

—— (1998) *University Research in Transition*, Paris: OECD.

Okamoto, K. (1994) *Lifelong Learning Movement in Japan,* Tokyo: Sun Printing.

Okitsu, Y. (1996) 'Adults in Japanese Higher Education,' *The Studies of The Japan Institute of Labor* no. 12.

Roudou Mondai Research Center (1996) *Daigakuintou ni okeru Syakaijin no Jiko Keihatsu no Genjo oyobi sono Shien no Arikata* (The Present State of Self-Development Activity by Non-Traditional Students and its Support System), Tokyo: Japan Institute of Labor.

Yamada, T. (ed.) (1993) *Shogai Gakushu no Chiteki Network* (Intelligent Network for Lifelong Learning), Tokyo: Gakkouhoujinn Keirikenkyuukai.

Yamamoto, S. (1998) 'Higher Education in Japan from the perspective of R&D,' in M. Hemmert and C. Oberlander (eds) *Technology and Innovation in Japan*, London/New York: Routledge.

11 New Zealand

The impact of market forces in the quest for lifelong learning in New Zealand universities

Roger Boshier and John Benseman

From 1984 until 1999 New Zealand was embroiled in a radical experiment in free market economics. The simultaneous embrace of lifelong learning and market forces was at the root of the problem. In 1984 new-right ideology contained two elements. The neoliberal element was committed to the free market and wanted to substitute it for the state. The second, a neoconservative element, was fundamentalist and espoused conservative moral values (anti-socialist, anti-feminist, anti-Maori). It abhorred 'dependency' on the state and claimed to speak the 'truth' and, most astonishingly, to eschew 'politics' (Prebble, 1987).

Prior to 1986, New Zealanders aged between fifteen and twenty-five were making a median income of $14,700 a year. By the year 2000 the same group were making $8,100 and youth suicides were higher than in comparable countries. As well, living standards had plummeted and 70 per cent of households were worse off than counterparts ten years earlier. 'Efficiency' and the 'free market' meant the already disadvantaged had been even more seriously jeopardized (Peters *et al.* 1994). The particular interpretation of lifelong learning in New Zealand was not a benign plan for educational reform, concerned with access and equity. Rather, it was a troubled, contested and sometimes mean-spirited programme which was not orientated towards the needs of increasingly impoverished sections of the community.

Policy before and after 1984

In the 1960s and 1970s New Zealanders such as George Parkyn (1973) Arnold Hely (1967) and Denny Garrett (1972) were elaborating a tapestry of lifelong education for UNESCO while others, such as Renwick (1975), were in Paris laying the groundwork for recurrent education. New Zealanders were fascinated by the way Faure (1972) and others wanted a broad conception that embraced informal and nonformal as well as formal settings. This became the centrepiece of the 1972–5 Norman Kirk Labour Government initiatives in adult education and also sparked books and reports with titles like *Towards A Learning Society* (Boshier 1980) and *Lifelong Education* (Simmonds 1972). In New Zealand adult education, the 1970s are now widely regarded as halycon years.

In the early 1980s the groundwork was laid for a radical New Right revolution that would puncture the utopianism, optimism and commitment to the public good nested in Faure and its New Zealand exemplars. In one year, government funds for adult education would be cut by 78 per cent (*Access* 1996). A New Right programme for radical change was launched in 1984. Every aspect of New Zealand life – including education – would sail under the flag of marketisation. Or, in many cases – such as the Workers Education Association (WEA) – sink, almost without trace.

By 1987 influential members of the government treasury department had decided education was a commodity to be guided by the principles of the free market. These became the basis of reports and Acts of Parliament (the Education Act 1989, the Education Amendment Act 1990, the Education Amendment Acts (4) 1991). There was to be a shift from the liberal human-ist ethos of the 1970s to a technocratic ideology.

Reports laid the foundations for the most radical changes since the 1877 Education Act that had established a national education system (Butterworth and Butterworth 1998, Peters *et al.* 1994). Few of the personnel invited to serve on these enquiries or of the submissions received represented the ethos of lifelong education. Adult educators were notably absent. None of the criticalists – either in New Zealand or abroad – were invited. But there were extensive consultations with the captains of industry and rightwing Business Roundtable.

Two assumptions were now nested in the New Zealand language of lifelong learning:

1 Education is a private good. Consumers who want it to maximise wealth, status or to secure the good life should pay.
2 Competition is inherently good. It causes individuals and institutions to perform at an optimal level and the education system to be efficient.

Policy changes were made by the Education Act (1990), under the banner of Learning For Life. Universities and other tertiary institutions were bundled together. Tertiary Education Institutions (TEIs) became profit centres or *enter-prises*. The discourse was executed with the same bombast that characterised other parts of the free market agenda. There would be a cult of efficiency, a level playing field, and competition pitting state-funded agencies against each other and the educational newcomers: the Private Training Enterprises (PTEs). D. C. Savage – former head of the Canadian Association of University Teachers – saw these developments as

> an unprecedented invasion of university autonomy and attack on acade-mic freedom by the central government . . . The protagonists wanted to see universities become private institutions . . . which would downplay collegial structures in favour of a managerial approach used by private corporations . . . this led to enormously increased bureaucratic control.
>
> (Savage 2000)

In addition, there was a deliberate attempt to substitute the language of business for that of the university. Students became clients, institutions fought one another for market share, and Vice-Chancellors were now increasingly termed Chief Executive Officers.

After 1984, many came to observe what came to be called 'The New Zealand Experiment', but few drew attention to the decline in literacy and numeracy rates, the escalating expulsions from school, the deepening problem of Maori underachievement, the confusion of demoralised and underpaid teachers, the dismissal of large numbers of skilled educators and restructuring of their institutions, and the emergence of an underclass (Kelsey 1995).

Universities could not escape the reach of reforms. The notion of 'academic freedom' was perceived as being under threat and critics such as Bruce Jesson (1999) claimed New Zealand was being overwhelmed by a 'cult of finance'.

Literacy crisis

Generations of New Zealanders had prided themselves on being highly literate but, in the mid-1990s, there was clear evidence literacy levels were lagging, particularly in some social groups (OECD 1997).

The *International Adult Literacy Survey* was conducted in New Zealand in March, 1996. Three types of literacy – prose, document and quantitative – were measured using a task-based methodology which required respondents to perform tasks of the kind encountered in daily life (such as reading a train or bus timetable, interpreting parts of a newspaper or reading instructions from a bottle of medicine). In brief, the results showed:

- Over a million New Zealanders (out of a population of 3.8 million) had a minimal level of competence in all three domains. Within this group, 20 per cent of New Zealand's population was found to have 'very poor' literacy skills (the lowest on a 5-point scale), meaning they could be expected to experience 'considerable difficulties in using many of the printed materials encountered in daily life' (Ministry of Education 1996).
- Most Maori and Pacific Islands people were functioning below the level of competence required to 'effectively meet the demands of daily life' (Ministry of Education 1996). On document and quantitative literacy, 70 per cent of Maori and 75 per cent of Pacific Islanders failed to meet the minimal level of competence (level 3 or higher). Between 40 and 45 per cent of Pacific Islanders were at the lowest level of literacy.
- Within the labour force there were 'stark contrasts' (Ministry of Education 1996) between employed and unemployed New Zealanders. Almost half the unemployed were at the lowest level of literacy (level 1) in each domain. Retired people also performed poorly in all areas.
- New Zealand compared well with other countries on prose literacy but

in terms of document literacy, several countries did better, including Belgium, Canada and Germany, while the Netherlands and Sweden did considerably better. Only Ireland and Poland had scores lower than New Zealand on document literacy. Concerning quantitative literacy (the ability to do simple arithmetic tasks) all countries scored significantly better than New Zealand except Ireland, the UK, the USA and Poland.

Two discourses greeted these results. In the first, apologists for marketisation pressed for an even more radical restructuring of education. Market forces have not had enough time to do their work. More market means better literacy. The second discourse, shaped by adult literacy activists, cited the results as evidence of crisis in adult education.

Participation of non-traditional students

Non-traditional students (from groups which have had disproportionately lower rates of participation) in New Zealand include Maori, Pacific Islanders, older people, women, immigrants, those from low socio-economic families and from some rural areas. The Education Act 1989 made a specific commitment to these under-represented groups.

Various studies of the participation of adults in New Zealand adult and higher education demonstrated that participants were a socio-economic elite. Even the Workers' Educational Association (W.E.A.) was largely unable to attract workers or, for that matter, people without a university degree. It seemed that 'to those that hath, more shall be given'. Once off the educational train, it was hard to clamber back on. All over the world, reaching the 'hard-to-reach' is a continuing preoccupation, and clientele analysis or participation surveys (e.g. Johnstone and Rivera 1965, London *et al.* 1963, Statistics Canada 1985) attest to the difficulty of attracting lower socio-economic groups into education. Outreach programmes or other sustained efforts can work but, once resources are withdrawn, the familiar patterns of old return. More than ever the task is to 'get the bloody numbers' in the enrolment economy (Roberts 1983).

Faure (1972) envisaged a learning society where providers of formal education would no longer have a monopoly on learning. Education and learning would be diffused throughout society and become the preoccupation of all. Much would be learned about psycho-cultural barriers that inhibit participation and institutions would have to put out the 'welcome mat' and remove barriers to participation.

Faure's utopia has not arrived. Although more New Zealanders have recently participated in education that occurs in formal and nonformal settings, the composition of the student body has not changed well-established patterns. The working class and disadvantaged groups are prominent by their absence. In general, participants have already 'supped well at the font of schooling'. Where non-traditional students become involved in post-school education, it is still in disproportionately lower numbers and invariably in the lower, less prestigious subjects and institutions. Such a situation can be seen as a form of 'educational inflation'. Non-traditional students have progressed relative to former generations, but have made little headway in relation to their more privileged contemporaries.

Learners in formal settings

In the mid-1970s less than 3 per cent of New Zealanders had a degree and most people learned what they needed to know at work, from mates or over the farm gate. 'University' was a privilege enjoyed by few, although numerous working-class families benefited from policies that led to the admission of mature-age students after the Second World War. Adults aged twenty-one or more could gain automatic entry, even without the requisite University Entrance exam. In recent years there has been a steady increase in the number of non-traditional students admitted to universities. This is partly a consequence of government and university policies, but also because of enrolment desperation induced by the radical commitment to market forces.

Enrolments in tertiary education increased by 8 per cent from 1993 to 1998 (Ministry of Education 1999 p. 84). In 1996 11 per cent of all New Zealanders had a university-level qualification and 14 per cent had a non-university tertiary education (OECD 1998 Table A1.1). Although this represented a rise in the rate of participation overall, it was lower than in comparable OECD countries. There was also strong evidence that those typically identified as non-participants were not showing up in numbers that signalled a change in historic patterns. Participation increased, but the underclasses were not showing up in anything other than their usual numbers. However, by the turn of the century, there were more mature-aged students enrolling in tertiary institutions. For example in 1998 over half (57 per cent) of first year tertiary students were aged twenty years or over and nearly a third (31 per cent) were over thirty years of age (Ministry of Education 1999 p. 19).

Maori

Under the country's founding document, the Treaty of Waitangi, there is a commitment to achieve equitable participation for Maori, as signatories of that treaty, in all elements of New Zealand life, including education. *Learning for Life Two* (Ministry of Education 1989), which provided the policy background for the Education Act 1989, stated that 'full participation by Maori in the spirit of the Treaty of Waitangi is an important objective of post-compulsory education and training system' (Ministry of Education 1989 Section 2.2:13). Along with Pacific Islanders, the Maori population is disproportionately young, but both have increased their involvement in tertiary education over the past decade: Maori by six times the number of a decade

Table 11.1 Percentage of New Zealand tertiary students by ethnicity compared to total percentage in the New Zealand population, 1990 and 1998

Ethnic group	1990		1998	
	NZ pop. % of total	% of students	NZ pop. % of total	% of students
European/Pakeha	82	84.7	71	70.7
Maori	12	6.8	14	12.6
Pacific Islanders	4	2.5	5	3.8
Asian	1	3	4	9.5
Other	1	2.9	6	3.4
Total	100	100	100	100

Source: Ministry of Education 1998 p. 27.

ago and Pacific Islanders by four times. Even so, neither has achieved a rate of participation matching their distribution in the total population (see Table 11.1).

Because of market forces it has become expensive to undertake higher or tertiary education in New Zealand. Even a relatively low-level Diploma in Eco-Tourism from a polytechnic costs over $NZ10,000, and learning to be an aircraft pilot can cost over $NZ100,000. Although there has been some improvement in the participation rates of Maori and Pacific Islanders relative to their presence in the total population (from 1990 to 1998), they are still below average and these groups tend to be over-represented in 'low-status' programmes. Maori and Pacific Islands participation rates may have started to decline because the costs of enrolment have a more adverse impact on poorer groups (Taskforce for Improving Participation in Tertiary Education 1999).

Older adults

In the past most students came into tertiary education directly from high school. By the year 2000 this was changing and there were more older students. Whereas 2.7 per cent of the population aged over twenty-five years were involved in tertiary education in 1990, in 1998 this had risen by 60 per cent, when 4.3 per cent of those over twenty-five were involved in education. The Ministry of Education (1999 p. 26) claimed the 'growth in the number of students aged 40 or more has been particularly strong in the 1990s, with these students making up 15 per cent of all students in 1998 compared with 11 per cent in 1990'.

Women

Historically, women had significantly lower rates of involvement in tertiary education than men and were largely confined to traditionally 'feminine' areas such as teaching, home science and health. By the end of the twentieth century, the participation rate of women was higher than men in all age groups. For example, in 1998, 30 per cent of men aged eighteen to twenty-four years and 4 per cent of those aged over twenty-five were enrolled in tertiary education, while the comparable figures for women were 34 per cent and 6 per cent (Ministry of Education 1999 p. 26). This change is reflected in the fact that 70 per cent of the increase in enrolments since 1990 were women.

Much of this increase has come from two kinds of women: those returning to study after having children and older ones wishing to upgrade their skills. Fewer women than men have completed postgraduate qualifications but, given their growing dominance at the under-graduate level, this pattern is likely to change in the near future. Overall, New Zealand women also had a higher rate of programme completions than men (Ministry of Education 1999 p. 46).

Immigrants

In most Western countries recent immigrants are typically under-represented in tertiary education, and this was usually the case in New Zealand. Indeed, Pacific Islanders, who constitute a large proportion of New Zealand's immigrant population, are notable by their absence from formal educational settings. Recent changes in immigration requirements have meant that a larger proportion of immigrants (especially from Asia) have higher qualifications. While there is a dearth of data on this issue, a few studies (see Kong 1997) and anecdotal evidence suggest that many immigrants have difficulty getting overseas qualifications recognised in New Zealand, and enrol in local tertiary programmes (see the large increase of Asian tertiary students in Table 11.1 above) or work outside their area of expertise. In June 2000 the Labour government announced a funding package to bring immigrant doctors' qualifications in line with New Zealand requirements as a result of the doctors' increasing agitation and claims that they had been misled into believing that they would be readily accepted into the local medical profession.

Lower socio-economic groups

Although there is no data using direct measures of socio-economic status (SES), inferences can be drawn from the backgrounds of students and recruitment patterns for schools. Parental income still exerts considerable influence on the likelihood of children attending tertiary education. In 1998, only 19 per cent of all tertiary students' parents had an estimated annual taxable income of less than $NZ 28,080, while 65 per cent came from homes with incomes over $NZ 50,751 (Ministry of Education 1999 p. 29). This pattern was strongest among students attending universities. In addition, students from low-income homes were more likely to need student loans than their high-income counterparts (Taskforce for Improving Participation in Tertiary Education 1999 p. 9). Low SES households included disproportionately higher numbers of Maori and Pacific Island families, although when SES factors are controlled for their participation rates are very similar to other ethnic groups (ibid.).

Data on participation rates from schools throughout New Zealand in 1997 showed that only 8 per cent of students entering university were from low decile schools (levels 1, 2 and 3), compared with 52 per cent of students from decile 8, 9 and 10 schools (New Zealand Vice-Chancellors' Committee 1998 Table 2.17). The gap between the schools has been increasing, with a 20 per cent reduction in bottom level (deciles 1–3) schools from 1994 to 1997. This gap also applies to other tertiary institutions.

Rural adults

Despite the withdrawal of subsidies and the profound restructuring of agriculture, New Zealand is still an important producer of dairy, meat and fruit products. Yet there has been a steady decline in population in rural areas and a drift of people to the north of the country, especially to Auckland which now accounts for over a third of the total population. As a consequence of this depopulation, and of hard financial times in most rural areas, there has been increasing financial pressure on tertiary providers (mainly polytechnics) located in the small to medium-sized population centres. With the reduction in the number of school-leavers in many rural regions, there has been a subsequent fall in enrolments in tertiary education in these areas (Ministry of Education 1999 p. 21).

Learners in nonformal settings

Histories of adult education in New Zealand (see Boshier 1979) as well as books providing an overview of provision (such as Boshier 1980, Benseman *et al.* 1996) place particular emphasis on the importance of non-formal (or 'out-of-school') settings for education. Twenty or thirty years ago the settings that attracted most analysis were community groups, the workplace, political movements, trade unions, arts organisations and such-like. There were some small scale proprietary schools – such as Pitmans for typing – and every town had a music teacher working out of his or her home. But otherwise private or 'for-profit' establishments were almost nonexistent.

Today, providers of education in nonformal settings are a visible, controversial and vibrant feature of the educational landscape. There are large number of nonformal providers, many run in conjunction with another business (e.g. a sewing class attached to a fabric shop; a ski school offshoot of a chairlift business). Others are stand-alone operations. While they manifest many of the characteristics of nonformal settings, in Schroeder's (1970) typology of adult education they are Type 1: established for the purpose of educating adults. In a learning society there would ideally be 'horizontal integration': interaction between formal and nonformal settings (Boshier 1998). But in New Zealand, formal providers compete with nonformal groups, and private training establishments (PTEs).

By 2000 there were over 800 of these formally-registered providers owned by private citizens or organisations. Most were either limited liability companies or trusts, and there were also some Maori organisations and incorporated societies. Because of their linkage with the New Zealand Qualifications Authority it was possible for a New Zealander to get a Nanny Certificate, a Diploma in Horticulture or Eco-Tourism or, if he or she found the America's Cup regatta tedious, a Diploma in Surfing. All from a private for-profit provider and often at a very considerable cost.

About a third of the PTEs claim to have a Maori orientation and 5 per cent a Pacific Island focus. Although PTEs are increasingly teaching degree programmes, most were dominated by programmes for the unemployed (Training Opportunities Programmes and Youth Training Programmes) with funding from Skill New Zealand.

PTEs catered to disproportionately higher numbers of Maori (28.7 per cent in 1998) and Pacific Island students (9.5 per cent) but, unlike their tertiary counterparts, their students were spread more evenly across the age range (Ministry of Education 1999 p. 20). Given their increased prominence, there is a surprising lack of information about PTEs and their students.

'Whare wananga'

This Maori form of tertiary institution is unique. Although they offer programmes under the same qualification 'umbrellas' as other tertiary institutions, *whare wananga* constitute a totally Maori learning environment with Maori management. They are considered an important alternative to mainstream provision. Most students attending *whare wananga* are Maori, which means they are in a majority and in an environment which is supposed to cater to their culture and needs as learners.

Accommodating non-traditional students

New Zealand universities were built on a British model and, apart from times of war or other unusual imperatives, were consciously elitist. Student recruitment was not an issue. Most students were youthful school-leavers. Mature adults or non-traditional learners hovered at the campus fringe – attending 'night classes' – usually in the Extension Department. Today, most of the drive to involve non-traditional students arises from Equal Educational Opportunities policies. Many institutions are actively attempting to recruit non-traditional learners. Hence, the University of Auckland set-up a Taskforce for Improving Participation in Tertiary Education (1999).

After the November 1999 election of a Labour government, there was a renewed emphasis on 'equal opportunities' with a 'Closing the Gaps' policy. This aimed to 'support and strengthen the capacity of Maori and Pacific Island communities, particularly through education, better health, housing and employment and better coordination of strategies across sectors, so that we may reduce the gaps that currently divide our society and offer a good future for all' (New Zealand Government 1999). By July 2000 government departments (including Education) were forming plans to implement the Gaps policy. There was a parallel commitment to strengthen the equity principles in the Treaty of Waitangi.

Fostering access

In the past New Zealanders appeared to accept the fact only 2 or 3 per cent of the population would gain a university degree. These days policy analysts and university administrators are scrambling to build 'mass' participation and commitment to postsecondary education. Because of the elite traditions of New Zealand universities, however, it is no easy task to build a welcoming climate for non-traditional learners. Some of the initiatives described below were borrowed from overseas, while others have a distinctive New Zealand twist.

Bridging programmes

Many non-participants lack formal entry qualifications. Bridging programmes (such as 'New Start') are increasingly seen as an integral part of tertiary provision. They help achieve equity policies and secure students for the enrolment economy that drives tertiary education funding. Some programmes are geared to specific qualifications (e.g. nursing, commerce, teaching), while others are more generic. Most award a qualification and completion is usually the equivalent to school qualifications. Some programmes are aimed specifically at under-represented groups (especially Maori and Pacific Islanders). Most students in bridging programmes come from non-traditional groups.

Adult open entry

New Zealand has long had an important alternative route of entry to tertiary education. Any adult over twenty years of age (previously twenty-one as the official 'age of majority') is able to enter any tertiary level programme unless there is a specific level requirement (as, for example, in medicine and dentistry). A typical entry statement reads 'Need Sixth Form Certificate or be over twenty years of age'. Educational institutions often counsel these students to do a study skills programme. What began as a response to post-war needs is now an instrument for open-access. Of course, once admitted, the over twenty year old has to pay the now considerable fees!

Recognition of prior learning (RPL)

Debate about the desirability and practice of this strategy has ebbed and flowed for the past decade. More recently the RPL concept has been expanded to include *recognition of current capability* (RCC) which acknowledges the ability to perform requisite skills, rather than restricting recognition to the completion of comparable educational programmes. These strategies have considerable appeal to non-traditional students, although they have not been utilised uniformly across the educational spectrum. Most institutions are reluctant to recognise RPL, let alone RCC.

Cross-institutional credit transfer

As with RPL, this practice varies considerably, and many mainstream institutions do not recognise programmes offered by competitors. When cross-credit is permitted, it is often at a lower level of recognition. Where qualifications are recognised by the Qualifications Framework, there is no difficulty in transferring them among institutions, but universities do not use the Qualifications Framework. Hence, problems can be encountered when transferring course credits from one university to another.

Staircasing

Known elsewhere as 'laddering', 'staircasing' enables learners to collect lower credentials en route to a 'higher' qualification. For example, a full year study at undergraduate level can result in a certificate. Two years' study in a diploma and three further years earns the learner a full degree. A post-graduate diploma can be awarded after one year full-time study, or turned into a masters degree after two years and then developed into a doctoral qualification. This strategy is popular with mature-age students who can stop at any point or readily build on previous qualifications. Nonformal settings are a vital part of staircasing.

Secondary Tertiary Alignment Resource (STAR)

This national programme enables secondary schools to 'purchase' tertiary-level programme that they do not normally teach. STAR enables students to undertake courses and get workplace experience that helps when they leave school. Almost all STAR students study at polytechnics and make up approximately 6 per cent of the total enrolments for those institutions (Ministry of Education 1999 p. 41).

Adult basic education

The 'Training Opportunities Programme' (TOP), 'Skill Enhancement and Commissioned Youth Action Training' are funded through Skill New Zealand, but provided mainly by Private Training Establishments, employers and polytechnics. Aimed at unemployed people with low levels of schooling, these programmes have entry into further education and training as one of their desired outcomes. In 2000 approximately a quarter of the participants in these programmes went on to further education, usually in polytechnics or PTEs. Given that there was no education for the unemployed fifteen years ago, these programmes have been a significant development.

Distance education

Prior to 1984, New Zealand had a correspondence school, and government or university extension workers typically worked with people in remote areas. In addition, Massey University, and later the Open Polytechnic, developed enviable reputations in correspondence and extra-mural provision. These days the number of institutions offering distance education has increased but, despite the creativity of the providers, the overall amount of distance provision has actually decreased (Ministry of Education 1999 p. 26).

What government statistics do not detect are New Zealanders taking online courses offered by Canadian, British, Australian and other foreign agencies. There is a frenetic scramble to develop web learning and education, often in association with other universities overseas. Discourses constructing these developments range from techno-utopian bombast that echoes the 'market forces' discussions of the 1980s through to concern about what individuals sitting at keyboards means for collectivist forms of learning preferred by Maori.

The now largely discredited Green Paper (Ministry of Education 1997) on tertiary education in New Zealand was infused with techno-utopianism. Some critics (Peters and Roberts 1999, Boshier *et al.* 1999, Wilson *et al.* 1998) raised critical questions, including the problem of US dominance of the Web and what it means for small countries like New Zealand.

Special structures

Many traditional educational institutional providers faced challenges – particularly from Maori and Pacific Islanders – over their inability to cater for the cultural and social diversity of learners. Maori have developed programmes for the pre-school level (*kohanga reo*), primary education (*kura kaupapa Maori*) and, to a lesser extent, at secondary and tertiary levels (*whare wananga*). Central government has been reluctant to increase the number of tertiary level *whare wananga* for fear of a Pandora's Box effect on funding demand. This has led to innovations which provide culturally supportive structures within existing institutions.

Separate departments of Maori Studies and Pacific Studies have existed for some time, but recent developments provide greater cultural autonomy and flexibility across entire institutions, For example, at the University of Auckland the *Whare Wananga o Waipapa* operates as a distinctively Maori form of education. It enables Maori staff and students to mix, and creates diverse qualifications by opening access to papers (or subjects) across traditional disciplinary structures. Moreover, with access in mind, many Maori *iwi* (tribes) have links with educational groups in their areas so as to influence programmes.

Market forces, labour and struggle for meaning

By 2000 New Zealand was struggling with forces Reich wrote about in *The Work of Nations.*

> Each nation's primary political task will be to cope with the centrifugal forces of the global economy which tear at the ties binding citizens together – bestowing ever greater wealth on the most skilled and insightful, while consigning the less skilled to a declining standard of living.
>
> (Reich 1992 p. 3)

Globalisation and 'market forces' had eroded the need to stay home and made it easier for talented people to seek fertile soil elsewhere. Post-1984 reforms radically altered the nature of the State. Some groups were empowered, most were marginalised. By and large, Maori, Pacific Islanders and other low-income groups suffered from reforms but some saw erosion of State power and ability to compete in a global economy as a vehicle for self-government. For 500,000 New Zealanders the answer to the 'New Zealand Experiment' lay in Australia – just over two hours flying time 'across the ditch.'

Employment and demise of the welfare state

By the middle of 2000 the Labour government was dismantling the Employment Contracts Act which had left a legacy of insecurity, especially for unskilled and other low-level workers. An unfettered labour market coupled with increasing technological demands had left most New Zealanders worse off financially than a decade before. This is because of what Hazeldine (1998) labelled 'selfish-shit' capitalism. With the number of unskilled and semi-skilled jobs in decline, there were fewer employment niches for people with low levels of education, and this renewed demands for literacy training. Turning fifty-five became a 'point of no return' for many workers who had lost jobs.

New Zealand had been the first country to give votes to women. Michael Savage, the Labour Prime Minister who erected a welfare state amidst the wreckage of the 'slump' or depression of the 1930s is still widely regarded as a saintly figure (much like Canada's Tommy Douglas). Yet, at the end of the twentieth century, New Zealand was leading the race to dismantle the welfare state. State assets were sold and government services reduced to a point where there were few blue pages in the back of the phone book. Neoliberals acted as if everyone would be better off if there was only a minimal government, or even none at all. This has led to a situation where government 'expects individuals to provide for the bulk of their needs via the market, their family, or voluntary agencies and charities' (Kelsey 1995 p. 2). With the social safety net in collapse, there was an increasing divide between those who could afford to pay for private services and those who had to wait in increasingly lengthy lines for state services.

The increasing cost of education was excluding many, especially those with the fewest resources. With tertiary students accruing debts in excess of $NZ80,000 for their studies, there was a demand for education to lead to employment. Debate about tertiary education was dominated by a human capital discourse. Many young people questioned the value of 'investing' in education, especially at lower levels where 'taking a course' did not necessarily lead to a job.

Lifelong learning as amoeba

In New Zealand lifelong learning tended to render invisible any obligation on the part of educators to address social conditions. It was nested in an ideology of vocationalism. Learning was for acquiring skills alleged to enable the learner to work harder, faster and smarter, and thus enable their employer to better compete in the global economy (Savage 2000). Lifelong learning also denoted the savvy consumer surfing the Internet and selecting from a smorgasbord of educational offerings. Learning was constructed as an individual activity. Lifelong learning is an amoeba-word that flows around, divides and forms entities that bear little relationship to the old. As a term, it slid easily from the tongue of Ministers of Education, captains of industry and university Vice-Chancellors – few of whom have ever heard of Faure (1972).

Lifelong learning also became a slogan to buttress formal education. Hence, under the heading 'lifelong learner' Auckland's UNITEC urged learners to find the 'right tertiary education partner' (*Futurework* 2000 p. 19). The New Right gutted *lifelong education* of its emphasis on equity, civil society and participation and, instead, deployed *lifelong learning* as part of the cult of finance.

In universities the effect of the post-1984 reforms was to:

- create vigorous competition for students which, because of the funding formula, demanded enrolments and led to a decline in standards
- escalate university (and tertiary education) fees and the burden of student loans; higher education was no longer a right-of-citizenship

- create a fast turnover of Vice-Chancellors who appeared under increasing pressure from the need to reconcile the realities of marketisation and the faculty need for security and commitment to the public good
- evoke a 1991 'study right' for school-leavers which discriminated against mature age learners; for adults, it was a case of study denial (Findsen, 1996)
- accelerate student debt and, along with the cult of finance, encourage both private and public providers to charge outrageous fees; the academic performance of students having to work to service large loans while studying became a major concern
- shrink funds available for research done by university faculty members who had to compete with agencies such as crown research institutes; internal university research funds tended to favour hard sciences; social science which was not part of the 'cult of finance' attracted diminishing levels of support
- erode conditions of work as administration was devolved to faculty members and student-staff ratios deteriorated (Jesson, J. 1999)
- erode trust, conviviality and collegiality as competition between university units escalated
- create a state of crisis; management from above, intervention by government and inability to secure willing, energetic and enthusiastic applicants for senior administrative positions, along with too many visions and mission statements, sapped energy and morale.

Conclusions

During the last fifteen years of the twentieth century, education in New Zealand went through unprecedented changes. The promised economic miracle did not arrive and, when Labour Prime Minister Helen Clark assumed office in December 1999, options were constrained by the excesses of the previous fifteen years.

There was a widespread consensus that the New Zealand Experiment had failed and things had to be done differently, even among members of the departing government. After the December, 1999 election the Quality Public Education Coalition (*Newsletter* 1999) noted

The last few weeks have seemed like a breath of fresh air. Springtime after a long cold winter perhaps. There is a feeling of relief among many in education that quality, opportunity, professionalism and equity might take a front seat, with the ideology of the last decade relegated to the back seat.

(*Newsletter* 1999 p. 1)

The future of lifelong learning was in doubt. Hence, in the 21 December 1999 speech, the new Labour-Alliance government announced that 'a competitive model in tertiary education has led to unsatisfactory outcomes in terms of both the quality and appropriateness of the skills produced . . . The present competitive model in tertiary education will be abandoned'. A Commission would be created to rebuild a 'collaborative and cooperative tertiary sector'.

Now the question is: can lifelong learning be rescued? Universities will have to articulate a vision for the public good founded on respect for New Zealand's history and heritage, trust in university faculty members and an understanding of the anarchist-utopian tradition in adult education (with its celebration of the do-it-yourself or farm-gate ethos).

Even demoralised adult educators showed signs of life by organising *Kotare,* a radical education centre that resembled Highlander Folk School (Benseman 1999). There were formidable challenges. Because of the depth of the post-1984 transformation, it would not be just a matter of turning back the clock. Social problems had become a priority and social cohesion was for the first time listed as one of the fundamental underpinnings of a strong economy. Radical individualism and techno-rational notions of lifelong learning would be jettisoned.

The Labour government commitment to build a more caring society provided an opportunity to reclaim lifelong learning and infuse it with a sense of community and possibility, once the leitmotif of Aotearoa. Universities serious about lifelong learning needed to find remaining members of a vanishing species: adult educators. If ever there was time to reach for old copies of the Faure (1972) report this was it. Educational policy needed a postmodern flourish: looking backwards but at the same time going forward.

References

ACCESS (1996) *Special Issue: Adult and Community Education in Aotearoa New Zealand: An Emerging Identity* vol. 15 no. 2, Auckland: University of Auckland School of Education.

Benseman, J. (1979) 'Continuing education clientele: present realities and future possibilities', *Continuing Education in New Zealand* vol. 11 no. 1.

—— (1992) 'Participation revisited: who gets to adult/community education 1970–1990?' *New Zealand Journal of Adult Learning* vol. 20 no. 1.

—— (1999) 'Kotare: building a radical alternative in New Zealand adult education', paper presented at the Australian Adult Learning Association *Crossing Thresholds* Conference, University of Melbourne.

Benseman, J., Findsen, B. and Scott, M. (eds) (1996) *The Fourth Sector: Adult and Community Education in Aotearoa New Zealand,* Palmerston North: Dunmore.

Boshier, R. W. (1970) 'The participants: a clientele analysis of three New Zealand adult education institutions (Part 1)', *Australian Journal of Adult Education* vol. 10 no. 3.

—— (1979) *Adult and Continuing Education in New Zealand, 1851–1978: A Bibliography,* Vancouver: Adult Education Research Centre and International Council of Adult Education.

—— (ed.) (1980) *Towards a Learning Society: New Zealand Adult Education in Transition,* Vancouver: Learningpress.

—— (1998) 'The Faure report: down but not out', in J. Holford, C. Griffin and P. Jarvis (eds) *Lifelong Learning in the Learning Society,* London: Kogan Page.

Boshier, R. W., Wilson, M. and Qayyum, A. (1999) 'Lifelong education and the World Wide Web: American hegemony or diverse utopia?' *International Journal of Lifelong Education* vol. 18 no. 4.

Butterworth, G. and Butterworth, S. (1998) *Reforming Education: The New Zealand Experience 1984–1996,* Palmerston North: Dunmore.

Faure, E. (Chair) (1972) *Learning to Be,* Paris: UNESCO.

Findsen, B. (1996) 'University-based adult and continuing education in New Zealand – trends and issues', *ACCESS* vol. 15 no. 2.

Futurework (2000) 'Where will you go in the future?' Auckland: UNITEC (recruitment brochure).

Garrett, D. (1972) 'Report on the Third UNESCO World Conference on Adult Education (Tokyo, 1972)', *Continuing Education in New Zealand* vol. 4 no. 2.

Hazeldine, T. (1998) *Taking New Zealand Seriously,* Auckland: HarperCollins.

Hely, A. S. M. (1967) *UNESCO and the Concept of 'Education permanente',* Wellington: National Council of Adult Education.

Horton, C. (1976) *University Extension Participants: Their Characteristics and Attitudes,* Hamilton: University of Waikato.

Jesson, B. (1999) *Only their Purpose is Mad: The Money Men Take Over New Zealand,* Palmerston North: Dunmore.

Jesson, J. (1999) 'Virtual technologies and academic labour: more questions than answers', in M. Peters and P. Roberts (eds) *Virtual Technologies and Tertiary Education,* Palmerston North: Dunmore.

Johnstone, J. W. C. and Rivera, R. (1965) *Volunteers for Learning,* Chicago: National Opinion Research Center.

Kelsey, J. (1995) *The New Zealand Experiment,* Auckland: Auckland University Press and Bridget Williams.

—— (1999) *Reclaiming the Future: New Zealand and the Global Economy,* Auckland: Bridget Williams.

Kong, M. (1997) *Continuing Education Issues for Chinese Professional Immigrants,* unpublished M.Ed. dissertation, University of Auckland.

London, J., Wenkert, R. and Hagstrom, W. (1963) *Adult Education and Social Class,* Berkeley: University of California Survey Research Center.

Ministry of Education (1989) *Learning for Life Two,* Wellington: Ministry of Education.

—— (1996) *Adult Literacy in New Zealand: Results from the International Adult Literacy Survey,* Wellington: Ministry of Education.

—— (1997) *A Review of Tertiary Education,* Wellington: Ministry of Education.

—— (1998) *New Zealand Education Sector: Profile and Trends,* Wellington, Ministry of Education.

—— (1999) *New Zealand's Tertiary Education Sector: Profile and Trends,* Wellington: Ministry of Education.

New Zealand Government (1999) http://www.govt.nz/news.detail

New Zealand Vice-Chancellors' Committee (1998) *Statistical Collection 1998*, Wellington: New Zealand Vice-Chancellors' Committee.

Newsletter of the Quality Public Education Coalition (Inc.) (December, 1999) vol. 3 no. 5.

OECD (1997) *Literacy Skills for the Knowledge Society: Further Results from the International Adult Literacy Survey,* Paris: OECD and Human Resources Development Canada

—— (1998) *Education at a Glance: OECD Education Indicators*, Paris: OECD.

Parkyn, G. W. (1973) *Towards a Conceptual Model of Lifelong Education,* Paris: UNESCO, Educational Studies no. 12.

Peters, M., Marshall, J. and Massey, L. (1994) 'Recent educational reforms in Aotearoa', in E. Coxon, K. Jenkins, J. Marshall and L. Massey (eds) *The Politics of Learning and Teaching in Aotearoa-New Zealand*, Palmerston North: Dunmore.

Peters, M. and Roberts, P. (eds) (1999) *Virtual Technologies and Tertiary Education*, Palmerston North: Dunmore.

Prebble, R. (1987) 'Foreword' to R. Douglas and L. Callan *Towards Prosperity: People and Politics in the 1980s, a Personal View*, Auckland: David Bateman.

Reich, R. (1992) *The Work of Nations*, New York: Vintage.

Renwick, W. L. (1975) *Recurrent Education: Policy and Development in OECD Member Countries: New Zealand*, Paris: OECD.

Roberts, N. (1983) '"Get the bloody numbers": raising the response to continuing education courses', *New Zealand Journal of Adult Learning* vol. 15.

Savage, D. C. (2000) 'Academic freedom and institutional autonomy in New Zealand universities', paper presented to the Association of University Staff [http//www.aus.ac.nz]

Schroeder, W. L. (1970) 'Adult education defined and described', in R. M. Smith, G. F. Aker and J. R. Kidd (eds) *Handbook of Adult Education,* New York: Macmillan and the Adult Education Association (USA).

Simmonds, E. J. (Chair) (1972) *Report of the Committee on Lifelong Education*, Wellington: New Zealand National Commission for UNESCO.

Skill New Zealand (1999) *Brief for the Incoming Minister of Education*, Wellington: Skill New Zealand.

Statistics Canada (1985) *One in Five*, Ottawa: Statistics Canada.

Taskforce for Improving Participation in Tertiary Education (1999) *Report*, Auckland: University of Auckland.

Wilson, M., Qayyum, A. and Boshier, R. W. (1998) 'World wide America: think globally, click locally', *Distance Education* vol. 19 no. 1.

Index

Abrahamsson, K. 87, 89, 94–5
access to HE 3, 4, 7, 9, 61, 94, 110, 152, 166–7, 177, 209; academic credentials 13, 14, 21, 62, 76, 77, 78; admission criteria 17, 22, 84, 86, 92, 132, 135; alternative entry routes 41–2, 49, 50, 52–3, 56, 57, 84, 85, 87, 92, 93, 104, 105, 119, 144, 153, 154, 157–8, 199–200, 221, 226; aptitude for study 62 (tests 85, 87, 92, 95, 135); attempts to widen 71, 139; barriers 70–1, 76, 77, 79, 80, 105, 111, 136, 144, 175, 185–90, 196, 202, 222, 223, 226, 230; before mass education 12–13; and courses in high demand 135; courses for, inadequate 76; and social groups 7, 69–71; ICT courses 9; inequalities 69–70, 75–6; institutional differentiation 16–17; legal regulation of entry 27; numbers interested in widening 64; unequal *see* gender, ethnicity, social class; vocational route 15, 22, 57, 58
adult education 3, 21, 49, 71–2, 75–8, 84, 103–4; 213; barriers to 80; learners' insecurity in universities 77, 78, 80; funding of 19, 73; gender disparity 77; mass access 4; and national competitiveness 72; participation rates 73–4 (target 77, 78); scale of 75; tradition of 182
adult learners 13, 14, 22, 38, 67–80, 83, 89, 90, 94, 97–8, 139–40; age 75, 76, 84, 91, 96, 102, 106, 149, 155–6, 162; definition 105, 155; neglect of 104; numbers 139, 149, 160–2, 182 (older 60); participation rate 116; performance 80; policy towards 103–5; subjects studied 90, 96; value of mixed-age groups 98; women 139
Agélii, K. 87, 88, 98

approaches to teaching/learning 6, 12, 31–2, 33, 79, 98, 101, 209; holistic 80; more complex 185
Australia 5; academic staff, role of 185; access to higher education 185–90; autonomy of learners 185; critical cusp for HE 175, 187; curriculum 177, 185; Dawkins Reforms 175–6, 177, 181; demography 181; equity 177, 178, 181, 182, 188; federal government/state role 175; flexibility of provision 177, 184, 185; higher education, demand for 173; ICT 18, 176; immigrant groups 182, 190; indigenous people 174, 175, 182–3; Karpin Report 180; knowledge society 173, 178, 190–1, 192; labour market 173, 177, 178, 186, 189–90; language variety 174; *Learning for Life* (West Review) 180, 189; learning society, progress towards 184–5, 190–1; lifelong learning 178–81, 187, 190; literacy 177; market forces 189, 191; nation in transition 173–92; Open Learning Australia 182; overseas students 173–4, 176, 182; partnerships with industry 176; part-time study 177, 182, 186, 191; private higher education 175, 177–8; rhetoric and reality 191–2; rural areas, students from 174, 175, 183, 187–8, 191; school completion rates 188–9, 191; social class 174, 175, 183, 184, 187–8, 191; student body, diversity of 184, 185; student finance 176, 180, 186, 188; Technical and Further Education sector (TAFE) 21, 176, 177, 183, 184, 185, 186, 189; technical institutes 175; tradition of adult education 182; under-represented groups 174, 183; vocationalism 176,